MW00577736

A HISTORY OF
IRISH MUSIC

LARRY KIRWAN

FORTY-SEVEN BOOKS
NEW YORK CITY

Larry Kirwan
blk47@aol.com
www.black47.com

A History of Irish Music/ Larry Kirwan. -- 1st ed.
ISBN 978-0-9639601-1-3

Larry Kirwan's journey through Irish music is a memoir, a love story, a history of modern Ireland and thus unique. Irish music was ever the nation's chief export, but here one of the finest proofs of that fact takes us on a vivid, beautifully written adventure through that great Irish product, roots, trunk and branch.

Tom Keneally, author of *Schindler's List*

Larry Kirwan calls it A History but I call it THE History of Irish music. Once more this Renaissance man presents us with another extraordinary work of art. No matter whether you are of the Galway Bay sentimental mold or of the passionate and patriotic Kevin Barry persuasion this book is for you - a metaphysical toe tapper chock full of poetry, witticisms, proverbs, laughs and the occasional tragedy. Give yourself plenty of time for you will not want to go to bed without finishing it. The History of Irish Music is impossible to put down.

Malachy McCourt, author of *A Monk Swimming*

Larry Kirwan's A History of Irish Music is a penetrating portrait of the artist as a musician, storyteller, historian, songwriter, immigrant, researcher and autobiographer. Kirwan's magisterial command of Irish music allows him to dig beneath the facts and explore its soul. This engaging, enlightening and insightful book is a must for anyone interested in the ongoing evolution of Irish music in particular and the music industry in general. Best of all, it's a rockin' good read!

Peter Quinn, author of *Banished Children of Eve*

From Wexford town to New York, from folk to punk/new wave, from the fervour of youth to the consideration of maturity, from politics to polemics, Larry Kirwan invests his subjective view of Irish music with a keen eye for detail and a deft turn of phrase.

Tony Clayton-Lea, *Irish Times* music critic

You don't have to be Irish to fall in love with the book and the heritage it celebrates. Larry Kirwan is a master musician, journalist, playwright, poet and mesmerizing storyteller. From the ancient pipers of the Celts to the Irish Rockers of today, this book takes us all on a journey through time. It is an invaluable guide for appreciating the endless varieties of music created from a culture that has enriched the world.

David Amram, composer, multi-instrumentalist, author

I love reading and learning, especially the history of Ireland, of music and of my friends. In Larry Kirwan's A History of Irish Music all my passions are rolled into one book. Whether in writing or in person, Kirwan's style is the same: genuine, laced with humor, illuminating and as accepting as a politically active bandleader can be. This book is full of seminal people, moments and music set against the backdrop of an Ireland undergoing political, religious and economic quakes. The shores change to America, the song remains the same, on the cutting edge of music in America Kirwan tells it as he experienced it, firsthand. I loved it.
John O'Brien, Co-Publisher/Editor Ohio Irish American News, Author

Warning: This is not your teacher's history book. In fact Larry Kirwan's, A History of Irish Music, is not a book at all, it's one hundred percent pure vinyl. Just set the needle in the groove, kick back and let it take you on a wild musical ride through the history of Irish music and every musical venue from Kielty's pub in Wexford town to a sweat filled Paddy Reilly's on Manhattan's East Side. Kirwan's been rocking and rolling his way to this particular masterpiece for about forty years…the jammy bastard.
Colin Broderick, author of The Orangutan

Initially an erudite and thoroughly engaging illumination of a long-lost Ireland, A History of Irish Music expands much further as Larry Kirwan takes the reader on a fascinating journey through his lifelong obsession with music. A veritable cornucopia of evocative tales detail Larry's discovery, love of and sometimes personal connections with many of the great and good of Irish and Celtic music from the last six decades.
Sean McGhee, Editor R2 Magazine

Larry Kirwan's relationship with Wexford, a town as old as Ptolemy, and the cradle of some of the best contemporary writers in the world – John Banville, Colm Toibin, Eoin Colfer – is beautifully delineated in A History of Irish Music: his evocation of the town, from the vantage of exile, mirrors Joyce and Dublin, though the poet and song writer in Kirwan sieves 'the thorny outlines of a culture that doffed its cap to no one' with a lyrical tempo which brings the fast changing world of his youth alive.
Tom Mooney, Editor Wexford Echo

Larry Kirwan is like a sports commentator who has actually played the game he is calling. As the frontman for Black 47 he is an insider who can write like an outsider. A History of Irish Music is part autobiographical, but never veers far from its central message that the island of Ireland, and its music, have been intertwined and intertuned for as long as anyone cares to remember, and that the world has benefited beyond measure as a result. This is a great story, and it is told by a musician and singer who can add consummate writing skills to his considerable repertoire. A great read that hits all the high notes.

Ray O'Hanlon, Editor *Irish Echo* and author of *The South Lawn*

A History of Irish Music is a fascinating and unique memoir and sociological history of modern Irish rock by Black 47's Larry Kirwan. Larry takes us from his youth in Wexford and the birth of Irish rock via the Beat scene and the Showbands through his emigration to NYC and his vantage point as a band musician seeing young Irish bands like Horslips and U2 trying to crack NYC for the very first time. Larry's own musical history is also fascinating through his time with Major Thinkers, Turner and Kirwan of Wexford and finally Black 47 – NYC's house band and how Larry revolutionized the percipience of what Irish music was in the eyes of America.

John Murphy, publisher of *Shite & Onions*

Jamming with the Saw Doctors, drinking with Shane MacGowan, catching Christy Moore on good nights and not so, hearing Rory Gallagher live and in person in Ireland--and coming to Americkay to become, with his mates Black 47 and get one of their best songs onto Sons of Anarchy! Now the man's a very well reviewed playwright, a revered and admired solo songwriter and performer, a novelist and SiriusXM radio dj personality. Is there nothing Larry Kirwan, the Irish master of all media, won't achieve? And begawd the man's still a Major Drinker down all these bloody wild years! I know, I saw him onstage at that final Black 47 gig at BB King's, lifting shots and pints to beat the band! So now he's come out with this fine roaring kinghellbastard of a read, A History of Irish Music! And we're all going to lift our pints and read along, Black 47 lilting away behind us. Damn straight we shall! Good health to you Larry--write on!

Bill Nevins, poet, political activist & author of "Heartbreak Ridge"

How can we know the dancer from the dance?
W.B. Yeats

INTRODUCTION

This is a very subjective history of Irish music as I witnessed and experienced it. I regret that so many worthy bands and singers have not been included, but there's only so much you can see or experience. Hopefully this book will encourage readers to explore the full spectrum of Irish music.

A History of Irish Music is in many ways inspired by *Celtic Crush*, my weekly SiriusXM Satellite Radio show. In the course of three hours I play roughly 40 songs and comment on many of them. As everything is improvised, I'm forced to recall long ago concerts, encounters, and opinions. These recollections often provide the raw fodder for this book. Over the show's ten years I've come to understand just how much all our lives are intertwined with music. Inevitably, musicians experience music in a different way - not necessarily a better one. For better or worse, this is a musician's view.

What really struck me is the sheer idealism – or foolhardiness - of musicians. We set out to play and create music without the least guarantee of success or financial security. At best, those of us lucky enough to make a living arise each morning like characters in a Beckett play, hoping to fail just a little better – for good gigs are scarce and great songs don't come easily. And that's the sunny side, the rear view mirror of most working musicians displays a string of casualties, often the more sensitive and talented of our peers.

Music is never created in a void and I've tried to outline the relevant social and political Irish climate. Religious conservatism, both north and south of the border and in the Diaspora communities, is a defining factor, and musical innovation seems to occur when it is challenged. The "National Question," as it used to be called, is often a spark for creativity; but a longing for modernity and a thirst for outside influences provide their own fertile soil.

There are so many people to thank: Tom Schneider for his encouragement and gimlet eye, Patrick Flood for his design, Mike

Farragher for his foreword, and all those who contributed help and friendship including Donal Gallagher, Andy Irvine, Ollie Jennings, Mike Scott, Jack O'Leary, Caroline Ironside-Crowe, Susan Connolly, Pierce Turner, Sean McGhee, Stephen Travers, Paddy Reilly, Jim Lockhart, Phil Coulter, Jack Warshaw. But in the end this book is a tribute to every Irish musician who ever picked up an axe and entered the arena. Whether standing or felled, you came to better understand the ineffable difference between the dancer and the dance.

Larry Kirwan

January 201

FOREWORD

Anyone who is taken by surprise that Larry Kirwan would write a book of Irish musical history obviously hasn't been paying attention. The man has been educating generations of Irish Americans--and any American for that matter--about Irish history for the last 25 years through the music of Black 47. I know I act on behalf of an entire middle-aged population when I tip my hat to him for fusing reggae, punk, and Hip Hop and translating my culture into a language I could more easily understand. That action has inspired a generation of artists, poets, writers, and musicians to find their voice, including me.

Standing on its own merits, *A History of Irish Music* would make an impeccable, meticulous chronicle of Irish and Irish American music throughout the years. He takes us to the middle of the town square on Market Day in Wexford during the Fifties to hear the earthy tones from the throat of a tinker woman named Margaret Barry. In a blink of an eye, we are then introduced to the full-throat throttle of Dropkick Murphys' Ken Casey, who has redefined Boston and its sports teams with his brand of Celtic Hardcore blaring over social media in this new millennium. Along the way, we are introduced to the madcap showbands that traversed through Ireland to interpret the popular music for music fans not yet plugged into television. Though the scenarios couldn't be more disparate, they are watermarks in the evolution of how Irish music has been transmitted to the masses over the years.

A History of Irish Music might have a shipping container full of facts and figures crammed into a textbook you might find in the hallowed halls of Trinity College but this isn't just history--it's HIS story. What makes this book so endearing is that it has been written from a fanboy's giddy perspective. There's the story about Larry steadying himself like a pimpled schoolgirl against the wall, overcome with awe as Blues great Rory Gallagher asks him for a lift home after leaving the concert hall a smoldering wreck behind them. He writes about being hypnotized by the blistering guitar on Them's "Baby Please Don't Go" that blared over Radio Luxembourg and how he'd wait patiently by the radio with a tape recorder to capture the song for obsessive consumption later that evening. Let me pause for a second to allow the YouTubers reading this to do a Google search on the words "radio" and "tape recorder"...

In recreating the birth of Celtic Rock, he reveals the humorous and heartbreaking ups and downs of the rock star life through his bespectacled and jaundiced eyes. One moment, he is getting pissed on free champagne backstage at a Horslips show and in another he's getting teary eyed at the urinal on the closing night of CBGB's.

Larry starts and ends many of the chapters with the lyrics of the greatest songs of our culture. The call to arms of "The Patriot Game" is juxtaposed with the depiction of carnage in Phil Coulter's "The Town I Loved So Well" with brilliant effect, creating an artistic statement in and of itself. Larry slips in the odd lyric from his own fabled oeuvre into the mix and though he is far too modest to admit it, he's proving to the rest of the world what every Black 47 fan knew all along: his songs stand proudly against any tune penned by an Irishman.

I'd harvest a kidney for a small stack of tickets to some of the shows that Larry Kirwan has seen throughout the years and details inside these pages. Van Halen opening for Horslips -- are you kidding me? He describes squinting through the mist coming off the rain-soaked coats of an audience crammed into a small Dublin folk club to hear the unrepentant Christy Moore belt it out before he found fame with Planxty and Moving Hearts. My life was forever changed when I saw Black 47 and The Saw Doctors wipe the floor with fans during a legendary gig at Tramps in NYC back in 1990 and I was thrilled to relive the gig through the lead singer's eyes in these pages!

Larry's hawk eye for detail and sly sense of humor guide the narrative but of course, you couldn't wash down a great Irish story without a few shots of sadness down yer gullet for good measure. You almost have to cast your eyes away from the page while the author looks on helplessly as the pharmacological pitfalls of a rocker's life claims one hero after another. His unflinching depiction of the soul wrenching sadness an immigrant feels when he walks the streets of his hometown and realizes that he no longer belongs there will be all too familiar to anyone who moved onto America or England for a better life.

So pour yourself a few fingers of whiskey, crack the binding, fire up the auld Kindle or iPad, and prepare yourself for a whiplash musical journey that starts on the next page!

Mike Farragher
Staff Music Writer, Irish Voice and IrishCentral.com and author of the "This Is Your Brain on Shamrocks" Series

December 2014

CHAPTER ONE

The Islands

If it's all so far behind me why does it seem like yesterday
The lark in the morning, your auld lad tossin' hay
The ferry in the harbor dancing jigs upon the waves
The day I turned my back on you and the islands

Seven years I stayed away though I wrote from time to time
Down all those dancing days your eyes haunted mine
But Bainbridge was the sweetest whore, took care of my demands
Bade me turn my back on you and the islands

I brought you petticoats of silk, a diamond from the Deuce
No price too steep to pay for your commitment
To lie once more beside you and roll you in my arms
That's why I came back home to you and the islands

No smoke from your chimney
Your yard was choked with grass
They said you'd upped and gone to the mainland
One mentioned that you'd met someone
Now lived in Dublin town
Grown tired of haunting dreams on the islands

Now it's all so far behind me but it seems like yesterday
The lark has quit the heavens, no one bothers savin' hay
I am a tourist in my hometown, an acquaintance once a friend
Since I turned my back on you and the islands

(Larry Kirwan)

Larry Kirwan

T he country and town were different. The former
was heavy and slow and moved to a stately
relentless shuffle; it had its own laws and was
rarely forgiving should you cross certain boundaries never
clearly delineated.

The town, on the other hand, was noisy and
effervescent, its main street throbbing like some jazzed-up
Breughel. Wexford was split into so many fiefdoms, cantons -
call them what you will - it still takes my breath away. Some
were no more than a warren of narrow laneways, others an
assembly of broad streets, each boasting a different accent,
alternate constitution, and step on the social ladder; all were
policed by volunteer militias more than eager to enforce local
expectations and to chastise those who offered the least slight,
real or imagined.

The country was heartily suspicious of the town and
sucked in its breath on first sighting of an urban spire or
factory chimney. Cyclists, for that's how most "culchies"
traveled in those days, dismounted and unhooked the clips
that restrained their wide, unfashionable trouser-hems.
Those lucky enough to travel by car or bus kept their eyes set
firmly ahead for fear of receiving the finger from marauding
bands of adolescent townies off to rob orchards or hunt
rabbits - mongrel dogs, younger brothers and even the
occasional baby in a pram in tow.

The town rarely wasted a thought on the country or
its people. And why would it? If they knew what was good
for them, culchies watched their step when gracing Wexford's
medieval streets, and though they no longer tipped their cloth
caps to their urban betters, they kept to themselves: the
womenfolk shopped in stores where they were known, the
men drank in pubs where they were tolerated – sitting in
clumped groups at corner tables, undistinguished as
Vincent's potato pickers, never occupying barstools or other
such favored tavern real estate. And when their children
attended the Christian Brothers or the Mercy, Presentation
and Loreto Convents, they rarely spoke up for fear their
broad vowels and thick accents would provide an occasion of

2

fun for the boys and girls from the dank lanes and back
streets; rather, they clustered together in support groups,
those from Rosslare or Kilmore in the South of the county
blending uneasily with those from Oylegate or Barntown in
the North or West. In truth, they had little in common
beyond the bond of the land and an antipathy for the sharp
tongue of the perfidious townie.

I was the exception. I mixed easily with both groups.
Though I lived with my maternal grandfather at 9 Lower
George's Street in the heart of the old town – a once
prestigious address though most of the grand old houses had
already been converted to flats – I spent much time on my
paternal grandfather's fine 100 acre farm just outside the
town limits.

Back then Ireland was very paternalistic. Inheritance
of property passed through eldest sons and, in the manner of
kings and pontiffs, Irish grandfathers rarely retired. The
crown prince of some collection of boggy fields might
languish well into his 60's before finally coming into his own
as the coffin of his father was shouldered to the church
mortuary.

Though the farm at Ballinagee was barely a couple of
miles ride from George's Street, my grandfather, Laurence
Kirwan, also owned a much larger property in Tacumshane
on the shores of the South Atlantic near Carnsore Point, the
exact South-East Corner of Ireland. This was a forlorn, if
somewhat romantic, spot bordered by a mile or so of our own
dramatic beach. It might just as well have been ten miles for
one could walk 'til one dropped along this graveled, sandy
expanse - the Saltee Islands in view - without encountering
another human, the wind harsh and salty having touched no
land since Antartica.

Why romantic? Well, tragic might be a better word
for, from time to time, small ships ran aground in the gale-
force storms that racked those waters. It was muttered by
those from surrounding areas that, in bygone days, the
natives of Tacumshane placed lights on rocks and sandbars to
lure vessels aground – all the better to loot them. What truth

3

there is to that, I don't know. But rumor and tales of yore are strong in that part of the world. It's also said that a high rate of mental illness afflicts the area because of inbreeding, though the inhabitants appeared sharp enough in all their dealings with me. Still, it was a different acuity to that of the townies, for they moved slowly but deliberately down Tacumshane way, answering inquiries in their own good time as if their minds were occupied with more important matters.

Laurence Kirwan had built a fine house on this property nestled between the pounding Atlantic and the shores of Our Lady's Island Lake; yet none of his sons wished to move there. Though beautiful in its own way, it was a windy and lonely spot at the end of a rutted road. People rarely ventured there except an occasional academic or American looking for permission to examine an old outhouse. The locals claimed that John Barry, founder of the American Navy, had been born in this tumbledown cattle-shelter before his family moved to a more genteel residence in nearby Ballysampson. Barry himself apparently had soon tired of the charms of the general area for he bolted to Philadelphia and prominence in his early teens.

Laurence Kirwan was an unromantic man and cared little for such rumors. To his way of thinking Barry's purported birthplace was a decent enough shelter from the wind for the hundreds of cattle that he kept on this farm. His bullocks were free to roam as they saw fit across the sandy banks and flatlands of this demesne for 9 months of the year. Then, on late spring mornings at the crack of dawn, we would drive them with much hullabaloo up narrow country roads to the lush grasslands of Ballinagee where they would fatten themselves through the summer before being shipped for slaughter to Birkenhead on the outskirts of Liverpool.

Being the eldest son of the eldest son I was expected to, and did, spend much time down in Tacumshane. From an early age I cottoned on to the fact that I wanted no part of cattle dealing or farming in general; but I did love that part of the country, its barely mitigated wildness, the stinging salt sea wind, and the oldness and cool indifference of the earth

4

beneath my feet. I was interested too in the people. Some of them brought to mind the earth itself: stolid, wise and patient. Those employed by my grandfather were suspicious of me at first; no doubt they feared that I might report their conversations. There had been much talk of the Land Commission breaking up the big farms and apportioning acres to the agricultural laborers; those views were occasionally bruited when they would halt for scalding tea poured from battered flasks, or a gaze at the ever-changing outline of the Saltee Islands. I wouldn't have even known how to report such treason to my grandfather for he was remote as those islands himself, only interested in surveying and counting his cattle, ever watchful that they never strayed down onto the treacherous beach with its shifting gravelly tides.

With time the men got used to my own silent presence, stoically encouraging me to help with the thinning of beet, snagging of turnips, weeding of potatoes, moving the cattle from favored spots to less grassy areas, and all the other monotonous tasks that went into keeping the farm up to my grandfather's Everest of expectations.

By the same token, that's when I began to notice that these people had their own music and songs that I never heard in the town. Long-form accounts of ancient battles, old woes and unfulfilled longings shoehorned into shanties, elegies and *aislings* that ambled along in perfect harmony and counterpoint with the whistling wind. They would hum these stories whilst going about their labors. I had to be careful and pretend not to listen, pick up a stray verse or two and then hope that they might add to my store of knowledge on some further day. It would take years before I could ask outright to hear, say, the third verse to some rambling epic for they might clam up and return to their thoughts, seeing me for what I was: a little townie spying on them and siphoning off their heritage. I learned how to size up their moods, for occasionally they would be expansive and wryly interested that I showed the least concern in what they had to say or sing about. More often than not, though, they were suspicious and shy and would tell me to bugger off, go seek out such knowledge from local experts such as Liz Jeffares of Kilmore or Paddy Berry of Duncormick, both of whom knew hundreds of "them bloody auld" songs.

Blushing to high heaven, my tail between my legs, I'd retreat behind some ditch or wall and leave them to their mumbling. Shuddering with suppressed fury at their guffaws, I'd try and decipher the dismissive words they employed about me; more often than not this would prove difficult for their gruff guttural tones were often miles beyond my comprehension. This was not just a matter of diction, for the people of that general area of Forth and Bargy had at one time their own distinctive language, *Yola*, a mixture of Middle English, French, Gaelic, and Flemish; and, though it had expired a hundred or more years previously, there were still odd words of the old tongue used locally – especially when the boss's grandson was snooping.

Many years later, while living in New York's East Village, with the drug dealers' cries and stray gunshots erupting below my window, I cracked open the first pages of Daniel Corkery's *The Hidden Ireland* and with a start recognized that as a boy I had stumbled upon my own surviving corner of that archaic world. It was fast disappearing even back then. Television would put the final nail in its coffin, but what a privilege and a prickly joy to have brushed up against this dissolving universe, however fleetingly, as it seeped off into the shadows.

Round about that time, I was making my first painful steps onto the stage. Too young to play at dances, I found that there was somewhat of a novelty market for Dylan/Donovan clones at the Sunday night variety concerts held in various country parish halls. No money changed hands for these feverish outpourings of tweenage folk-rock angst, but one could be plucked from home by a committee member, driven to somewhere in the back of beyond, given tea and a ham sandwich after one had less than wowed various widows, spinsters and a bored-out-of-his-skull parish priest, and then driven home, the tepid applause still tinkling in one's ears.

On one such occasion I encountered the redoubtable Mrs. Liz Jeffares backstage. I knew her by reputation and was both literally and figuratively blown away by a performance that had the old ladies leaping from their chairs and the parish priest stirring from his coma. It wasn't just that she was a wonderful *Sean Nós* (Old Style) singer; it was more that she inhabited her songs in a manner akin to the Mississippi blues musicians. Floored I may have been but I was not without some seeds of courage; when her admirers had dispersed I sidled up to her and inquired what would be the chances of her sharing with me the words of *The Rocks of Bawn*.

Though she had been the essence of jollity when surrounded by her fans, she sized me up in what seemed like a very mercenary manner. I feared she was about to tell me to shag off, but instead she took me by the hand and said she'd gladly swap me the words of this "auld come-all-ye," as she described it, if I would reciprocate by sharing "that new bit of a stave by the quare fellah from England with the long hair." It took me more than moments to establish that the song she was interested in was *Little Red Rooster* by the Rolling Stones. She said it was ten times better than *The Rocks of Bawn* any old day of the week - "leaves it in the tuppence-ha'penny place," if I remember her actual words. "It's way more to the point too," she added, "and a far sight easier to remember." I was astounded that she would actually have heard of The Stones, let alone have an appreciation of something so modern, but everyone listened to the "wireless" back then; and as for her love of the song, well that makes a lot more sense now too, for Liz Jeffares was a farming woman and well used to observing her own rooster lording it over the hens in her haggard.

Laurence Kirwan died in 1970. He never cared for music and would have been aghast if he had known that I'd make my living from such a precarious occupation. His one piece of advice to me was "always own your own property –

no matter what happens, they'll find it hard to throw you off that." His only wish was that Ballinagee be kept as a working farm. Whenever back in Wexford I will drive miles out of my way to avoid its 100 acres of memories, each square inch now cemented down with flimsy modern houses towering over its former lushness. I do go down to Tacumshane occasionally. It has long had new owners but they never put any pass on a redheaded solitary stranger roaming the deserted beach, humming old tunes while gazing across the dunes at a heap of stones where John Barry was supposedly born before he set off for fabled Philadelphia.

The Rocks of Bawn

Come all ye loyal heroes and listen on to me.
Don't hire with any farmer till you know what your work will be
You will rise up early in the morning from the clear day light till the dawn
And you never will be able for to plough the Rocks of Bawn.

My shoes they are worn and my stockings they are thin
My heart is always trembling now for fear they might give in
My heart is always trembling now from clear daylight till the dawn
And I never will be able for to plough the Rocks of Bawn.

Rise up, gallant Sweeney, and get your horses hay
And give them a good feed of oats before they start away
Don't feed them on soft turnip sprigs that grow on your green lawn
Or they never will be able for to plough the Rocks of Bawn.

My curse upon you, Sweeney boy, you have me nearly robbed
You're sitting by the fireside now, your feet upon the hob
You're sitting by the fireside now, from clear daylight till dawn
And you never will be able for to plough the Rocks of Bawn

I wish the Sergeant-Major would send for me in time
And place me in some regiment all in my youth and prime
I'd fight for Ireland's glory now, from the clear daylight till dawn
Before I would return again to plough the Rocks of Bawn.
                                        (Traditional)

CHAPTER TWO

Vinegar Hill

The sun was settin' the rocks on fire
The fields blisterin' with the heat
When the militia came marchin' through our town
Knockin' sparks off the little streets
The priest watched them from his front door
The sweat sparklin' on his skin
When they burned his little chapel down
He grabbed his missal and his gun

I must go down to Wexford town
Where the lightning cracks the air
And the people sing of freedom
They've banished all despair
The coward dies a million times
The freeman dies just once
So here's to you, revolution,
May your flame keep burning 'til
We meet our Armageddon
Up high on Vinegar Hill
                    (Larry Kirwan)

Wexford town didn't give a goddamn what anyone thought of it. In the current inter-connected world I've often wondered if it still feels the same. Back then the old town was self-contained and though it devoured news it was relatively unconcerned with the outside world. Stretching lazily outwards from the Slaney River, Wexford was flanked by two railway stations, no less – the North received passengers from Dublin, while the tearful South dispatched emigrants to nearby Rosslare Harbour where they caught the boat to Fishguard in Wales and then on by British Rail to London.

It was a rare family that didn't have relatives in London, Birmingham, Liverpool or a hundred other burghs throughout the UK. Wexford rarely gave a nod of the head to Dublin except to send a few of its brightest sparks up to molder in the civil service. When all was said and done, where would you sooner be? In some stuck-up provincial capital or across the pond in "the big smoke" where the shillings were plentiful, the biddies divine, the fashions the latest, and should bad luck hound your steps, wouldn't there be plenty of others with whom to raise a glass and douse your fractured dreams and sorrows?

Wexford had taken on all comers and subsumed Celt, Viking, Norman, Cromwellian, Hessian, Victorian and ultimately the English retirees who treasured its stolid citizenry, once inexpensive real estate and relatively mild temperatures. Henry II had done penance in Selskar Abbey for the murder of Thomas a'Beckett, Cromwell's roundheads had slaughtered its Catholic heretics, while a couple of doors down Lower George's Street, Bagenal Harvey and his revolutionaries

10

had held a celebratory dinner party after capturing the town in 1798. I hope the food was delicious for it was to be a short-lived triumph - they were all hung from the bridge when the English Redcoats retook the town soon thereafter. But that's neither here nor there; there's nothing quite like a tumultuous history to bequeath the old town's inhabitants a certain sense of themselves.

And Wexford, through thick and thin, has bustled along with a studied air of self-assuredness. Could that have stemmed from a general lack of interest in its hinterland? The town had been walled since the Viking days and gazed outwards over a broad estuary towards the sea. Nor did it confine its interest solely to nearby Britain or even Europe, no it set its cap to the world in general. Up until the early 20th century, when the harbor silted up, it had been a busy commercial port with trading routes to Scandinavia and the Low Countries, its ships even tacked way past the treacherous Bay of Biscayne into the Mediterranean and onwards deep into the Black Sea.

My own great-grandfather, Capt. Thomas Moran, had gone down in his three-master, with all-hands lost, off Lands End while returning from Odessa; and my father would sign on as a cadet with Reardon Smiths of Cardiff and spend the Second World War dodging German U-boats before crisscrossing various oceans for much of the rest of his life. These two and the many like them added their store of foreign experience to a town that already considered itself cosmopolitan; and like many before them they brought back the music they had heard in foreign ports and sowed its seed in the fertile lanes and back streets.

One rarely heard jigs and reels in Wexford but, in the course of a stroll down the narrow winding Main Street, you could encounter Puccini, Verdi, Gilbert &

11

Sullivan, Jimmy Kennedy, Paul Robeson, Buddy Holly, Elvis Presley, Lennon & McCartney and whatever was current on Radio Luxembourg or the BBC.

Jimmy Kennedy was a favorite of my father's and the sailors who frequented their own pubs near the quays, alas now bereft of schooners and steamers but not of memories and traditions. These men would have considered the slip jigs of Kerry and the fluid ornamental reels of Sligo about as cultured as the chants they had heard up the Congo River. Yet, it was a rare night you passed by one of these establishments and didn't hear a song written by the sophisticated Kennedy from Portstewart, Co. Derry. Not surprising, I suppose, since he wrote over 2000 of them, and they had been recorded by everyone from Vera Lynn to Elvis. When I first ventured with my guitar into these smoky dives as a teenaged accompanist for singsongs, the participants would gaze at you as though you might hail from a different planet were you unfamiliar with the chords of *South of the Border, The Isle of Capri* or *Red Sails in the Sunset*.

Need I mention that a little known quartet from Liverpool, while toiling away in the dingy nightclubs and strip joints of Hamburg, often crooned *Red Sails* in between Little Richard and Chuck Berry rockers? Not surprising really since this greatest of rock bands had distinct Irish connections, as do so many Liverpudlians. Three of the mop tops boast Irish descent. Then again the 'Pool was within spitting distance of Dublin and soaked up so many Irish immigrants during the famine years of 1845-47. Most of the poor unfortunates fleeing the country crossed over to Liverpool first to catch the coffin ships that would transport them to the US. Many, too weak or impoverished to go further, stayed on to man the factories and sweat shops springing up

12

throughout Lancashire in the bleak dawn of the industrial revolution. Wexford had its own distinct links with the birthplace of the Beatles. My grandfather's bullocks, indeed most Irish cattle, were shipped to nearby Birkenhead for slaughter; while a packet ship ran twice a week from Wexford to Liverpool carrying many from the back streets and lanes to seek their fortune and a new life in smoky Lancashire.

In fact when the Beatles hit the big time in early 1963, one of our local musicians, Aidan Ffrench, sent a demo tape to his cousin, George Harrison. Their grandfather, John Ffrench, had taken that emigrant boat to Liverpool in the 1890's carrying their musical genes with him. I can't remember if George ever replied; it matters little now, both cousins have passed on to the great Rock 'n' Roll band in the sky. Still, it's hard not to wonder if the Ffrench musical genes are once more stirring in some guitar-loving Liverpool or Wexford youth.

Apart from the occasional victory in the All Ireland Hurling Final, there was one event that united both Wexford town and country – the Rebellion of 1798. This heroic, but ultimately brutal insurrection, was to lead to a great store of songs that were shared by both townie and culchie. The shock waves from the French Revolution in 1789 belatedly reached Ireland, leading to the formation of the United Irishmen, a secret republican organization. The Irish were so enamored of their French comrades that they cut their hair short in the Parisian manner leading the English to brand them as "croppies." One of the most beautiful songs of the Wexford Rebellion, the Croppy Boy, would gain its name from this quirk of fashion.

Larry Kirwan

The Croppy Boy

*It was early, early in the spring \
The birds did whistle and sweetly sing
Changing their notes from tree to tree
And the song they sang was Old Ireland free.
It was early, early in the night,
The yeoman cavalry gave me a fright
The yeoman cavalry was my downfall
And I was taken by Lord Cornwall*

*As I was going up Wexford Street
My own first cousin I chanced to meet
My own first cousin did me betray
And for one bare guinea swore my life away.
And as I mounted the platform high
My aged father was standing by
My aged father did me deny
And the name he gave me was the Croppy Boy.*
(Traditional)

Ever aware of a seething Irish resentment and
now conscious that both Presbyterian and Episcopalian
had joined their Catholic neighbors in the ranks of the
United Irishmen, the English feared that Napoleon
Bonaparte might use Ireland as a base for invasion. In
1798 they resolved to lance the boil. They encouraged
local militias to ride herd on the people with the idea of
strangling any revolution before it could gather steam.

Martial law was declared in many areas and in
particular County Wexford with its integrated
population of Protestant landlords and Catholic tenant
farmers. Awaiting the arrival of a hoped-for French
expeditionary force, the United Irishmen bade their

14

time: landlords hid their caches of firearms in cellars and
outhouses, while the tenantry concealed their traditional
long pikes in the straw roofs of their cabins.

It was the hottest summer in memory, but oddly
enough, the spark that ignited the insurrection came
from a conservative priest who had spoken out against
the United Irishmen and all secret organizations. A
militia unit searching for arms in a farming area of
North Wexford, set fire to the small church of Father
John Murphy in Boolavogue. P.J. McCall wrote the
following verses that even in my time could still raise
the blood of both town and country.

Boolavogue

*At Boolavogue as the sun was setting
O'er the bright May meadows of Shelmalier
A rebel hand set the heather blazing
And brought the neighbours from far and near.*

*Then Father Murphy from old Kilcormac
Spurred up the rocks with a warning cry:
'Arm! Arm!' he cried, 'For I've come to lead you
For Ireland's freedom we'll fight or die!'*

*He led us on against the coming soldiers
The cowardly yeomen we put to flight
'Twas at The Harrow the boys of Wexford
Showed Bookey's regiment how men could fight.*

*Look out for hirelings, King George of England
Search every kingdom where breathes a slave
For Father Murphy of County Wexford
Sweeps o'er the land like a mighty wave.*

(PJ McCall)

15

The song had a special resonance in 9 Lower George's Street for my grandmother's people were related to General Thomas Cloney, the only leader of the Rebellion to survive. Cloney, an independent type, happened to be riding back to his farm in Moneyhore in North County Wexford when he encountered the first band of rebels led by Father Murphy. Apparently he was of two minds about revolution but, tired of local sectarian needling, threw in his lot with the rebels and soon became a leader. He fought in most of the major engagements including the bloody Battle of New Ross.

Taken captive after the defeat at Vinegar Hill, in a twist of fate, he was secreted off by a neighboring Protestant militia commander with whom he'd quarreled and who wished to "deal with him privately." While the other leaders were being hung from Wexford Bridge, Cloney awaited his own execution; but in the general chaos that engulfed the countryside his enemy could not make it back to the isolated barn where the general was imprisoned. In the interests of calming the country, the commander-in-chief of English forces, Lord Cornwallis, declared a moratorium on executions. After a period of imprisonment, Cloney lived to a ripe old age, a rebel to the end. Some of his relatives - seeking a more stable life - emigrated to the US, changed the spelling of their name, and begat the singer Rosemary Clooney and actor, George.

In the local Christian Brothers school we only learned of the gallant heroes and their ultimate defeat. Our lessons and heritage of songs did not reflect the sectarian violence unleashed on both sides, especially in the town of Wexford which changed hands twice leading to the murders of Protestants first and then, on an even greater scale, Catholics. Eventually, both town and country were "pacified" by the English army and local militias; their modus operandi included hanging or banishing to penal colonies anyone suspected of "croppy" sympathies.

Because of the ferocity of reprisals and general shame over sectarian brutality, people throughout the county shunned the subject of '98, as the insurrection was called. But in the late 19th century, PJ McCall, a nationalist songwriter, began to collect the memories, along with snatches of folk poetry and song that the older people were prepared to share. Even then he found that many Catholic tenant farmers and laborers were reluctant to speak to a stranger. But he was a persistent type and used the tales to craft powerful anthems that were sung at concerts, drawing rooms and pubs throughout both town and country.

Another poet and songwriter was John Keegan Casey. A revolutionary himself, he died at the age of 23 after suffering much deprivation when jailed for his part in the Fenian uprising of 1867. Although like most Wexford people I was raised on, and love, McCall's work; despite its power, however, there can be an element of journalism or agitprop that sometimes date his songs. Casey, however, had that rare touch of the poet for *The Rising of the Moon*, though written 150 years ago, has a strange contemporary power that still moves audiences whenever I sing it. I don't think Casey ever even visited the county but he certainly summed up the exhilaration and majesty of the tragic times that unified both Wexford town and surrounding countryside.

The Rising of the Moon

Oh, come tell me Sean O'Farrell, tell me why you hurry so?
"Hush a bhuachaill, hush and listen", and his cheeks were all
aglow,
"I bear orders from the captain - get you ready quick and soon
For the pikes must be together at the rising of the moon"

And come tell me Sean O'Farrell where the gathering is to be?
"In the old spot by the river, quite well known to you and me.
One more word for signal token - whistle out a marchin' tune,
With your pike upon your shoulder at the rising of the moon."

Out from many a mud wall cabin eyes were watching through
the night,
Many a manly heart was beating, for the coming morning
light.
Murmurs flashed along the valley to the banshee's lonely
croon
And a thousand blades were flashing by the rising of the
moon.

All along the singing river that black mass of men was seen,
High above their marching numbers flew their own beloved
green.
"Death to every foe and traitor! Whistle out a marching tune.
And hurrah, me boys, for freedom - 'tis the rising of the
moon!"

(John Keegan Casey)

18

CHAPTER THREE

Wexford Town

*My family lived in Wexford town, stopped traveling and
settled down,
Though my father kept a horse and car, we lived within the
town,
The people there misunderstood, or they did not know our
ways,
So with horse and car, back on the road, I began my traveling
days.*

*My father was called the Fiddler Dunne, and I'm a fiddler too,
But although I often felt his fist, he taught me all he knew,
I know I'll never be as good, and yet I feel no shame,
For the other things my father taught, I am proud to bear his
name.*

*He taught me pride and how to live, though the road is hard
and long,
And how a man will never starve, with a banjo, fiddle or song,
And how to fight for what I own, and what I know is right,
And how to camp beside a ditch on a stormy winter's night.*

Larry Kirwan

_O times were good and times were bad, and people cruel and
kind,
But what I learned of people then, has stayed within my mind,
I'll honor friends with all my heart, do for them all I can,
But I've learnt to go the road again, when they spurn the
tinker man._

_O Wexford is a town I like, but the traveling man they scorn,
And a man must feel affection for the town where he was born,
I know one day, that I'll go back, when my traveling days are
done,
And people will begin to wonder, what has happened to the
Pecker Dunne._
                                           (Patrick "Pecker" Dunne)

Fair Day was a great occasion although the
institution was already on its last legs in my
childhood. Farmers would drive their cattle,
sheep, pigs, and whatever else they wished to sell into
squares around the town. There they would encounter
cattle dealers, the like of my grandfather, along with
jobbers and farmers who would peruse their stock and
make early low bids - for you never knew who might be
in wretched straits and eager to strike a bargain; as the
day grew older all hands would repair to the
surrounding pubs until everyone was both desperate
and oiled enough to actually make a deal. Then out to
the square to make sure they were talking about the
same livestock, and once more back to the pub for the
settling drink, the spit in the palm before the binding
handshake, and then more drinks to wash down that
covenant.

The hullabaloo was tremendous. The lowing of
cattle, the drovers cursing as a frightened bullock hoofed
it down a narrow laneway, the whack of ash-plants off

20

the beast's back and rear end, the bark of dogs, the cries of children, and all the regular sounds of the town amplified to match the Fair Day's heightened adrenalin. To add fat to the fire, toss in the traveling singers, instrumentalists, storytellers, cardsharps, sweet sellers, matchmakers and every manner of trickster and shleeveen known to man - and a few known only to women. Some of these colorful souls were tinkers, now better known as travelers, a less specific, if more politically correct, name.

I have a memory of the great Margaret Barry, a tinker-woman who sang and played the banjo. I was very young and it was on the occasion of a big inter-county hurling match, another great social occasion. Maggie was a legend the length and breadth of Ireland and my maternal grandfather, Thomas Hughes, hoisted me on his shoulders so that I could catch a glimpse of her. A large crowd had gathered around this simple woman who exuded a strange air of stoic dignity as she gave forth with a song called *The Galway Shawl* that I only really became familiar with years later in the Bronx. Her voice was strong and cut through all the clutter; her Cork accent exotic, each word enunciated and delivered with clarity and restrained passion. People hung on her every syllable, and despite the noisy throng of passers-by, she had summoned an oasis of calm within the half-circle that arced around her. Talk about word of mouth; Margaret Barry had played so many fairs and match days that she was a household name, though considered too crude to be heard on the national *Radio Éireann* from which we got much of our news and music.

I loved fair days, but match days were their equal. They unleashed a wildness that took the old town by the scruff of its neck and shook it free of its slumbering

nonchalance. Wexford adored its hurlers, especially
when it seemed as though they might defeat their
archrivals, the mighty Kilkenny, and reach the All
Ireland Final. The cries of the vendors, the surge of
expectant faces up lanes and back streets towards the
Gaelic Athletic Park, the repressed excitement that
would erupt during sixty gasping minutes of belting and
pucking the *sliotar* up and down the grassy pitch,
hurleys splintering, blood spouting, with no thought of
personal safety by any participant – all of this inspired
the people to shrug off the patina of feigned
respectability imposed by church piety or latent
Victorian propriety. Suddenly you'd come face to face
with the old hidden Gaelic Ireland - the thorny outlines
of an ancient culture that doffed its cap to no one.

Many Irish people disdained this whiff of the
past, were embarrassed by it; while others relished the
temporary exultant freedom it bequeathed them. For
there was a madness to it, a license to be oneself and not
the controlled, quasi-English, modern person that
priests, teachers, and respectable society extolled and
expected. Though this anarchic other self could lay
dormant and unheeded for years, you never knew what
might ignite it. An old lyric that touched the heart or
some sudden frantic reel that set feet tapping often
provided the necessary spark. In a novel of mine,
Rockin' The Bronx, I write of such a moment in a staid
dancehall on Jerome Avenue in the Kingsbridge section
of the Bronx when the band breaks into a fevered
version of *King of the Fairies* as originally performed by
Horslips. The tune, or rather, the unhinged performance
unleashes a frenzy of mad dancing that breaks down the
normal social barriers and results in the beginning of a
relationship that would upend the life of the protagonist.

22

I've often felt that the Irish people were ill suited
to the two great religions foisted upon them – Jansenist-
tinged Catholicism and Calvinist Presbyterianism. Not
that there aren't good qualities in either faith, but the
gloomy, hell-fearing, pre-destined, puritanical nature of
both, to my mind, sits uneasily astride the skittering
spirit of the earthy Celt. Add the fading, genteel
Victorianism that lacquered Irish culture in my
boyhood, and the end result was an almost tangible
sense of repression that rattled around the lanes and
back streets of Wexford. There was the occasional rebel,
of course, but for the most part one accepted this foreign
conditioning, and none but the occasional alcoholic anti-
Christ or anti-clerical Marxist questioned it. I suppose
that's why I treasured the rare flashes of the hidden
Ireland; they might have been disturbing, even
threatening, but they were also liberating and exultantly
rewarding.

Patrick "Pecker" Dunne was born in Mayo but
raised in Wexford, as the song at the top of the chapter
states, but he had quit the town because of slights, both
real and, perhaps, imagined. Still, he always returned.
You would have forgotten about him, and then there
he'd be on the Main Street, brooding, playing, sneering,
singing, challenging the sedate citizens of Wexford to
question his allegiance to the town. He was a fine big
tinker man with a full head of black curls and a
particular independent way about him - an exotic cross
between a Mexican bandit and Zorba the Greek, yet he
reeked of that old hidden Ireland. He was as proud as a
summer dawn and exuded an air of devil-may-care that
signaled you might listen if you wished, but that he
didn't give a goddamn, one way or the other. He never
spoke in between songs, and while singing his eyes
glared off into the distance or followed his big fingers up

and down the banjo neck; then from out of nowhere
some notion would strike him and he'd sweep the
crowd with a piercing, if oddly disinterested, look.

I never spoke to him though I logged in many the
hour watching him, listening to and soaking up his
music. He wrote *Sullivan's John* - one of my favorite
songs ever. It tells the story of an outsider who joins the
tinker band and witnesses the hunger, displacement,
despair, violence, but also the rugged freedom of the
traveling life. There's a quality to it that's Dylanesque –
but it's more likely that the man from Hibbing,
Minnesota, appropriated this DNA from the Irish folk
songs and murder ballads that he immersed himself in;
like all great revelatory songs it allows you a front-row
glimpse of another world, wonderful to behold but
hardly one that you'd want to permanently inhabit.

Sullivan's John

Oh Sullivan's John, to the road you've gone
Far away from your native home
You've gone with the tinker's daughter
For along the road to roam
Ah, Sullivan's John you won't stick it long
Till your belly will soon get slack
You'll be roamin' the road with a mighty load
And a toolbox on your back

I met Katy Caffrey and her neat baby
All behind on her back strapped on
She had an old ash plant in her hands
For to drive her donkey on

Enquiring in every farmer's house
As along the road she passed,
Oh, where would she get an old pot to mend
And where would she buy an ass

There's a hairy ass fair in the County Clare
In a place they call Spancil Hill
Where my brother James got a rap of a hames
And poor Paddy they tried to kill
They loaded him up in an ass and cart
While Kate and Big Mary looked on
Oh, bad luck to the day that I went away
To join with the tinker band
(Patrick "Pecker" Dunne)

I never saw Pecker let his guard down. If he was
drinking or distracted you might get a peek into his life
but only for a split second before a curtain was drawn. I
don't think I even heard him speak all the times I saw
him performing on the Main Street, but one night I came
upon him outside Kielty's Pub just above Corn Market,
mere yards from my grandfather's house. He was
counting his money before entering. Kielty's was one of
the few pubs in Wexford that tolerated travelers; I
watched Pecker stride in to slake his thirst. It was a
warm evening and the door was open. Though very shy
I couldn't resist; I stuck my head in around the corner
and peered into the shadows.

He had bellied up to the bar and was ordering a
drink. A silence had descended on the house for the
Pecker was by this time a national figure. The great John
Huston had even cast him in a movie called *Sinful Davey.*
He neither looked left nor right but took his drink while
staring straight ahead. Eventually, a murmur arose,

someone pointed at the boy standing in the doorway and I ran for it. The Pecker never even glanced around.

As a Dublin wag once put it, "Wexford is famous for two things – strawberries and knackers." The latter is a pejorative name for travelers. It wasn't one that was employed in the Wexford of my youth. Indeed, tinkers were quite accepted within the town, and if one tended to keep ones distance, it was because they considered themselves a people apart. There was a feeling that a great wrong had been done to them – either by Cromwell or the hardships of the famine – that caused them to take to the roads. Our housekeeper, Miss Codd, called them "God's children" and wouldn't hear a bad word said about them.

My grandfather too respected them. Indeed, he was fond of them, for their love of stately memorials gave him the chance to sculpt ornate figures that his usual customers would have considered gaudy or too expensive. I often came upon him in his dusty office poring over pictures of statues and vaults, a slew of tinker men peering over his shoulder. He claimed that they had "a sense of the majesty of death." They also paid cash, often in advance, a fact that no doubt endeared them to him even more.

At a time that was very poor by today's standards, you could say that the tinker provided a valuable service. In a town more class conscious than Calcutta, even the lowest people on the Wexford social scale could look down on tinkers who no doubt had their own pecking order. Nothing was wasted back in those days. Clothes were handed down from sibling to sibling and when worn out were converted to cleaning rags – unless, one had a tinker. Ours was Mrs. Connors, a very decent woman, who arrived on our doorstep every month or so. We kept a bag of discards under the stairs, and Mrs. Connors would cart this off while calling down eternal protection on the household from all manner of saints and martyrs.

And yet, though we lived in close proximity to them, we knew little of the tinker world. They had their own language, or means of communication, called *Shelta* and could employ this to keep you at arm's length should they need to communicate in your presence. Most people had little interest in them anyway. They were just a fact of life, and decades could pass without you having any meaningful intercourse with them. For the most part they kept to themselves and were rarely seen in groups outside their camping grounds except when they ventured into town for weddings and wakes.

They had one major failing – the drink! For whatever reason, they appeared more susceptible to its darker side than the settled people of the town and this often led to communal feuding and fighting. Then again, that may be a perceived prejudice for God knows there were many instances of alcohol-fueled domestic and communal violence within our own townie ranks. Nonetheless, once you noticed a crowd of tinkers gathered, you tended to give them a wide berth for fear of the outbreak of a sudden battle.

At the age of thirteen or so I came upon one such gathering that was to change my life. On my way back from the Christian Brothers school to my grandfather's house, I often took a diagonal shortcut through the church grounds. This allowed me to come out on James Gate Street opposite Kielty's public house. To my surprise the narrow thoroughfare was jammed with tinkers, while even more of them spilled out the doors of the pub. I was of two minds whether to cut back through the church grounds or work my wary way through this foreign assemblage. However, they

appeared peaceful and would have cleared an instant
pathway for me in any case because they rarely tolerated
townies in their midst. But none of them paid the least
attention to me, all eyes were on the door of the pub,
then a hush descended upon them.

For once I was able to take their measure. They
were dressed in their Sunday best, and since none wore
black armbands I deduced they were celebrating a
wedding. I worked my way down the street until I
could catch a glimpse of what entranced them. One or
two looked at me suspiciously, but I pretended not to
notice and made as if to just push my way past. Then I
came upon a bunch of their children, all of whom were
holding hands; I settled uneasily amongst them and
followed their gaze.

A thin man dressed in a light brown suit, shiny
with grease and wear, sat on a flagstone with his back to
the pub doorpost. He had much drink taken, still his
eyes were clear and of the palest blue. A large bottle of
Guinness propped between his legs, he was patiently
waiting for total silence. One or two people still
muttered beneath their breaths, while a number of
others hissed, "whist," and glared at the offenders.
There was a drama to the affair and I could sense that a
tension existed between the gathering and this person
whom they obviously respected and perhaps even
feared.

He was tall for a tinker, and his long legs
stretched out over the path into the gutter. There was a
hawkish look to the man - his nose long and aquiline
dominated a leathery face that had seen the wear and
tear of many a wet winter's night. His hair, naturally
oily, seemed the color of dirty snow. He could have
been a young looking sixty or an old forty. His fingers
were long, and stained from tobacco, the tops of his nails

yellow. He held the bottle with one hand while the other rested on the filthy street. When he tossed his head back, a bitter pride creased his eyes; then he closed them, and the crowd stiffened and held its breath. He began to sing and the mournful tale changed my life. I had never heard its like. His voice was racked with the pain of experience in a way I've never heard since. It stayed in my brain for many years until one day in New York I put on a CD by Davy Spillane. My heart almost stopped when I heard Sean Tyrell sing and I was transported back across the years to the scene outside Kielty's. Some of the words were different, and I had added others to add sense to the story, but it was definitely descended from the same song – the same pain. It spoke of a woman called Molly Bán (white or blond) and of the great love one man had for her, how she left him in the still of the night for another, and how he would never get over the loss.

The song seared me, for it revealed that love was much more than the facile smiley-teary thing I had witnessed in countless movies at the Abbey Cinema or read about in books from the County Library. Love, I discovered, had much more in common with tragedy and heartbreak than happiness and contentment. Great love always has a cost, and unless one stumbles upon it at the exact right time and place, that price will be exacted to the fullest.

I added an instrumental section, a bridge, a verse and a closing line of my own for the song had taken on new dimensions while nestling in my memory. I was unafraid to do so because one night another man of traveler stock had lectured me about the necessity of such an action in the Eagle Tavern in New York City. Eddie Furey said, "Unless you give back to a song, it just gets stuck in time and withers away." I took him at his word. I had little choice in the affair and, anyway, there's always Davy and Sean's beautiful version should one need to hear the accepted, and perhaps original, version.

What matter! While that hawk-faced man sang, I was united with those tinker people. It only lasted four or five minutes at the most; still, I never sing this song but I'm swept back to the gathering outside Kielty's Pub and the sense of wonder that long dead tinker-man bestowed upon me all those years ago.

One Starry Night

One starry night as I lay sleepin'
One starry night as I lay in bed
I dreamed I heard wagon wheels a creakin'
When I awoke, love, I found you had fled

I'll search the highways, likewise the byways
I'll search the boreens, the camping places too,
I will inquire of all our people
Have they tide or tidings or sight of you

For it's many a mile, love, with you I've traveled
Many's the hour, love, with you I spent
I dreamed you were my love forever
But now I find you were only lent

I'll go across the sea to England
To London or to Birmingham
And in some public house I'll find you
Lamenting your lost love back home

I'm drunk today, I'm seldom sober,
A hadnsome rover from town to town
When I am dead, my story ended
Molly Bán, a stóirín, come lay me down

One starry night as I lay dreaming
One starry night as I lay in bed
I dreamed I heard wagon wheels a creakin'
Now that you're gone, love, I might as well be dead
                              (Traditional with additional
                    lyrics and melody by Larry Kirwan)

CHAPTER FOUR

Courtin' In The Kitchen

Come single belle and beau, unto me pay attention
Don't ever fall in love, 'tis the devil's own invention
For once I fell in love with a maiden so bewitchin'
Miss Henrietta Bell out of Captain Kelly's Kitchen

With me toora loora lie, and me toora loora laddy
With me toora looral lie, and me toora loora lady

(Traditional)

Neither my grandfather, Thomas Hughes, nor my Uncle Paddy sang to themselves which was very unusual in those days. Most people unselfconsciously hummed, whistled, lilted or simply belted out whatever song or tune that was on the tip of their tongues. There was no stigma whatsoever about this in Wexford; indeed, people were noted for their vocal offerings on the street, although at the same time, one did not wish to make too big a deal of it for fear of seeming boastful or, even worse, being labeled " a feckin' eejit."

My Uncle Paddy seemed to have no interest whatsoever in music; this was strange in itself, and would have caused much raising of eyebrows if he'd made any kind of big deal about it. But he knew better. There was a fine line between an acceptable oddness and the avalanche of scorn that attended sheer idiocy. Paddy was indeed the far side of odd but, due to his innate canniness, no one ever accused him of straying anywhere in the vicinity of out-and-out eejithood. Our housekeeper, Miss Codd, considered him more of a "street angel and a house devil," for she often felt the wrath of his tongue should an ironed shirt display a crease or his tea not be heated to the particular degree desired. Then again, that lady had a way with words and, though at times a shade narrow-minded, she perennially hit the nail on the head when a cool insult or sharp retort was required.

She had no notion of the term obsessive-compulsive with which Paddy would be tagged nowadays, but she was keenly aware that he was a large-sized pain in the arse who was ferociously moody and would brook not the slightest interference with his daily, weekly, and annual rituals. A creature of habit, he was more predictable than an East Village junky, and I could set my clock to the split second on his arrivals and departures from the big barracks of a house on George's Street.

He was, I suppose, impatiently awaiting my grandfather's demise for he worked and chafed under the old man's thumb in their headstone yard opposite the North Railway Station. This was a frigid place for at

least nine months of the year, and when the wind blew –
as it often did – clouds of lime and dust would arise
from the stone, the fine particles of which would end up
in your eyes, nose and particularly the back of your
throat; it goes without saying that the occupation of
stonecutter was one that could knock the fullness of joy
out of any man. Uncle Paddy did not bear his burden
with a lot of equanimity and there was a nagging
tension between him and my grandfather that from time
to time flared into outright hostility and even fisticuffs.

When I strayed into drinking myself at the
geriatric age of seventeen, I was staggered to find that he
was an extremely popular person in the bar of The
County Hotel – a haven of alcoholism frequented by
bank clerks, businessmen, publicans, teachers,
detectives, down-at-heel gentlemen farmers and a
hodgepodge of others whose only unifying characteristic
was that they considered themselves a social step or two
above the local riff-raff.

Paddy Hughes was considered "a character"
amongst this intrepid band of solace seekers: one who
listened to his acquaintances with a detachment that
bordered on the ironic or sarcastic depending on the
time of night and how deep he was into the four large
bottles of Guinness and two balls of malt that he
consumed religiously three hundred and sixty three
nights of the year – on Christmas Night and Good
Friday he consumed the same amount of Guinness at
home but refrained from the whiskey for some reason or
other, though I doubt it had anything to do with religion
or the good fellowship of the season. At the bar of The
County Hotel, he could be silent for hours amid the
bantering and slagging but, at a strategic lull in the
conversation, he would deliver a *bon mot* the like of
which would have the other patrons spluttering into

their drinks and howling with glee. And yet, he never hummed, whistled, sang or lilted in public or private. As Paul Simon put it, he was indeed "a most peculiar man."

I have a feeling - though unsubstantiated - that my grandfather quit singing whistling and humming after my grandmother died. He certainly knew a lot about music ranging from the grand operas of Puccini through the lighter fare of Gilbert & Sullivan, all the way down to the most banal come-all-ye. A devotee of Count John McCormack, he had witnessed the great tenor perform on many occasions. He very sadly confided in me, however, that he was forced to admit that Enrico Caruso had the beatings of the Count when it came to sheer vocal horsepower, not to mention sweetness of tone. This was by no means a popular or accepted opinion in Wexford, for people back then took their opera seriously, and McCormack was a national icon on a lofty plateau where Roy Keane, Charles Haughey, Christy Moore, U2 and various moving statues would later hang their hats.

Whatever about singing, whistling and humming, my grandfather made no bones of his regret that he never mastered a musical instrument. He blamed this both on the supernatural and a family by name of Kelly who lived close by when he was growing up in the town of Carlow. As a teenager he had come into possession of a fiddle and used to practice it late at night when the other members of his household had gone to bed – decent enough of him, I suppose, though I personally can't imagine sleeping through the scrapings and stutters of a neophyte fiddler. On one such night, he dropped the fiddle with fright when he heard the blood-curdling tones of a lady down the lane apparently in deep and dark despair. With his hair standing on end, he didn't even stoop to pick up the damaged instrument but hightailed it upstairs, and leaped beneath the blankets quicker than a West Side hooker. The next morning he was informed that old Mr. Kelly had passed away in the night and that the Banshee always paid a howling visit to that particular branch of the Kelly clan immediately before one of their number departed this mortal coil. Bad luck to the old moaning biddy! Had my grandfather not quit the instrument I might have been a fiddler of note today.

Miss Codd, our intrepid housekeeper, on the other hand, sang away with abandon in the kitchen and in every other part of the house too. In fact, I could always pinpoint her exact location by cocking an ear for her dulcet tones. She adored music, and by sheer osmosis, I picked up much of her vast repertoire. She was an appreciator of ballads and come-all-yes who knew every word of such standards as *The Boys of the County Armagh, The Homes of Donegal, Moonlight in Mayo,* you name it. That being said, she was not without appreciation for Elvis, Jim Reeves and "anything decent with a bit of a go in it," as she was wont to say. She also encouraged my own singing and would listen with great attention and no little sympathy as I labored to wrap my fingers and voice around the chords of some Beatles song.

What masters of the odd chord the boys from Liverpool were and what a world of music they opened up to me. 'Twas from them I learned to value the nuanced beauty of major, minor and diminished sevenths and all other such shadings that I employ in my own songs. As Mister Lennon once put it, "as soon as we learned a new chord, mate, we wrote a song around it." Ah, but you had a large sized touch of the poet too, Johnny, there's no denying that.

36

Miss Codd was my first audience. I would hear her pause in the hallway as I was belting out a Four Tops or Byrds favorite; shuffling from one high heel to the other, she would respectfully await my tortured conclusion before waltzing into the room and delivering *Paddy McGinty's Goat* or *Courtin' in the Kitchen* in a soaring soprano with more swoops and swoons than the Coney Island Cyclone. Over the years I ceased to distinguish any dichotomy between her old-fashioned repertoire and my own yearning for modernity, which leads me to conclude that this formidable lady was a major influence on my very catholic musical tastes.

The days of whistling, humming, lilting and outright belting were fast coming to an end, however, though we whistlers, hummers, lilters and belters were unaware of such an impending disaster. Everything, in fact, was changing because of the introduction of television. It wasn't exactly that the new medium snuck in by shelter of night. Far from it; we were all well aware of its insidious pleasures, though not of its effects.

A number of the more prosperous households could already receive BBC-TV whose rays seeped over the sea from England; these upscale houses were easily distinguished by the large pitchfork-like aerials mounted on their chimneys. Reception, however, was mixed at best. Then, in 1962, the Irish government introduced *Raidió Teilefís Éireann* (RTE), its own homegrown station. The day had been much anticipated, and as the anointed first broadcast time of 6pm approached, the country lurched to a halt. Those who had not purchased a television rented one, while the great unwashed who could not afford such luxury stood transfixed five and six deep in the streets around the windows of the newly minted television rental stores.

I can no longer remember the name of the first program broadcast on RTE, but I vividly recall the overwhelming favorite in the house on George's Street. Every week both my grandfather and uncle gazed in rapt attention, and with a regard akin to awe, as Mister Ed, a loquacious American horse, talked his way into our affections. Even Miss Codd used to poke her head around the dining room door to catch a glimpse of this equine wonder – this was a rarity for, given her position in the household, she did not dine with us or sit by the fire of an evening. Indeed the only other time I had witnessed her take her ease with us was while craning her ear to a distorted broadcast from Vatican Radio while awaiting news of the death of Pope Pius XII.

No one foresaw the effect television would have on Irish life, perhaps because the social niceties of talking, visiting, gossiping, whistling, singing, lilting and other forms of self-expression and entertainment appeared to be embedded bone deep in our national psyche. What threat then from these first broadcasts - a mere three hours a night? No matter what the content of the mostly American imported programs, they were ushered in at 6pm with the a toll of a bell and the recitation of the Angelus – a fact that must have thrilled our Southern Protestant brethren while, no doubt, providing ammunition to the Rev. Ian Paisley whose rabble rousing career was just afoot in the North of Ireland.

One, however, should have taken note that people had begun staring at the official rigid screen-saver during the day while listening to the accompanying classical music. The addiction became more pronounced as the years passed when people would justify the buying or renting of a TV set by

stating, "sure won't I be saving money by staying in at night rather than wasting it at the pub or the pictures."
  If the house on George's Street came to a full stop for Mister Ed, it slithered to a more stately pause for a weekly Sunday afternoon performance by Seán Ó'Riada and Ceoltóirí Chualann. Ó'Riada had only recently gained fame as the composer of the epic soundtrack to *Mise Éire* – a film that concerned the founding of the Irish State. The footage of the struggle that culminated in the War of Independence 1919-1921 was stirring in itself, but Ó'Riada's music had an even profounder effect.
  I can well recall being marched from the Christian Brothers School across town through the narrow streets to the Abbey Cinema. As happens when hundreds of boys are unexpectedly liberated from their disciplined drudgery, spirits were high and the stately Abbey rocked from the racket of short-pantsed high jinks. Yet, within seconds of the lights dimming, we were awed into silence by the majesty of the music.
  Ó'Riada had led a rather quixotic life. Born in County Limerick, his boyhood was drenched in traditional Irish music. From an early age he showed signs of musical promise and received formal classical training. A rebel of sorts, he had fled Ireland for Paris with the intention of becoming a composer. Living the bohemian life in a garret, he wrote a number of pieces in a formal European style. Eventually, his wife, Ruth, tracked him down and talked "some sense into him," as a colleague of the time stated, although it's also reported that he said to her, "I'd rather be breaking stones in Ireland than be the richest man living in Europe". In any event, he returned with her to Ireland chastened, if hardly straightened, became musical director for the

Abbey Theatre and began to cast old Irish melodies in a classical setting.

Nothing had prepared the country for the sheer beauty and power of these somewhat shop-soiled tunes when they soared within Ó'Riada's dramatic orchestral arrangements. Melodies that we had come to accept as almost white noise background to our everyday lives now came thundering out of the Abbey Cinema's house speakers in the flickering darkness. The grainy black and white footage added to the effect as we watched familiar heroes stride across the celluloid, mostly to their doom.

Many lives were affected by Ó'Riada's music for *Mise Éire* – mine for definite! In fact, it could be argued that a spark was struck in certain hearts that would become a fire ten or more years later in the resistance to British rule in the North of Ireland. Whatever about such speculation, Ó'Riada became an instant and unlikely national hero.

I suppose that's why my grandfather, uncle and I religiously watched Ó'Riada's series of shows on RTE every Sunday afternoon. I still get an almost physical sense of contentment when I recall those occasions. Miss Codd was responsible for serving up three meals a day, except on Thursdays and Sundays when she was free to come and go as she pleased from 2pm onwards, thereby skipping six o'clock tea which became my dilatory responsibility. I can only imagine how serving up the other nineteen meals per week could drive someone to distraction – and to top it all, Uncle Paddy was a picky and unpredictable eater - much given to shoving a plate load of food away and on occasion striding out of the room with a muttered, "nine hours a day of freezing my arse off in that bloody yard and then to be expected to eat this load of tripe!"

This would occasion our aggrieved housekeeper to fire her dishrag at the sink, in a manner not unlike Roger Clements' fastball, before racing up the three flights of stairs and slamming her bedroom door almost off the hinges. A deathly silence would follow, broken only by the rustle of my grandfather's newspaper or the gnash of his dentures as he stoically ate and read on. For my part, I would stare at the far wall and mentally pick my way through some song or other, for I had learned the hard way that silence was a virtue on such occasions. I wonder now why I've always failed to employ this strategic tactic in my own adult dealings with outraged ladies.

Paddy never misbehaved on Sundays. Perhaps that was because Miss Codd pulled out all the stops for the dinner that was served on the stroke of 1pm. And, no doubt, her culinary strivings have something to do with my pleasant memories of Ó'Riada's traditional Irish programs on RTE. There were no surprises with Miss Codd's menu choices. Her *piece de résistance* was roast lamb; this delight would be followed on successive Sundays by roast pork and roast chicken and then back to lamb again and so on, and so forth, and so fifth, as John Lennon might say. All of these dishes were served with roast potatoes, boiled carrots and turnips.

The one divergence from this regime was the addition of a tangy green mint sauce with the lamb. Dessert, which we called "sweet," was an undistinguished pudding that she concocted from pieces of stale bread left over from the week. This concoction had need of much sugar and jam, I remember, but whatever its taste, the heavy sogginess of the dish put a certain contented seal on the occasion. Then, while taking tea and perhaps a Jacob's biscuit or two, all three of us would loll in our armchairs and watch the great

41

Ó'Riada haul traditional music out of the bog and onto the concert stage.

To my memory, never a word was spoken between us regarding the shows, although we watched all of them with a dull fascination that I later recognized in porn addicts. Was it Ó'Riada's national reputation, his genius, the novelty of hearing traditional music on Irish television, or could it have been some form of patriotic statement, because my grandfather and uncle shared a fervent, if covert, belief in the Irish Republican cause? I don't know and I wish I'd asked. Uncle Paddy wouldn't have even entertained such a question from a "trumped up know-it-all," the like of me. My grandfather, however, spoke to me of many things – some of which I had no desire to hear, especially when he was drinking – but as with many matters, I have left it too late, for they're both long gone and little remembered.

I had no idea at the time that Ó'Riada had an interest in and experience of so many different forms of music. Apart from being a fine pianist, I've heard it rumored that he even tried his hand playing drums with various *Céilí* and Jazz bands. I am told that he longed to be accepted for his classical European type compositions, but one would not have known any of this from the Sunday afternoon programs. He usually played harpsichord, and to the best of my memory, was surrounded by a group of musicians that included an uilleann (Gaelic for elbow) piper, a couple of fiddlers, a flautist, and a bodhrán player (the hand-held Irish goatskin drum). This was a far cry from his soaring, thundering *Mise Éire* music and yet was unlike anything that I'd ever heard before.

All three of us in the room were familiar with *Céilí* bands, and there were some great ones; yet, these were essentially dance ensembles who tended to use trap drums and a piano for rhythm with various accordions, whistles, fiddles and the like going at it hell for leather with the noble intention of getting everyone in the hall up on their feet and stomping through *The Walls of Limerick, The Siege of Ennis* and any number of other set pieces.

Ó'Riada's *Ceoltóirí Chualann* was austerity personified compared with the general jubilance of the *Céilí* bands. To my mind, he had incorporated the ideas of some of the great jazz groups, particularly those of Miles Davis, for there was a quality of silence throughout Ó'Riada's offerings that I later came to recognize in *Kind of Blue*. Now I had never even heard mention of Miles at the time, although Satchmo - Louis Armstrong - was a god in Wexford, and I have no idea if Ó'Riada ever caught wind of the stormy, mercurial Davis either. He didn't need to, for I'm of the mind that times breed and breathe certain atmospherics, as it were. In the 1970's, many people in downtown Manhattan sang in a style that became popularized by David Byrne of Talking Heads. I certainly did, and it was through no influence of Mr. Byrne's; I know that because I was at CBGB's during the Heads' first Bowery appearance and noted David's yelping style which I had already heard from the like of Tom Verlaine of Television among others.

Ó'Riada conducted *Ceoltóirí Chualann* in an intense but very unfussy manner. He would often begin a piece with a couple of nods for tempo, then a handful of chords on his harpsichord; an instrument, say the pipes, would play a melody for a verse or two before being joined by a fiddle in unison, or occasionally harmony or counterpoint; both might then take a break whereupon the flute would take up the melody and be

43

coupled with a tin whistle, until eventually all of the instruments would enter to finish off the piece. But there was a restraint that we were unfamiliar with and a lack of melodrama. The slow pieces were indeed soaked with regret and longing, but it was of a dry-eyed character almost startling in those days.

Ó'Riada resisted the urge to spice any arrangement with dance-hall style theatrics. His climaxes were always controlled, and I wonder now if he had fallen under the influence of Yeats' dictum that "poetry should be as cold and passionate as the dawn." Or perhaps all great artists instinctively understand this "secret rule" and know how to put it into practice. As I write this and mention Yeats, I am aware of a veil of my own slipping away and am beginning to understand why all three of us sat so rapt on those Sunday afternoons; by stripping away all the extraneous calcification, Ó'Riada's music offered us a glimpse of a hidden place where it was possible to experience contact with the authentic Irish soul.

I had no idea that one day I'd become friendly with Paddy Moloney who was the piper with *Chualann*. In fact, long before Ó'Riada disbanded the group, some of the members under Moloney's leadership recorded as The Chieftains. There are times when I listen to the Chieftains, particularly in their quieter moments, when I'm reminded of the austere splendor of Ó'Riada's ensemble, but times change and great bands can neither afford, nor wish to, stand still. And yet, there's a living direct line between the Chieftains and *Ceoltóirí Chualann*. Do yourself a favor and listen to *Mná na hÉireann* by The Chieftains. This is Moloney's arrangement of a poem by Peadar Ó'Doirnín set to music composed by Ó'Riada – with *Chualann* it was usually sung by a guest vocalist, in particular Seán Ó'Sé.

Either way it's a magnificent soulful melody. With no disrespect to Ó'Riada, I often wonder if he didn't adapt it from some old Irish tune, for it seems to be of a different time and space, and touches me in a way that no contemporary melody does. Then again, perhaps that's pure envy speaking, for I am equally moved by Puccini's *Nessun Dorma*, and that wasn't conceived back in the mists of time either.

The other innovation that Ó'Riada introduced was the now much maligned *bodhrán*. Of course, *bodhrán* playing has been refined over the years and certain musicians can extract almost symphonic sounds from this rudimentary instrument – take a listen to John Joe Kelly of Flook, for instance. But Ó'Riada, probably because he had been a trap drummer, had the *bodhrán* up front, and central to the rhythm of *Chualann*. This prominence would horrify many contemporary traditional outfits, but there's an earthiness to *Chualann's* arrangements, a powerful drive that still sets them apart from the vast majority of the traditional ensembles that have come since. Listen to *Live at the Gaiety* for the open-skinned power of the performance. I believe Peadar Mercier had taken over *bodhrán* duties at this stage and he is the center of the band in much the same way, dare I say it, as John Bonham was in Led Zeppelin.

The singer on that particular night was Sean Ó'Sé. A trained tenor who knew his stagecraft, it's interesting to hear how he contains any staginess or theatrics as he sublimates himself to Ó'Riada's influence. And yet, there are heartbreaking moments of loss and longing that he coaxes forth, particularly on *Carrickfergus*. This beautiful Irish blues later became so abused and hackneyed that it would only be attempted by the very drunk late at night in pubs when a surfeit of pints had put paid to any notion of taste.

45

But listen to the rendition on *Live in the Gaiety*
with alternating verses of English and Irish. Was it
Ó'Riada or Ó'Sé who initially combined the translated
English lyrics with the original 18ᵗʰ Century 'Do Bhí Bean
Uasal', ('There Was a Noblewoman'), written by the poet
Cathal Buí Mac Giolla Gonna. Rumor has it that actor
Peter O'Toole sang the English lyrics to Dominic Behan
who may have written the second verse. Whatever the
origin, the mood in the Gaiety in 1969 is somber and
takes us back to a different time; indeed one forgets the
live setting until there's a distant whoop on the line,
"I'm drunk today but I'm oft times sober…" It's one of
those magical moments when you're yanked from the
past into the present and not without some pleasure.

I remember no such moments back in the house
on George's Street as Ó'Riada's music was transforming
three very disparate people. Two of them have long
since passed on, so I'd have to hazard a guess as to what
they were thinking. But I only have to summons those
balmy afternoons to prove that music allows us to
transcend our venal settings and limitations, and puts us
in touch with things that we can otherwise only dream
of.

Carrickfergus

I wish I was in Carrickfergus,
Only for nights in Ballygrant
I would swim over the deepest ocean
The deepest ocean for my love to find
But the sea is wide and I cannot swim over
And neither have I wings to fly
If I could find me a handsome boatman
To ferry me over to my love and die

My childhood days bring back sad reflections
Of happy times I spent so long ago
My boyhood friends and my own relations
Have all passed on now like melting snow
But I'll spend my days in endless roaming
Soft is the grass and sure my bed is free
Oh, to be back in Carrickfergus
On that long mountain road down to the sea

But in Kilkenny it is reported
On marble stones there as black as ink
With gold and silver I would support her
But I'll sing no more now till I get a drink
I'm drunk today and I'm seldom sober,
A constant rover from town to town
Ah, but I'm sick now, my days are numbered,
Come all ye young men and lay me down

(Traditional)

CHAPTER FIVE

Brennan On The Moor

'Tis of a famous highwayman
A story I will tell
His name was Willie Brennan,
And in Ireland he did dwell
And on the Kilworth mountains
He commenced his wild career,
Where many a wealthy gentleman
Before him shook with fear.

And it's Brennan on the Moor,
Brennan on the Moor.
Bold brave and undaunted
Was young Brennan on the Moor.

One day upon the highway,
As Willie he went down,
He met the Mayor of Cashel
A mile outside the town:
The Mayor he knew his features;
"I think, young man," said he,
"Your name is Willie Brennan;
You must come along with me."

Now Brennan's wife had gone to town,
Provisions for to buy,
And when she saw her Willie,
She began to weep and cry;
He says, "Give me that tenpenny,"
As soon as Willie spoke,
She handed him a blunderbuss
From underneath her cloak.

Then with his loaded blunderbuss,
The truth I will enfold,
He made the Mayor to tremble,
And robbed him of his gold;
One hundred pounds was offered
For his apprehension there,
So he with horse and saddle
To the mountains did repair.

(Traditional)

Wexford to Carrick-on-Suir in Country Tipperary is scarcely more than fifty miles and can be accessed in an hour or thereabouts on the broad main roads that became ubiquitous in Ireland after the country's integration with the European Economic Community. Back in the early '60's though such a trip would have taken closer to three hours. It would have been an adventure of sorts and one not taken lightly – sandwiches would have been packed along with a thermos filled with hot, sweet tea. To make an event of it, a stop for dinner might have been planned for the return journey, usually at a hotel restaurant in Waterford or New Ross, as much to crown the day's proceedings as to break the journey.

I took a number of such trips between these two very different towns with both of my grandfathers. Laurence Kirwan often traveled this route to buy cattle from a friend, John Kehoe, who ran a butcher's shop in Carrick, while Thomas Hughes occasionally erected a headstone in the local cemetery.

Both were stately drivers who tended to run with the flow of traffic. Although men of very different temperaments, they would be astounded by the current phenomenon of road rage. Both could be rather taciturn until either fueled with whiskey or inspired by a good conversation, and each placed a high premium on courtesy, as did most people of their generation. Thus, should a car be moving slower than their normal cruising speed of forty or so miles per hour, they were inclined to remain in its wake and use the opportunity to gaze upon whatever sights the countryside afforded them – and many were available to the seasoned eye.

Each would without question or comment pull over to the grassy verge so as not to alarm an approaching herd of cows; or if the animals were traveling in the same direction, they would nudge their cars past bespattered behinds with due deference. Speed, as you can tell, was not of paramount importance; rather they considered themselves guests on the road who should behave accordingly; they would eventually get to their destination, and if they were delayed for minutes or even hours, then so be it – the road, after all, had much to offer.

Both randomly picked up hitchhikers and would engage them in detailed conversation; this presented little problem because it was considered the responsibility of the passenger to gauge the mood and inclination of the driver and keep him entertained. One could learn much from these travelers, as they were usually locals who only needed to skip a couple of miles up the road. They would relay pieces of information - never to be found in books - regarding skirmishes in the political or personal arena, the idiosyncrasies of the inhabitants, appearances of ghosts or Virgins (spiritual and otherwise), and the general lay of the land, as it were.

Both grandfathers would listen intently to these facts, incorporating them into their own knowledge of the area, usually vast in and of itself. Even now, when speeding down one of these main drags, a forgotten fact or rumor will prick my memory, and sure enough I'll look out and notice some fairy *rath*, or a tree upon which some patriot was hung, or a house that boasted some scandal in a previous century. I often wonder if the younger inhabitants of the area have any notion of these facts, although their seniors surely do; for conversation was highly valued back in those days – although the entertainment quotient was important, chat was also a way of sharing knowledge, a treasure back in a time when earthly riches were scarce.

As the shadows lengthened on the way home, it was not rare to have a Volkswagen passenger-van whiz by like a rocket on the narrow roads. Packed to the gills with men wearing suits, the vehicles were usually top heavy - a tarpaulin lashing down amplifiers, suitcases and a kick drum to the roof rack. These were the showbands speeding to ballrooms in every town, village, back of beyond and middle of nowhere. It's difficult to explain the phenomenon of these very particular musical outfits now, or their vast appeal; suffice it to say they were a unique brand of homegrown Irish entertainment and in many areas the only form thereof.

Just as Rockabilly sprung from the social conditions of the Southern US states in the mid-1950's, in a somewhat similar, if less original, parallel so too did showbands emerge in the Ireland of that era. Rural areas in general, and most urban centers too, were plagued by emigration. The country had stagnated under the protectionist policies of successive governments since the formation of the Irish Free State in 1922. Conversion to a Republic in 1948 did little to improve matters. Hundreds of thousands had already emigrated by the early '50's when the floodgates opened anew with many heading to Eisenhower's USA, but most taking the boat to the UK then in the midst of reconstruction after World War Two.

Social conditions in Ireland were stifling – the Catholic Church had a lock-hold on the country with the ecclesiastical authorities calling the shots – indeed, in 1951, Dr. Noel Browne was forced to resign as Minister for Health for daring to propose a Mother and Child scheme that would have guaranteed free pre-natal care and comprehensive health coverage for all children up to the age of fifteen. Though Irish infant mortality rates were appallingly high, this Act was deemed to be contrary to Catholic social and moral teaching; the real apprehension of the church authorities appeared to be that such usurpation of civil authority would eventually lead to the introduction of state approved contraception and even abortion.

Dr. Browne had already caused much unease in ecclesiastical circles by what was considered his heavy-handed, though successful, campaign to eradicate the curse of Tuberculosis in the country. Against this backdrop of civil and ecclesiastical strife, showbands seemed to appear from nowhere; but, as ever, the roots of any music, no matter how unoriginal, spring from deep within a community's conditioning and culture. Immersed as it was in the social life of the country, the Catholic Church could not help but play a role in the rise of showbands.

Showbands, though, owed much of their origins to the American big band. The Glenn Miller Orchestra, among others, had become popular in Irish urban areas during World War Two with such hits as *In The Mood* and *Moonlight Serenade*; Miller's tragic death in an air crash in 1944 only added to his legend. Thus, in the post-war years each Irish town sported some modified form of big band which might contain a section – drawn from the local marching brass and reed band - of saxophones, trumpets and trombones; these would be augmented by a couple of string players, and a set of trap drums allied with a piano for rhythm. Like their American counterparts, all members - except for the vocalist - sat and read their notated parts from music stands.

In 1958, however, a band from Donegal, the Clipper Carlton, kicked aside their stands, stood up and revolutionized entertainment in Ireland. Not only did the Carlton stand up but they danced – or, at least, moved in syncopation, thereby originating the infamous "showband shuffle." Some were horrified at this lewd innovation, but not the young who had already been introduced to Elvis the Pelvis on radio, nor the emigrants who returned from London every Christmas

and summer with Eddie Cochran, Buddy Holly, Gene
Vincent and Bill Haley 78's and 45's.

Up until then, bands tended to play within a
twenty or thirty-mile radius of their own localities, but
the Clipper Carlton quit their day jobs, toured the
country and caused a sensation. In a matter of years, the
only musicians still sitting were those too inebriated to
stand up. The new combos were called showbands
because they put on a show, and the better the show, the
more people turned out to see them. Fired by the
success of the Clippers many other outfits began to
extend their radius from home. This led to them cutting
their numbers to more manageable proportions, for how
many musicians and their instruments could fit in a
Volkswagen van.

A pruning of sorts occurred that ultimately pared
showbands down to sax, trumpet, trombone, drums,
and the newest innovation - an electric guitar, for it was
hard to swivel like Elvis without Scotty Moore licks
driving you, or sound like Cliff Richard, his British
imitator, without Hank B. Marvin's tremolo pealing
behind you. Oh, and not to forget a bass guitar, for
pianos were notoriously out of tune in the parish halls of
Ireland; besides, if keyboards were your thing, to hell
with the big old clunky piano, bring on the recently
introduced sleek and portable Farfisa or Vox Continental
electric organ.

And so, the standard showband was born, with a
lead vocalist thrown in. More often than not, however,
an instrumentalist often stepped forward and took on
those duties - as with Brendan Bowyer, trombonist and
most famous of all showband lead singers. Do I sound a
tad biased? Well, not really, though they were from
nearby Waterford city. Through dint of the excitement
caused onstage by Bowyer during his hip-shaking Elvis

imitations, the Royal were soon acclaimed the number one showband in the country. They had a huge following in Wexford: the Parish Hall would be packed so tight it was literally impossible to move once on the dance-floor. This may sound somewhat restrictive but it had its advantages, for, in essence, it was how many of us got our first taste of sex – at least, with another person. Once you had succeeded in enticing a young lady onto the floor for a set of dances, you had little choice but to hold on for dear life and be melded to her for the next ten or twelve minutes. Thus did Brendan Bowyer endear himself to a whole generation of horny adolescents and play a major part in introducing the sexual revolution to Ireland.

What kind of music did showbands play? Everything, and I'm not really exaggerating – having been a member of a couple of unheralded combos in the declining days of their era. Well, maybe not everything, but certainly any tune that had entered the Top Twenty as counted down every Sunday night on Radio Luxembourg. There was but one caveat: the song had to be danceable, but it was a rare tune that Irish audiences could not jive, waltz, foxtrot, shuffle or just plain stagger around to. Thus, no matter how deplete of musical chops, one quickly became familiar with rock, jazz, swing, folk, polka, tango, shimmy-shimmy, Watusi or whatever else was heard on those golden Sunday nights on "the station of the stars" – beamed all the way across Europe from the Royal Duchy of Luxembourg.

Those of us laboring in the trenches didn't put much pass on it at the time, but showband members received a very sound grounding in music because of the sheer variety of genres that one had to at least gain a smidgen of proficiency in. This may have had something to do with the technical prowess and sheer musical eclecticism of such showband alumni as Van Morrison, Rory Gallagher, Tommy Makem, Pierce Turner, Henry McCullough of the Joe Cocker Band and Keith Donald of Moving Hearts. For unlike those who got their start in garage bands and mostly tended to play in the keys of E and A, or folkies who could turn to a capo, a showband "head" – as he was commonly known - had to know his way around every key in which a Top Twenty song was performed. Added to this, Irish horn players preferred, whenever possible, to play in the keys of C, F and G, necessitating that we guitarists match them a tone lower in the finger twisting chords and scales of Bb, Eb and F.

And oh, those horn players! In my brief showband stint I chafed beneath their technical expertise, antediluvian sound (to my then untutored ear), not to mention their idiosyncratic behavior and sheer snobbishness towards anyone even remotely connected to "a hunk of wood with six strings hangin' off it." But when we came to form Black 47, I had, at least, a rudimentary idea of how horns should sound, where they should be positioned in a song, and which part of the pocket they should occupy.

But let us return to pristine Carrick on the banks of the lovely River Suir in County Tipperary. Though set amidst prosperous farmland, the small market town had suffered its share of woe from the curse of emigration. Two of its inhabitants, Tom and Paddy Clancy, seeing little future in post-war Ireland, set out to seek theatrical fame and fortune in America leaving behind their younger brothers, Bobby and Liam. They had grown up singing the Irish folk songs and ballads of the local Comeragh Mountains and been introduced to the *Sean Nós* vocal style of the Irish-speaking *Gaeltacht* in nearby Ring and Helvick Head in Co. Waterford.

Baby of the family and budding musicologist, Liam, was hired by Diane Hamilton - a New York friend of Paddy's - to traverse Ireland recording and notating the fast disappearing ballads and folk songs. It was while visiting Keady in Co. Armagh that he first encountered Tommy Makem, son of a well-known singer and song collector, Sarah Makem. The two young men immediately struck up a friendship united by their interest in preserving folk music; however, there seemed little future in knocking a living out of such an archaic pursuit in the Ireland of 1959, and so both Liam and Tommy, independent of each other, emigrated to the US within a month's span. Liam figured he would take a shot at theatre since both Tom and Pat had found some success on the stages of Greenwich Village. Tommy, the hardheaded and more pragmatic Northerner, sought industrial work in New Hampshire but injured his hand in a factory accident, whereupon he headed south to see what fortune might offer in New York City.

Acting work, as ever, was scarce enough, so for pints, shots and general craic the Clancy's and Makem began singing and exchanging ballads in the back rooms of the White Horse Tavern - where Dylan Thomas some years previously had one too many whiskeys - and the Lion's Head in Sheridan Square, home of journalists, communists, seamen, and sundry writers with various drinking problems. They fit in handily with the many folk singers who were migrating to the Village, among them Bob Dylan who claimed that Liam was the best ballad singer he had ever heard. They began to score dates in various uptown clubs and one bitterly cold day while visiting their manager, Marty Erlichman, they wore the four white hand-knit Aran sweaters that Mrs. Clancy had sent them as protection against the frigid New York winters. Erlichman, instantly recognizing a gimmick, insisted that from that moment forth they only remove those sweaters in the privacy of their beds.

With the release of a couple of albums of ballads and drinking songs, they were making a name for themselves in New York, Chicago and Boston when they were noticed by a talent scout and given a spot on the Ed Sullivan Show on March 2nd, 1961. As luck would have it, the headliner had to pull out and the boys substituted for fourteen glorious minutes before 80 million people. Practiced in holding a stage, confident, direct and with the actors' magnetic eye for the camera, The Clancy Brothers and Tommy Makem became an overnight sensation. John Hammond, who happened to be watching, signed them to Columbia Records for $100,000 – monumental money in those days – and an absolutely astronomical sum for the boys from Carrick and Keady. They achieved something else no less stunning: they changed the way Irish-America listened to music – kicking Danny Boy with his Irish Eyes Smiling along with Mrs. Murphy's Chowder and Paddy McGinty's Goat into the middle of Galway Bay.

The songs they performed were a revelation. They sang of highwaymen and rebels, patriots and hustlers, noble drunks, and floozies who would someday – given half a chance – turn into virtuous mothers. The Clancy Brothers and Tommy Makem were handsome and passionate, intense and patriotic, swashbuckling and celebratory. They had poetry at their fingertips, and the theatrical delivery to make the words on a page come dancing off the stage in a new and sparkling light. Makem was authoritative, powerful and earnest, while Liam had an ache in his voice and an infinitesimal silence between his words that still has the power to take one's breath away. Tom and Paddy, though sometimes overlooked because of the talent of the two youngsters, sang with a rare passion and a commitment to the material; they added two other ineffable qualities: consummate timing and the actor's power to make everything more than it actually is. As can happen, one moment of inspiration can meld together all the different qualities and characteristics that individuals bring to a group and bond them together into a sound. I'll let Liam Clancy describe such an occasion. "Brennan on the Moor was a famous old ballad but it was sung mournfully. We were in this apartment in Greenwich Village and I was sitting on this couch that had springs in it. And I said 'Let's try and belt it out like the Highwaymen. Get the sound of galloping horses." And so he sang while bouncing up and down on the springs creating what he considered the sound of a galloping horse. That allegorical horse would soon carry the foursome into musical history with a definitive stop at Carnegie Hall.

Take a listen to the reissued *In Person at Carnegie Hall* from St. Patrick's Day 1962. It's as good a live recording as you're ever likely to hear. These guys were not only powerful and authentic, but like Jack Kennedy they recognized early on that presentation would be a key factor in the new television age. Many of the songs may seem hackneyed now from years of drunken bellowing and semi-parody in pubs, parties and festivals, but back in the early 1960's most of the audience was hearing them for the first time in crystal clear, passionate ebullience. The lusty *Bould O'Donohue*, the irreverent and patriotic *Johnston's Motor Car*, and a chilling rendition of Dominic Behan's masterpiece, *Patriot Game*. No wonder Bob Dylan was moved to lift the melody and sentiment of the latter, and harness it with his own questioning and still relevant, *With God On Our Side*. He'd have been less than human if he hadn't

seized this opportunity, and even if he never gave a tip
of his hat to the outraged Behan, the man from Hibbing
always acknowledged his debt to and admiration for the
Clancys & Makem.

They were completely unknown in Ireland until
played on Radio Éireann by Ciarán MacMathúna who in
1962 picked up a couple of their albums while visiting
the U.S. They swept the country overnight in the same
manner that The Beatles would conquer America shortly
thereafter. Indeed, by 1964 one third of all albums sold
in Ireland had been recorded by the Clancys and
Makem. They were so popular that the mighty
showbands even felt called upon to don *báinín* (white)
Aran sweaters and actually stop the dancing while they
performed a set of "Clancy ballads." Years later, when I
first made my foray into the showband world one of the
more popular numbers was a quickstep version of the
Clancy's *Bonny Shoals of Herring*. One can only imagine
what that grave purist Ewan MacColl would have
thought of this polka-like resetting of his flinty sea
shanty.

Back in the Ireland of 1962, some of the Clancy
songs were excruciatingly familiar, others merely rang a
bell while a handful, such as *Bonny Shoals of Herring*
were totally new. Regardless, the Clancys and Makem
swept the dust off all of them. They removed layers of
calcification from patriotic laments like *Roddy McCorley*
and *Kevin Barry*. By juicing them so jubilantly while
never tampering with their innate power, they cast these
songs in a new light. We had become vaguely ashamed
of them, especially after the botched IRA border
campaign of the mid-1950's. The Clancys and Makem
cauterized some of the innate danger and subversion,
thus rendering the old songs more respectable, and
ultimately acceptable, by placing them in a more

theatrical framework. An acquaintance of theirs said to me many years later in a Manhattan saloon, "You could see the shadow of the gunman behind the lads, but you were damn certain he had no bullets."

With the possible exception of the Northerner, Tommy Makem, the group was more patriotic than political. And if they mentioned the IRA in a song, it was more a good-natured quip as in *Johnston's Motor Car*; indeed, it's hard to think of these four warm-spirited men even thinking in terms of physical violence - and so they initially sang of 1798's *Roddy McCorley* rather than 1957's *Sean South of Garryowen*. Within Republican circles they were often criticized for this, and yet Liam did a better version of *Patriot Game* than anyone I've ever heard. This most bittersweet of protest and political songs featured as its subject Fergal O'Hanlon, Sean South's partner in the failed attack on Brookeborough RUC Barracks in County Fermanagh. The genius of the lyric is that instead of lionizing O'Hanlon, it mourns his loss while questioning the motives of those who sent him to his death. The Clancy Brothers and Makem might have laughed, lusted and exulted through most of their set, but the *Patriot Game* sent a splinter of the cold ice of realism through every hall during its performance.

Dominic Behan may have complained that Liam omitted the verse about "shooting down police," but then so did I when Black 47 recorded it on our initial cassette release in 1990. I wonder though, did the Clancy's and Makem even know about those lines. I definitely didn't, though I probably wouldn't have recorded them in any case, since Chris Byrne, the co-founder of Black 47, was a member of the NYPD at the time. But whether you use four or seven verses of *Patriot Game*, there is little doubt in my mind that it is one of the most complex and brilliant political songs ever written, and Liam Clancy chillingly brought it to life.

As often happens with overwhelming success and over-saturation of a product, there comes a backlash. The Clancys and Makem never lost their support with Irish-America – in many ways, they had become its voice – though that voice often seemed dated and out of touch as American cities went up in flames in the late 60's and urban blight took hold in the 70's and 80's. Eventually, Liam grew tired of being the "kid brother" to Tom and Paddy and set out on his own. He and Tommy Makem formed a very successful duo that appropriated the Clancy mantle, and when that partnership came to an end, I would run into Tommy a couple of times each summer as we headlined different stages at Irish festivals throughout the country. In fact, I said goodbye to him one last time at Chicago's Gaelic Park in 2006. Though weakened from a lingering illness, he was not unlike a legendary boxer that day, going three or four rounds until he was overcome by fatigue and had to leave. Yet he did so like the warrior he always was – on his feet and promising to return.

In Ireland we grew tired of the Clancys and Makem. It was more to do with us than them. As a country we were still coming to terms with modernity - finding ourselves while casting off English cultural imperialism; though truth be told that particular implant is lodged bone deep in the Irish psyche. Still by the mid-1960's we had grown wary of all outside influences; besides, many Irish people were never quite comfortable with the Clancy/Makem show-business staginess – there was a little too much Bing Crosby in Aran jumpers for a country that was about to come under siege from the recently ignited Troubles up North.

The backlash took a while to gain strength, but then it hit with such force that none but the brave or crazy would have risked the inevitable ridicule by venturing forth in a white wool sweater. We had need of homegrown heroes and we wanted them to be like us – unpolished and accessible. That group was already gaining popularity in the pubs of the capital; inspired by James Joyce's collection of short stories, they called themselves The Dubliners.

But The Clancy Brothers and Tommy Makem bestowed upon us a number of gifts – they jacked open the floodgates of a folk revival, they showed us how to entertain while still retaining a measure of profundity, and they encouraged us to dream and be more than we were. For that, we'll always be grateful.

The Patriot Game

Come all ye young rebels, and list while I sing,
For the love of one's country is a terrible thing.
It banishes fear with the speed of a flame
And it makes us all part of the patriot game.

My name is O'Hanlon, and I've just turned sixteen.
My home is in Monaghan, where I was weaned.
I learned all my life cruel England to blame,
So now I am part of the patriot game.

This Ireland of ours has too long been half free
Six counties lie under John Bull's tyranny.
But still De Valera is greatly to blame
For shirking his part in the patriot game.

They told me how Connolly was shot in a chair,
His wounds from the fighting all bloody and bare
His fine body twisted, all battered and lame
They soon made me part of the patriot game.

I don't mind a bit if I shoot down police
They are lackeys for war, never guardians of peace
And yet at deserters I'm never let aim
The rebels who sold out the patriot game.

It's nearly two years since I wandered away
With the local battalion of the bold IRA,
I'd read of our heroes, and I wanted the same,
To play out my part in the patriot game.

And now as I lie here, my body all holes,
I think of those traitors who bargained in souls
And I wish that my rifle had given the same
To those Quislings who sold out the patriot game.

(Dominic Behan)

CHAPTER SIX

Such a Parcel of Rogues in a Nation

Farewell to all our Scottish fame
Farewell our ancient glory
Farewell even to the Scottish name
So famed in martial story
Now Sark runs over Solway sands
And Tweed runs to the ocean
To mark where England's province stands
Such a parcel of rogues in a nation!

What force or guile could not subdue
Through many warlike ages
Is wrought now by a coward few
For hireling traitor's wages
The English steel we could disdain
Secure in valour's station
But English gold has been our bane
Such a parcel of rogues in a nation!

Larry Kirwan

> *Oh would I had seen the day*
> *That Treason thus could sell us*
> *My old grey head had lain in clay*
> *With Bruce and loyal Wallace!*
> *But pith and power, till my last hour*
> *I will make this declaration*
> *We are bought and sold for English gold*
> *Such a parcel of rogues in a nation!*
>
> *(Robbie Burns)*

There are artists all across the musical spectrum nowadays who could be labeled centrist, even rightwing, but it would have been hard to find such a politically challenged soul amidst the 1960's folk scene in Ireland or the UK. In those claustrophobic and incestuous circles, a familiarity with Marxism and the views of Trotsky was as *de rigueur* as a first class knowledge of the Child Ballads or the song collections of A.L. (Bert) Lloyd.

While Francis James Child was an American academic who provided much grist for the folksingers' mill with his *English and Scottish Popular Ballads*, published between 1882 and 1898; Bert Lloyd was a Communist Party member who traveled ceaselessly around the UK in the mid-1900s collecting songs and attempting to foster the arts in working class communities. Along with another confirmed Marxist, Ewan MacColl, he was responsible for creating a subgenre of folk music that became loosely known as *Industrial Folk*.

Lloyd and MacColl were friends and collaborators, but while both could more than hold their own with a song, MacColl was also a groundbreaking

66

songwriter and a riveting performer. His influence is still felt today, not only in the austere folk and traditional music that he himself cherished but also in *Celtic Rock, Paddy Punk*, and all manner of Irish music where dust is blown from the rafters and listeners are wont to shake a leg.

MacColl was born James Henry Miller to Scottish parents during the First World War in Salford, Lancashire – a burgh he would commemorate in one of his most storied songs, *Dirty Old Town*. Many people attribute that song to Shane MacGowan, so sensitive and apt is his signature rendition (although oddly enough, Joe Strummer had a strong hand in The Pogues arrangement, including the modulation in key Shane apparently disliked.) In fact, MacColl had a deep influence on MacGowan's writing style and many another too.

MacColl's mission was to capture the sights, sounds, environment and living conditions of his time, then set them in diamond hard lyrics within a barebones traditional setting. A generation later Shane set out to do much the same thing, but with the addition of electric instruments, combined with the rhythms and attitudes of the Irish pubs and punk clubs of London. I too am a bastard child of MacColl's, for I attempted something similar by using New York City and its many influences as my prism through which to view, and experiment with, Irish music.

I saw MacColl in the early 1980's at Folk City, a Greenwich Village club where Bob Dylan made his first professional New York appearance. It was magical, and ultimately touching, to finally hear the master live. Approaching the end of his career, at first MacColl seemed distant, older than I'd imagined, and a tad resigned. Perhaps he was coming to terms with his own

mortality and ambitions – for in the age of Ronald
Reagan it had become diamond clear that there would
be no revolution, no workers republic. Who knows
what was going through his mind, but it was apparent
that he was harvesting little satisfaction from the fact
that he had exerted such a tremendous influence on so
many musicians.

I had strayed far from folk music myself and was
a member of a "new wave" band, Major Thinkers –
green lightning streak in my hair and other such self-
conscious frills; to compound matters I was acutely
aware that I was floundering creatively. But as the
evening progressed, MacColl nailed me to the wall with
the sheer simplicity and power of his message. I
realized that I had become overwhelmed with the
"how" rather than the "what" of making music. My
message, such as it was, had been swallowed up by the
fashionable demands and constraints of the day. There
would be more awkward and futile years ahead before I
would get back on what I considered the right track, but
for better or worse, the old master sowed a seed that
night.

I had brought with me *Absolutely and Completely*,
an album I'd recorded with my boyhood friend, Pierce
Turner. It contained a version of MacColl's wonderful
Traveling People. We had taken his clear-eyed, severe
lament and turned it into a full-scale sonic assault
featuring the moog synthesizer – though, in general,
well received, one critic labeled our arrangement "an
electronic wasteland" and it wouldn't have surprised me
if the songwriter agreed. While I stood in line to meet
"Mister MacColl," as he was being addressed, a couple
of folk purists of my acquaintance sniggered at the sight
of the album – surely I wasn't about to insult the great
man with this puerile downtown deconstruction of his

classic. But, in the bloom and optimism of youth, I
really felt that he should know that his song had
inspired two sincere neophytes to our own idea of
greatness, no matter what anyone else thought of it.
And then it was my turn: I stuttered my feelings
and held out the album for his signature. He gave me
much the same look that Johnny Cash would years later
– it took less than a second but time clattered to a halt
under his X-Ray inspection.

I must have passed muster for he said not
unkindly, "I've heard of this. Send me a copy
sometime." Then he signed the album and politely
waited for me to say more. But what was there to say?
Eventually one of the impatient purists shunted me on.

The signed album was later stolen from my
apartment by a junky acquaintance and I never sent
MacColl a copy of our impassioned "electronic
wasteland." Who knows what he would have thought;
his wife, Peggy Seeger, said that he had opened up in
both social and musical matters in the last years of his
life.

Luke Kelly, soon to form the Dubliners, was no
less moved and even more influenced by MacColl. Born
on Sheriff Street in Dublin's inner city to a working class
family, though a promising student, he left school at the
age of 13 and took odd jobs before emigrating to
England four years later. Like many a Paddy, he
worked on the building sites and frequented the
immigrant pubs, but he also took up the banjo and
immersed himself in folk music and Marxism. Given
these influences, it's not surprising that he encountered
MacColl and began to study the art of folk singing under
his tutelage.

MacColl believed that a singer should so immerse
himself in lyrics and music that he could then dispense

with all ornamentation and self-aggrandizement and deliver the song straight from the soul. Luke never lost that message and became MacColl's greatest disciple. As a performer he simply oozed conviction and fixity of purpose. He had a head of wild red hair and a ready smile, but when he sang he expected silence – and for the most part he got it. I remember attending my first *Fleadh Cheoil* in Enniscorthy; it must have been around 1967. This was an annual national gathering of traditional musicians who would vie for various honors.

For the rest of us, *Fleadhs* were great big sprawling affairs – more notable for drinking and revelry than staid musical competition. At this particular event I was not yet a tippler - that would come soon enough. Still, I was enjoying the whole vagabond scene in the packed town square of Enniscorthy on a gloriously clear, sunny day – the very walls throbbing with music, good fellowship and liquor. Even though it's an ocean of years ago, I can still recall the "hushing and whisting" that spread from person to person, as we beheld a wild looking red-headed man - a banjo in his fist - being helped up on to the roof of a car. Almost reverentially the whispers swept the square, "It's Luke Kelly."

Though he may have consumed a small barrel of porter himself, he balanced expertly on the sloped roof of the car and, for a long moment, stood still as a statue and stared out at us. I came to recognize that stance in the many times I saw him perform down the years. If there was no actual verbal command from him, there was a real expectation of silence, and amazingly every drunk in that square heeded him. The hush swelled and spread outwards, enveloping those who either knew the man by acquaintance or reputation all the way down to people who wouldn't have given a goddamn if Jesus

Christ himself had hopped down off the cross and belted out a couple of verses of the *Hallelujah Chorus*.

I was stunned by the power of any man to still that unruly crowd, but it's only in retrospect that I wonder if Luke's imperious demand for silence was really his delving into the technique he had learned from MacColl. Or perhaps it was a combination of his shamanistic power over audiences allied with his inner search for the heart and soul of the song? Who knows? Bob Marley was one of the few others I've witnessed who seemed to combine the same outward power and introspection.

And then Luke began to sing *Kelly The Boy From Killane* and his words ricocheted across the same square that Father Murphy and his Pikemen had stormed through in 1798. It was one of those moments of revelation and I knew I'd never be happy if I didn't at least try to do the same myself some day.

Kelly From Killane

What's the news what's the news,
oh me bold Shelmalier
With your long barreled gun from the sea
Say what wind from the south brings his messenger
here
With a hymn of the dawn for the free
"Goodly news 'goodly news do I bring youth of Forth
Goodly news shall you hear Bargy man
For the boys march at morn from the south to the north
Led by Kelly the boy from Killane

Larry Kirwan

Tell me who is that giant with the gold curly hair
He who rides at the head of the band
Seven feet is his height with some inches to spare
And he looks like a king in command
''Ah me boys that's the pride of the bold Shelmaliers
Among our greatest of heroes a man
Fling your beavers aloft and give three ringing cheers
For John Kelly the boy from Killane

Enniscorthy's in flames and old Wexford is won
And the Barrow tomorrow we will cross
On a hill o'er that town we have planted a gun
That will batter the gateway at Ross
All the Forth men and Bargy men march o'er the heath
With brave Harvey to lead in the van
But the foremost of all in that grim gap of death
Will be Kelly the boy from Killane

But the gold sun of freedom grew darkened at Ross
And it set by the Slaney's red waves
And poor Wexford stripped naked hung high on a
cross
Her heart pierced by traitors and slaves
'Glory oh, Glory oh to her brave sons who died
For the cause of long downtrodden man
Glory oh to Mount Leinster's own darling and pride
Dauntless Kelly the boy from Killane

(P.J. McCall)

The effect on his audience was cathartic and
when he finished the last thrilling chorus he laughed
heartily at the huzzahs and thunderous applause; with a
shrug of his shoulders he took a slug from a bottle
handed up to him, then wiped his mouth with his

sleeve. His point made, he continued with *The Leaving of Liverpool* – a sea shanty The Clancy Brothers and Tommy Makem had made popular. The nature and structure of this sailors' work song gave us the freedom to join in with Luke, and we did so with gusto on the choruses – our voices reverberating around that square until you could almost see the beautiful Scouse girl on the banks of the Mersey that we were all leaving behind.

The Leaving of Liverpool

Farewell to you my own true love
I am going far away
I am bound for California
But I know that I'll return someday

So fare thee well, my own true love,
And when I return united we will be
It's not the leaving of Liverpool that grieves me
But my darlin' when I think of thee

I have signed on a Yankee Clipper ship
Davy Crockett is her name
Aye and Burgess is the Captain of her
They say that she's a floating hell

Farewell to lower Frederick Street
Ensign Terrace and Park Lane
For I think it will be a long, long time
Before I see you again

Oh the sun is on the harbour, love
And I wish I could remain
For I know it will be some long time
Before I see you again

No matter how many times I saw Luke over the years he always moved me. Yet, I prefer to think of him at that moment. I suppose it had something to do with the times: there was an air of possibility abroad, a sense that things were changing. Luke was emblematic of that change; though experienced in the hard ways of the world, on that lovely summer's day he seemed so young and beautiful. Looking back on his performance, it wasn't what he did – it was how he did it. Even as a callow teenager, I knew both songs well and was already tired of them. The Beatles, Dylan and Hendrix were pushing music outwards – and inwards – in ways that I could only applaud but not yet fully understand; their lethal and heady magic floated to me over the airwaves courtesy of John Peel on the BBC and a host of mad and irreverent disc jockeys on Radio Caroline - the pirate ship bobbing out there on the Irish Sea.

Luke, on the other hand, summonsed to life a revolutionary spirit that had lain dormant in Enniscorthy Town Square for almost 170 years. Like the many others present that day, I had no idea how he did it – nor did any of us care; we were transported by something that was achingly familiar and yet had been kept from us at arm's length all our lives. It was our own sense of Irishness – something feral that one never heard on the radio, a spirit that did not sit easy in musty Victorian parlors at sing-songs around out-of-tune pianos. Luke had sensed it in the square that afternoon when he adhered to MacColl's discipline that demanded he confront the truth of the song he was about to perform.

There were other occasions when I saw Luke bemused and almost hesitant to get on stage. As the years passed, the gatherings he performed at were often very rowdy – people were more interested in hearing their own voices than creating the space and silence he needed to delve into the heart of some lyric and find its truth. In the course of the night he always silenced them once, or even twice, but in the end what was the point in trying to contain a Niagara of noisy banality fueled by flashfloods of Guinness. And so, with a shrug of his shoulders, he'd harness their errant energy, but you could almost touch a thin shroud of despair that cloaked him no matter how much he beamed. After all, he was one of the lead singers in a popular and rowdy folk group and had to make a living.

My other favorite performance of this galvanic talent was much later when I had moved to Dublin and was attending a Showband Monday night out at the Television Club on Harcourt Street. Cahir O'Doherty (now a renowned ballad singer in Florida) and The Gentry was the featured band. Cahir had a tremendous Soul type voice and The Gentry were very hip and cutting edge by Irish standards at the time. In the midst of the dancing, Cahir announced that he had a special guest. Everyone assumed it would be some other showband luminary, instead out strode Luke, resplendent in a flower-power shirt and matching turquoise tight pants. This caused consternation for, although Luke did favor the occasional vivid color, he was after all a folk-singer and tended to dress in puritanical blue denim accord.

The shock did not stop there, for he instantly launched into a bluesy, boozy, Music Hall cum Soul version of *With a Little Help From My Friends* replete with cabaret style kicks as though he were auditioning for The Rockettes. And, oh my God, was he good – hilarious and having the time of his life. That was Luke – troubled and triumphant - ancient Ireland deep inside him exploding from the roof of a car in Enniscorthy, but always the rebel dismissing expectations while harnessing the power of Rock 'n' Roll from a stage in Dublin. Ireland was like that back then – a country unsure of itself, uncertain what to leave behind, but afraid to miss out on the waves of political, social and musical change that were roiling the rest of the world.

When Sean Lemass took office as Taoiseach (Prime Minister) in 1959 he set about sweeping away some of the stasis caused by the social and economic policies of his predecessor, the by then musty founding father, Éamon de Valera. Within months Lemass initiated *The First Programme for Economic Development*. Although it had a vaguely Stalinist ring, this bold policy had little to do with any socialistic leanings. In essence, it involved a drastic shift from the protectionist policies instituted by de Valera during the 1930's economic war with Britain. Tax breaks and grants were made available to foreign firms wishing to set up business in Ireland. In addition a sum of over £200 million was invested in an integrated program of national development. The upshot of this was that unemployment fell sharply and a rare sense of optimism began to spread through the country.

Emigration was still a fact of life, but some of those who had fled to the UK began to tentatively venture home. Previous to this, emigration had tended to be a one-way ticket – the best that could be hoped for was a rushed visit at Christmas and, with a bit of luck, a fortnight's holidays in the summer. Many of the 1940's and 1950's generation never returned – some through bitterness at the country and the politicians who had failed them, and many more because they had made better lives for themselves by creating their own little piece of Ireland in North London, Dagenham,

Birmingham, Coventry and a rake of other cities and towns whose names will always reek of emigration. The center of their world was the pubs they frequented. Homesick for familiar music and songs, they flocked to the establishments that employed itinerant ballad singers and musicians the like of Margaret Barry, Seamus Ennis, Michael Gorman and the incomparable Seosamh Ó'hÉanaí (Joe Heaney). Smithsonian Institute has done us all a great favor by releasing *Irish Music in London Pubs,* recorded live at the Bedford Arms in Camden Town circa 1964. It's a singular peek back in time and, though formal and occasionally stiff, one can sense the camaraderie, and how the uncompromising music helped to assuage the pain of dislocation.

A new generation of singers and players including Dominic Behan, Luke Kelly, and Andy Irvine amongst others gravitated to these pubs, sessions and folk clubs. There they added their own wizardry to the freewheeling, rougher ambience that infused traditional music in the watering holes of the Diaspora - a long way from the more prissy surroundings in which one would hear such music back in Ireland. There too they stood shoulder to shoulder with trade unionists and workers' rights advocates who had been emboldened by the Labor Party Government of 1945-1951 and who would soon take power again under the Harold Wilson administration in 1964. With the post-de Valera thaw loosening up things back in Ireland, ex-pat musicians began to hop on the boat train and head home on a more frequent basis. Along with their guitars and banjos, they took their songs, freedom of spirit, and new ideas along with them.

While in Dublin they gravitated to O'Donoghue's, a pub on Merrion Row. It was there that Luke Kelly

developed a friendship with Ronnie Drew, an actor,
with a voice akin to sandpaper being scraped across old
cement. Ronnie, amazingly, given his thick Dublin
accent, had spent some time in Spain teaching English
where he had picked up a rudimentary flamenco guitar
style. A noted wit, both funny and biting in the Dublin
manner, he was overheard telling stories at a party by an
actor named John Molloy who put him onstage at the
Gate Theatre with banjoist extraordinaire, Barney
McKenna. Molloy was to play a large part in the
formation and early success of The Ronnie Drew Ballad
Group and, oddly enough, in my own decision to take
up a musical career.

It's interesting just how incestuous the
folk/ballad scene was and how a few characters would
go on to seed an exceedingly strong and vibrant musical
movement that ranged all the way from austere
Traditional to ribald Celtic Punk. Ronnie, as it turns out,
was a regular listener to the *Ciarán MacMathúna Radio
Show* - the same person who introduced The Clancy
Brothers and Tommy Makem to an Irish audience. It
was on this show that he also first heard singers like
Dominic Behan and began to pick up his own repertoire.
Ronnie, Luke, Barney McKenna and Ciarán Bourke
began informally singing in a corner of O'Donoghue's in
1962. Seeking a more democratic name they changed
from The Ronnie Drew Group to The Dubliners on
account of Luke Kelly reading James Joyce's book of the
same title at the time.

O'Donoghue's became the center of the
Ballad/Folk world as the fame of the Dubliners grew.
Seosamh Ó'Héanai (Joe Heaney) from Connemara,
reckoned to be the leading *Sean Nós* (Old Style) singer in
the country, was frequently at the bar and would
contribute songs. It was from him that Ronnie Drew

learned *Seven Drunken Nights* – a song banned on Irish
Radio but picked up by the pirate station, Radio
Caroline, in 1967. Although edited down to five nights
for respectability's sake, the song propelled The
Dubliners onto the British charts with an appearance on
Top of the Pops. From there it was onwards to
international fame and as a consequence the discovery
of Irish Folk Music by so many people

Another who frequented O'Donoghue's was Jim
McCann who would much later join The Dubliners - but
before that he had a number one hit in Ireland with *The
Sea Around Us* by The Ludlows, written by Dominic
Behan. Behan himself was no stranger to the pub on
Merrion Row. Brother to world famous playwright,
Brendan Behan, Dominic is arguably the most influential
Irish songwriter of the 1960's. I'm always stunned by
the number of well-known songs that he has written and
often not received credit for. *The Auld Triangle* has
mushroomed in popularity since The Swell Season
version; I often think of Dominic's *McAlpine's Fusiliers*
by The Dubliners as being the fountainhead of Shane
MacGowan's repertoire, while *The Merry Ploughboy* and
Come out Ye Black & Tans can be heard in any Irish bar
across the US whenever people raise their voices – or
glasses.

Dominic even cracked the American charts with
his ballad, *Liverpool Lou* on the heels of the Beatles
success, and Yoko Ono declared that it was one of John's
favorite lullabies to sing to his son, Sean. Behan added a
hint of danger and controversy to the socialist leaning
Folk scene because of his ultra-nationalist beliefs and his
friendship with such Republican luminaries as his half-
brother, Cathal Goulding, then IRA Chief-of-Staff.

Another attendee of O'Donoghue's was Andy
Irvine, a young British musician, with a yen for Woody

Guthrie and traveling. He too had come under the influence of Ewan MacColl and came to Ireland to pursue an acting career but ended up immersing himself in traditional music. In O'Donoghue's he met Johnny Moynihan, a working class Dubliner with a love of *Sean Nós* singing and an interest in many musical cultures – he was the first person I ever heard play the Blues on a tin whistle. Irvine and Moynihan would go on to form Sweeney's Men, and along with Terry Woods, later of The Pogues, they recorded an eponymous first album that is still influencing Irish Folk Music

    I first came face to face with this Dublin bohemian Folk scene through playing on the same bill with The Dubliners at a Wexford Opera Festival Fringe event. John Molloy had become aware of the growing international status of the festival and had booked a grand finale concert for The Dubliners in a marquee tent set up in the back yard of White's Hotel, mere yards from my Grandfather's house on George's Street. Pubs back then closed at 11pm but, much to the delight of Wexford's revelers, an extension had been granted until an unthinkable 3am for the two weeks of the festival. To keep everyone happy – and more importantly, drinking - music had to be supplied from 9pm to 3am; one of the ways White's Hotel management filled up the time was to run heats for a talent competition over the course of the weeks with the winners competing at this grand finale concert while The Dubliners took a break.

    Although still in mid-teens, I was a veteran of many the parish hall variety show by then and so tossed my hat into the ring. My voice had deepened and I had been one of the stars of a recent Wexford Youth Club concert; it appeared to me, at least, that the years of singing my heart out for Miss Codd in the kitchen were paying off, and I was finally ready to claim my rightful place on the larger stage of life. Besides, I had perfected carbon copies of Donovan's *Catch The Wind* and *The Universal Soldier*. These two ditties propelled me to the final.

The huge tent was jammed and The Dubliners were on fire. I had never experienced anything like the raucous excitement; it streamed off the stage only to be ping-ponged back and forth between the band and audience. Until then every concert that I'd attended had been in the nature of a formal show that the audience might appreciate, or even marvel at, but definitely not participate in. This was like taking a session in the back room of a pub, magnifying it, shooting it up with adrenalin, and forcing the crowd to give back in proportion what the band was putting forth. None of this presented much problem, what with Luke Kelly rebelliously belting out *Dirty Old Town* like he was ready to burn the whole bloody place down, or Ronnie Drew inviting you up to *Monto* to check out the finest whores in Dublin; these verbal flourishes were all tied together with the barbed wire notes that Barney McKenna was coaxing from his spiky banjo. John Sheehan added a somewhat refined fiddle that sweetened the mix and added a rare melancholy that was never cloying. Ciarán Bourke on guitar and whistle cemented the arrangements and added the occasional song in Irish that made us all wish that we'd taken more time to familiarize ourselves with our native language while in school.

Each one was funny, irreverent and scathing, the way men with a sure command of words tend to be in pubs. And then when they took their break to a huge ovation it was the turn of the Wexford talent to strut their stuff. Oddly enough, I don't remember feeling nervous. I suppose it was because I'd received such a

great response during the heats; probably, too, I felt at
home with the Donovan songs and was finally coming
to terms with my new and deeper voice now that it had
completely broken. The fact that I wouldn't be wrecking
my chances with any of a number of young ladies from
the Presentation Convent, and now dolled up in the
front rows, didn't hurt either.

And sure enough you could hear a pin drop
during my introspective reading of *Catch The Wind* - the
place erupted when I finished. I had blown the previous
contestants away. Ronnie Drew, watching from the
wings, winked at me, but Luke bade me no heed as he
was tossing back pints with a bunch of the town's young
socialists. And so there was just one competitor after me
– Packie Hayden – who stood about 5 feet tall, and was a
local character and Elvis interpreter. I knew Packie's
stuff well from seeing him onstage at dances and variety
shows; however, I was never quite sure if people were
laughing at or with him. I liked him very much as he
was a very kind and thoughtful man who always made
a point of complimenting and encouraging me. As I
came off the stage he took me in a bear hug and told me
I was great.

Then he exploded from the wings and broke forth
into a riveting version of *Jailhouse Rock*. Within seconds
the audience was on its feet dancing as he moved
dervish-like across the stage. Small as he was he got
down on his knees in front of my heretofore adoring
fans from the Presentation Convent: then he leaped into
the crowd dancing amongst them before vaulting back
on the stage and doing a split that had the crowd
gasping, before he finished with his show-stopper, *Blue
Suede Shoes*.

The place was in pandemonium while I stood
white-faced barely able to draw a breath, such was my

shock and sorrow. The contest was decided on audience participation, and while I received a rousing shout and second-place for my efforts, it was no-contest. Packie had wiped the floor with me. The cheers were ringing in my ears, and the salt tears stinging my eyes as I sidled my way out of the maelstrom of celebration inside the tent and made my way through the cool October night back to my grandfather's big barracks of a house that loomed up the street. I was almost at the door when I heard his shout and the footsteps behind me.

"C'mere, young fellah, will you!" John Molloy was nearly out of breath from running. I wiped the tears away before turning around. He put his arm around me and gave me a hug. "Don't let what happened get you down," he said. "You have something. Ronnie himself says so."

"Thanks," I said and started to move on.

"Where are you goin'?"

"Home."

"What for?"

In truth, I didn't know. There was nothing for me there – just endless hours in my draughty bedroom staring at the peeling wallpaper. On the other hand, I couldn't face the embarrassment of people feeling sorry for me back in the tent. John Molloy, a great actor and man of the world, could see right through my glassy eyed defiance.

"C'mon," he took me by the arm. "The lads are about to go on, and I have to introduce them. They're always better the second set."

And they were. I stood in the wings of that stage. Packie Hayden, in his kind and gentlemanly way came up and said not a word but put his arm around me as we watched The Dubliners, perhaps the greatest Folk band, put on one of their luminous shows. Ronnie Drew winked at me again, and I thought I caught an impish smile from Luke. I learned something about the fraternity of musicians that night: you don't have to be the best to be a part of it – you just have to give your best. The rest will look after itself.

CHAPTER SEVEN

I spent a lot of time in that big draughty bedroom. There was no central heating back in those days. The kitchen was the one perennially warm haven in my grandfather's house; oddly enough, it contained both an electric and a gas cooker, why I'm not sure, for it meant more work for Miss Codd who fought an ongoing battle with grime, grease and decay, not to mention the limestone dust trailed in by the two men every time they came home from the stone-yard. The sitting room could be warm too, if you sat within a foot or two of the open fire; even at that proximity, however, your back would usually be frozen stiff from the icy wind that whistled up from under the door. On the bitterest of nights I'd throw an old overcoat across the gap between the floor and the door, but I had to be careful to remove it when retiring lest Uncle Paddy come a cropper on his unsteady arrival back from the pub.

My grandfather too was getting older, and the first signs of dementia were setting in though, at the time, I thought that was just a normal process of aging. We were very close but he could be tiresome, as the elderly often are to skittery adolescents; so despite the Arctic conditions I craved privacy and spent much time in my huge bedroom hunkered beneath sheets, blankets, quilts and old coats listening to Radio Luxembourg and the occasional American Forces Network program that elbowed its way through the murk of Irish atmospheric conditions. These latter shows were my favorites as you could often hear unalloyed the Soul and Blues music that was doled out to homesick American soldiers stationed in Germany. The signal was never strong and sometimes I'd be forced to stick my ear up against the cloth cover as a classic by James Brown, Joe Tex or some other luminary would wax and wane before succumbing to white noise and ghostlike intrusions from other faraway stations.

I didn't hear the song that was to change my life on AFN, however, for I remember the signal being crystal clear even though I was immersed in a book at the time. I was a voracious reader and had by this time almost exhausted the shelves of the County Library. I instantly looked up at the sound of those first bass notes; it was almost as if I knew that something monumental was about to happen. Then a scalding, trebly guitar ripped into one of the greatest intro figures, and I bolted upright in bed - no thought to the coldness of the night or the cross current of draughts from beneath the door and the creaky window frame. As if that wasn't enough, the voice that implored three times, "Baby please don't go..." before emoting "down to New Orleans..." almost swept the Brylcreem from my adolescent hair such was its pungent brilliance.

It was Van the Man and I hung on every syllable of the two minute, thirty-eight sizzling seconds of *Baby*

Please Don't Go. I jacked my ear into the cloth cover of
that dusty old Siemens radio for fear I'd miss the name
of this group. Imagine my astonishment, joy, and
patriotic exhilaration to discover that Them were not
from Liverpool, Newcastle or even accessible London,
but from Belfast scarcely 150 miles up the road.

I've been listening to Van Morrison ever since –
not religiously like some, I haven't even bought a CD of
his for nigh on twenty years; but he's like an old love
that you never actually broke up with - just drifted apart
from. And yet I only need to hear a sliver of a song and
I'm ready one more time to go to the wall for this East
Belfast wizard.

Still and all, I didn't even know his name in those
early Them days! Nor did I rush out and buy the 45
single of *Baby Please Don't Go*, although I did foot it
down to Andy Cadogan's Bicycle and Phonograph shop.
Andy did indeed have a copy, but it was already
"spoken for," he informed me gravely. I was stunned.
To the best of my knowledge the bloody thing had only
debuted on Luxembourg the night before. Another
Them fanatic lurked down Wexford's narrow streets and
back lanes. Though he declined to name this intrepid
audiophile, Andy did offer to spin the disc. I drank in
the 2minutes and 38 seconds of magic one more time
while Mr. Cadogan attended to his more profitable
business of flogging bicycles. He then carefully dusted
the vinyl, slid this work of art back into its sleeve and
gingerly placed it on the top shelf – no doubt to prevent
it from miraculously easing its way into my adolescent
overcoat pocket.

All was not lost, however, for back then I was a
veritable Steve Jobs at the forefront of technology. I had
worked a full summer picking blackcurrants, potatoes
and anything else that could be yanked from the earth,

and invested my savings in a sparkling new Grundig Tape Recorder. It wasn't long before I collared *Baby Please Don't Go* on a Decca Records Luxembourg show; I could now play and rewind this future classic to my heart's content.

This caused no little concern to my Uncle Paddy who hadn't even seen fit to acknowledge the glory of The Beatles but was now forced to endure "the howlings of this American anti-Christ," through headaches, hangovers and the many other tribulations of a gentleman leading the sporting life around Wexford town. When I informed him that the said singer was not only from the island of Ireland but East Belfast in particular, he stopped dead in his tracks and cast a suspicious eye over my freckled acned visage as if seeing me for the first time.

"And he's a black Protestant too?" He whispered in a most accusatory manner.

"He's not black!" I protested.

"If he's from East Belfast, he's black as the Ace of Spades!"

"I've seen a picture of him. He's as white as a bottle of milk."

"Jesus Christ, boy, what are they teaching you in that school of yours? You don't know what 'black' is?"

I was reluctant to admit my ignorance. I had up until then assumed black to be a color; however, I was summarily informed that it was really a pejorative adjective applied to our Protestant brethren, particularly those consigned to the Presbyterian hellhole of Northern Ireland. I shrugged off this piece of knowledge. It didn't matter to me if Van was a Holy Roller with turquoise skin who danced on the heads of a vast heavenly host and had forty-seven wives, most of whom were virgins. In for a penny – in for a pound, I was a

Them fanatic and religion had sweet damn all to do with it. Oh but in reality it did, as I was to discover later. Then again, what did I know - besides Them was on a roll.

Back in those days I used to devour both *New Musical Express* and *Melody Maker* and was a fountain of information on the doings of every band and musician that ever had designs on crashing the Top Twenty. Ray Whelan, our local newsagent, would allow me to stand in his shop and read one of these weekly tomes from cover to cover as long as I purchased the other. So, I was forewarned about Them's second single, *Here Comes The Night*, weeks before it was released. I prayed to high heaven that it would live up to the standard of their first opus, and oh, my God, for once I was rewarded - it was even better. That recording still fills me with awe, not to mention loneliness and loss. Written and produced by Bert Berns from the Bronx, this veteran who had worked with Sam Cooke must have been stunned when he heard the soulful maturity of Morrison's voice. Though just eighteen at the time, Van sang as if he had fallen into the black hole of despair and might never escape.

Where did this knowledge of pain come from? Well, Van was blessed that his father was a merchant marine and regularly brought home American Blues and Folk records. But there was something even more primal in his background. Old time religion! It was everywhere in East Belfast, and George Ivan Morrison's mother was a devotee. I could scarcely believe the fervor of that fundamentalist part of town when I was first taken there as a boy. The very streets pulsed with hymn singing on a Sunday morning as communal voices erupted in praise of their Savior across a sacred spectrum that ranged from spired churches to rickety evangelical shop fronts. Nor was there anything in the least tentative or knee-jerk about these outpourings, far from it; instead the normal service was two to three hours of propulsive amplified praise for Belfast's very fractured notion of the one true Protestant god – and a far cry from the much tamer, institutional Roman Catholicism that I bowed a knee to back home. Though Van has traveled many miles, both literally and figuratively, since those evangelical days, I can still hear an echo of that particular pious ebullience the moment he opens his mouth.

Morrison was never a bigot – musicians rarely are – but those streets of East Belfast were creased with an almost pathological anti-Catholicism; thus it was a long journey in attitude, if not miles, from his mother's fundamentalist kitchen to the sitting room of the McPeake family. Francie McPeake was the patriarch and had already written the classic *Wild Mountain Thyme (Will You Go Lassie Go)* when the very young Van arrived on his doorstep and heard for the first time the keen of the uilleann pipes. All the McPeakes played an instrument and learned the jigs, reels and slow airs handed down to them by their father. Van listened and assimilated these *Fenian* and *Taig* chants and would summon this knowledge when he made his own incursions into Celtic and Irish Traditional music many years later.

But with Them he was still the young R&B man, replete with shades, wailing away on his saxophone when he wasn't sending shivers through my spine with that voice of his. I could feel myself changing as I listened – and I could tell that Miss Codd sensed I was drifting away from her. For my sake she had overcome cultural difficulties with The Stones and Dylan but this "fellah from Belfast" was stretching matters: he wasn't just about words and melodies, he was dredging up forbidden sounds from the "foul rag and bone shop of the heart" – aye, and the soul too. I had persuaded her to watch Van emote *I Put A Spell On You* on some television broadcast. She listened dutifully; a silence thick as a curtain hung between us when he finished.

"He'd sing a lot better if he opened his eyes," she finally snapped and strode out of the room.

He strode right on out of Them too during an American tour. Their third single, *One More Time*, though I adored it, was a flop; their two LPs, *The Angry Young Them* and *Them Again*, acclaimed now, were not well received at the time. But America loved him; Morrison was more authentic than Jagger, besides he had written *Gloria* and every kid who ever played Rock 'n' Roll in a garage gained calluses from the three chords of that undecipherable, but subversively sexual, ditty. I still play it – at the end of a sweaty night it makes more than sense and brings me back full circle to a cloth-covered radio in a freezing Wexford bedroom when I had no idea of the journey I myself would soon set out upon.

But back then I was living the life through Van as he conquered America with *Brown Eyed Girl*, a song that still gets people up on the dance floor of barrooms the world over. And then it happened! I had moved to Dublin. It was late at night, I was ill and had gone to bed, couldn't sleep, turned on BBC Radio, was lying there in the dark when out of nowhere *Ballerina* began to play. I recognized Van's voice instantly, of course, but the track was so different than anything I'd experienced before. I didn't even know Van was still recording; he had seemed to vanish off the face of the earth. It was only later that I discovered he'd had contractual difficulties after the sudden death of Bert Berns. The talk was that the mob had somehow gained an interest in Van, they wanted more *Brown Eyed Girls,* and the obdurate little man from East Belfast had refused.

From the first notes of *Ballerina* I recognized its majesty. I drank in every syllable, every beat until I was almost intoxicated. And then it was over and the DJ mentioned that someone had sent him a copy of *Astral Weeks* "from the States," and he wasn't quite sure what to make of it.

I was living with Pierce Turner in a cold-water flat in Rathmines at the time and got him to buy the LP the next day. When Pierce returned, we played the album, both of us stunned by its austere beauty and originality, until we came to the transcendent Madam George. Jesus Christ, the bloody thing skipped and got stuck on the word "pennies" as in:

> *"And you know you gotta go*
> *On that train from Dublin up to Sandy Row*
> *Throwing pennies..."*

It was heartbreaking! We didn't know what the hell to do so wrapped up were we in the song and the album, and yet the goddamn thing skipped. We didn't want to bring it back; we didn't want to be without this revelatory work of art in case the magic it was weaving around us dissipated and never returned. Pierce hit upon a solution. He taped a silver sixpence to the top of the needle, and we returned to the beginning of the song. When it reached "pennies" again, the needle lurched infinitesimally around the pocket of the note for a millisecond and then continued. We were in heaven. To this day, whenever I play the song, I still hear that ghostlike wavering on "pennies" thought it obviously doesn't happen in its present cold digital format.

Apart from *Madam George,* I never think of this album in terms of songs – it's more like a symphony to me; it begins, I'm swept along in some kind of emotional

current and am still in motion minutes after the echo
fades on the last words, "I just don't know what to
do..." What a perfect lyrical ending, there's no
conclusion. It's a phrase that is relevant at all times of
your life and perhaps more so in the autumn than the
spring.

Madam George may be my favorite recording ever
– it's right up there, and most times surpasses *Like A
Rolling Stone*, particularly in more intimate and
thoughtful situations. I don't know whether Van
intended it (and I've often been totally flabbergasted by
interpretations of my own lyrics), but to me it reeks of
Belfast as a Caravaggio reflects Rome – not the Belfast of
today, mind you, but that of the mid- 1960's, that period
when time seemed to stand still right before the
Troubles re-ignited and changed everything. In
retrospect it seems inevitable that the
Nationalist/Catholic minority would demand civil
rights; after all, African-Americans had been doing so in
growing numbers since the beginning of the decade.
Belfast, however, appeared to be weighed down by a
brooding fatalism.

The little light that seeped through came from
music - in particular Them! That is not to say that life
did not go on; it did and it was fueled by the strict
Pentecostal and Jansenist beliefs. You could almost
touch the singular sexual repression lurking on the
streets of Belfast. That's what *Madam George* captures for
me: denial and alienation of many kinds; but also
humanity in all its shapes and sizes - accepted, rejected
and occasionally perverted - fighting back and
demanding recognition. I got to know many drag
queens and transvestites during my early years in New
York, beautiful and often tragic people, they were all

spiritual daughters of that great Belfast heroine, Madam George.

I never hear the song now without being swept back to the drizzly dark streets *in the cold hail sleet and snow,* and I never hear Richard Davis' mind-altering bass without perceiving in some compartment of my mind, *the clicking-clacking of high heeled shoes.* I never hear the swirling strings without recognizing the silhouette of a spectral figure up a darkened alley lounging in a doorway, the lit end of her cigarette exposing a rouged inviting face

Van seems so stolid, so very Ulster-like, when you see him up close or hear him speak. Little of the lyricism or romanticism that you associate with his songs is apparent. And then you play *Astral Weeks* and a vast soundscape unfolds before you - all influenced by those two revolutionary recording sessions in Century Sound Studios, New York City back on September 25th and October 15th, 1968. Thank you, Mr. George Ivan Morrison

CHAPTER EIGHT

The Curragh of Kildare

The winter it has passed
And the summer's come at last
The small birds are singing in the trees
Their little hearts are glad
Ah, but mine is very sad
Since my true love is far away from me

And straight I will repair
To the Curragh of Kildare
For it's there I'll finds tidings of my dear

The rose upon the briar
By the water running clear
Bring a joy to the linnet and the bee
Their little hearts are blessed
But mine is not at rest
For my true love is absent from me

All you who are in love
Aye and cannot it remove
I pity the pain that you endure
For experience lets me know
That your hearts are full of woe
A woe that no mortal can cure

And straight I will repair
To the Curragh of Kildare
For it's there I'll finds tidings of my dear
                    (Robbie Burns)

It's almost hard to imagine now just how
different Ireland was before television took it
by the scruff of the neck and shook it out of its
insularity. Change would have come anyway, but by
1967 we had gained a new self-awareness of each other
and of the world outside. Notwithstanding that RTE
shone a flashlight on the country in 1962, I still think of
the early and mid-1960's as a continuation of the cinema
era; and remember Irish people were huge fans of the
"pictures," as we called them. Many people went three
or four times a week. John Wayne and Humphrey
Bogart phrases were a part of our vernacular, so
television with its canned American shows fit right into
that scenario.

Gay Byrne and his Saturday night *Late Late Show*
had a huge and irreversible effect on the country. Byrne
himself was a comedian and actor who would probably
have emigrated to London and followed in the footsteps
of Eamonn Andrews a BBC broadcaster and celebrity.
Instead he was offered the first Johnny Carson style Irish
talk show. He had considerable skills, not the least of

which was an ability to empathize with people and tease
out their private life stories and experiences. Having
been interviewed by Leno, Letterman, O'Brien and
many other American television hosts, I can testify that
Gay Byrne was more than their equal.

Though foreign guests were frequent, it was the
Irish – both renowned and unknown – that stunned us.
Up until then, people whispered amongst themselves;
salacious details were shared and the speed which these
could spread was staggering. Yet we had never heard
ordinary people willing to talk aloud about their most
intimate affairs and in front of the whole country too.
Not only that, but for the first time we heard the
citizenry question the church and its ironfisted control of
the country. Such was the national repression we almost
expected these heretics to be struck down by divine
lightning bolts; with the result, the next day the whole
country would be reliving snippets of remembered
conversation from the show.

There would be protests too against this lack of
taste and respect; RTE would be deluged by telephone
calls, but for the first time the secular powers-that-be did
not buckle. In fact, they recognized that this furor was
good for business; get a guest on who complained
bitterly about the all-powerful Archbishop of Dublin,
John Charles McQauid, for instance, and you could be
sure the whole country would be tuned in the following
Saturday, if nothing else, to witness the consequences.
As the theme music of the show began, the anticipation
would not be unlike the moments before the throwing-in
of the ball at an All-Ireland Hurling Final - the whole
country would be sitting on the edge of its chair.

Television had some tremendously positive
effects on Ireland. As the lid blew off Northern Ireland,
people from the Republic got an actual glimpse inside

that sectarian police state. Up until then, unless you were from one of the border counties, you would never have set foot in "the North" and would have known very little about it, except through rumors or the lyrics of some pro-Republican songs. You would have heard the dreaded, whispered name of the B-Specials – a Protestant paramilitary force "employed" by the Northern state to ensure the inviolability of the border - a side occupation of these thugs, of course, was to keep the Nationalist/Catholic community under threat and thus less likely to demand full democratic rights. Still, these fascists had about as much relevance to the average person in the Republic of Ireland as the *Tonton Macoute* in faraway Haiti.

I was an anomaly. From an early age I had a deep interest in history and politics, besides which, it would have been hard to ignore my maternal grandfather's ongoing rant that we had "sold out the Northern Catholics for a 26 County Free State." To add fuel to the flame, I had cousins in East Donegal just across the border from Derry and visited on occasion. My uncle, Father Jim Hughes, a missionary priest home from the Philippine Islands for an extended visit, was not without his own interest in matters north of the border. He had an odd fixation on the Protestant firebrand, Rev. Ian Paisley and felt that this bigot might be a reincarnation of St. Paul. That wasn't as strange as it might seem, for Ireland in the early 1960's was a superstitious, off-the-wall country.

Once the Troubles re-ignited in 1968, TV cameras from around the world documented the jack-booted sectarianism of the failed Northern Ireland statelet that was an integral part of the United Kingdom. It should always be borne in mind that successive British governments, both conservative and socialist, condoned gerrymandering, discrimination and the treatment of Catholics as second-class citizens until the very pillars of Northern Ireland began to collapse in 1968. Modern Ireland, north and south, was born that year. Bernadette Devlin, a militant student leader and riveting personality, came down from Belfast, appeared on the *Late Late Show* and blew away the whole cover of state approved bigotry that London had allowed to fester for centuries.

As things worsened in the years that followed and the Provisional IRA set out to make Northern Ireland ungovernable, most people in the Republic either grew inured to the violence or tried to block out the almost endless carnage; still, in the early days of the Troubles, television opened our collective eyes to a reality that we too in the Republic had chosen to ignore.

In the years leading up to the television era, however, most Irish people peered out from behind a red-velvet Catholic curtain and looked askance at modernity. We knew what was going on in the rest of the world; we just weren't sure of its relevance. There was also a certain sense of inferiority. We had transitioned from being a favored colony of the vaunted United Kingdom to partitioned freedom. The six northern counties (four with Protestant and two with Catholic majorities) remained part of the UK while we in the southern twenty-six counties fought a brutal civil war in which many of the best and brightest leaders were killed.

The Catholic Church, which up until then had to tread softly under British rule, now stepped to the fore and, in coalition with conservative politicians from both Civil War sides, essentially took control of the country. Life in a Catholic theocracy was all most of us knew; though there were often murmurs of dissent, for the most part, people accepted the church's dominance in civil affairs and just got on with the ceaseless business of making a daily living.

Social habits had changed little since independence, and indeed since years before that. We were part of a busy, inquisitive, incestuous society; contrary to what is bruited around today, the pub was not the center of social life. Public houses were havens for hard-drinking men, women very rarely trespassed; in fact women did not for the most part drink much at all – a sherry or two at a wedding or wake. When Uncle Paddy got "caught" by the Garda Síochéna in a pub after an all night drinking session, the scandal that titillated the town and caused the event to make the front page of the local newspaper was that a married woman had been apprehended at eight o'clock on a Sunday morning in his and his cronies company. Her presence, of course, was not a civil offence but my uncle must have dreaded the expected scandal as he was found hiding in a wardrobe in an upstairs room of the pub. My grandfather was outraged by the event and predicted that the stone yard would lose "all our clerical customers and decent Protestants too." This did not happen but to Uncle Paddy's considerable chagrin he became known from then on around Wexford as – "the man in the wardrobe."

The nexus of most communal activity was the home – for those with social pretensions, get-togethers took place in musty parlors or sitting- rooms, while everyone else preferred their gatherings to be hosted in the heated kitchen. Thus when someone arrived with a parcel of stout or sherry, a session would ensue, and each person present would be called upon to entertain the gathering with some bars of a song; if you had "no voice whatsoever," then you had better be able to recite a dramatic poem or story. Everyone had to participate and a sacred silence would ensue while each person delivered his or her party piece.

Local celebrity was a big deal! Should someone, say, possess a sweet tenor voice, the word would eventually get out, and this budding Caruso would be called upon to sing at some local variety show. Should he prove popular, then he would make the leap to larger charity shows, and with a bit of luck go all the way to the vaunted *Tops of the Town* competitions in Wexford Parish Hall. These shows were extremely popular and would sell out in a day. It's no exaggeration to say that back in the pre-television era we were both very amused and entertained by each other.

The local Catholic clergy controlled Wexford Parish Hall, as they did every other such institution in Ireland. The construction of these fine premises had been financed by Sunday church collections from the faithful, and a local committee of upstanding and devout Catholics ran the halls - with a reverend father supervising. However, a certain populism reigned - unless you were hiring it for a speech by Nikita Kruschev, all you had to do was lay down a modest deposit and pay the remainder of the fee from the receipts of your event.

I can't remember who came up with the idea for the annual *Wexford Ballad Competition,* but it was a tremendous success from day one. Ballad groups flocked to our streets from all over the country. There was a series of heats throughout the week with the final on a Saturday night. The hall was full for each of the heats but packed to the rafters for the grand finale. Miss Codd attended each show, as did I, and everyone promoted their personal favorites. Mine was a group of three students from Dublin called The Emmet Folk after

101

the revolutionary, Robert Emmet. Miss Codd stood foursquare behind a family group from Slane, County Meath, by name of The Johnstons.

The Emmet Folk had endeared themselves to the local youth by sleeping overnight in a hay barn a mile out of town. They dressed semi-mod, had long hair and yet knew their traditional music; this is hardly surprising since they were led by guitarist Mick Moloney, a master of folk music currently lecturing at New York University. Their lead singer, Brian Bolger, was a native of Gorey, Co. Wexford and thus a local favorite. The other guitarist, Donal Lunny, was also an accomplished harmony singer and someone who continues to influence the course of Irish music to the present day. Their show-stopping song was *Curragh of Kildare,* written or collected by Scotland's national poet, Robbie Burns and subsequently transplanted to an Irish setting. Like many that night in the Parish Hall, I was overcome by the song's power, beauty and relevance – it was as if I had been looking at a diamond on my mantelpiece everyday and had never noticed it before.

I have to say I was biased against The Johnstons for the Emmet Folk had caught my imagination. Not that I didn't think they were brilliant. They had innate family harmonies not unlike those of The Roches whom I would come to adore later in Greenwich Village. Two girls, Lucy and Adrienne, fronted the group. They seemed slightly ethereal, slim and far-removed, but they sang like poised angels with just a hint of steel in their delivery. Their brother, Michael, played a twelve-string guitar and anchored them with a strong, if less striking, voice. Their big song was Ewan MacColl's *The Travelling People,* and their treatment of it was a revelation. MacColl's version was a hard-edged lament. The

102

Johnstons added a whiff of a contemporary Mamas and
Papas' influence that was far from unbecoming.

It was a tossup between the two groups but The
Johnstons edged it that night because of a deeper
commitment – they were family and winning meant
something more than it did to the three vagabonds in
The Emmet Folk who were already about to head off on
different life journeys. There was also a forthright
quality to The Johnstons – they delivered their songs
from the heart and I can still picture them onstage under
white lights reaching out to the back walls of the
jammed hall. The Emmets were more soulful and
introspective; they drew you in and bathed you in the
ancient pain of the protagonist in *Curragh of Kildare*. In
retrospect, it was a fair result though I felt aggrieved at
the time – my type of music had lost.

I can't for the life of me remember why I hadn't
participated in the first competition for I sang at every
local wake, wedding and dogfight; but, by Jesus, I was
determined to be a part of the second one. And why not
- The Johnstons had appeared a couple of weeks later on
The Late Late Show and blown the country away with
their version of *The Travelling People*. They were signed
to a record deal and the song topped the Irish charts
soon thereafter. Wexford, and its ballad competition,
was on the map.

The Emmet Folk dissolved within months. Even
on the Wexford stage there had been hints of tension,
and they went their separate, though cordial, ways soon
after returning to Dublin. Mick was heading deeper into
traditional music and Donal, whose tastes were very
catholic, cast his net to the wider fringes of the Dublin
folk scene where he hit upon The Spiceland Folk. Brian
and Mick Byrne were from Sheffield in England and
brought with them not only raffish charm and good

looks but some fine voices and a sound understanding of the dynamics of British folk music. Their father, Tommy, had been a famous boy soprano of the 1930's and had won the *Feis Ceol* (Competition) three years in a row; consequently, they were well versed in singing *as Gaeilge* (in the Irish language).

Perhaps fearing a quick dissolution, and wishing to maintain their separate identities, they became The Emmet-Spiceland Group and began making a name for themselves around the folk clubs and ballad pubs of Dublin.

Unaware of all these goings on up in the capital, and with an eye on The Johnstons' national success, I began laying the ground for a breakthrough at the next Ballad Competition. I had been playing solo in the pubs of Wexford when I received an invitation from Claire Rowe of The Southern Folk Four, now down to two members, herself and co-lead singer, Denny Hogan. Clare was a very attractive young woman and instant sparks flew between us that led, no doubt, to a blending of our voices. We did a sparkling version of Tim Hardin's *Reason To Believe*. This and other covers along with a couple of god-awful, melodramatic odes of mine caused us to stand out in Wexford where we were an instant success, though truth be told, the competition was sparse.

I must have sensed rumblings from Dublin for I felt that we needed some extra guitar firepower, so I brought aboard Declan Sinnott. Deckie, as he was known in those days, was a gangly adolescent, shy and retiring, but already showing signs of guitar virtuosity. There was friction within the group from the outset as each member had definite musical leanings and wasn't shy about promoting them. Ah, the passions of youth!

Emmet-Spiceland hit the Wexford Ballad
Competition like a tornado. Although steeped in
traditional music and even singing *as Gaeilge* the
beautiful *Báidín Fheilimí*, they were four handsome
dudes who looked and dressed as if they had stepped
straight off Carnaby Street. If I remember correctly, they
wore matching pink shirts, red velvet cravats, black bell-
bottom trousers and Beatle boots. Not only that but they
sang like larks and played their guitars as if they'd just
come from lessons with Segovia. Their set is still seared
on my brain, if not my soul; it also included a fiery four-
part harmony version of *Reynard The Fox*, the like of
which had my knees trembling at the thought of
following them onstage. But their coup-de-grace was a
song I'd never heard before.

The Lover's Ghost
*"You're welcome home again," said the young man to his
love,*
"I've been waiting for you many a night and day.
You're tired and you're pale," said the young man to his dear,
"You shall never again go away."
"I must go away," she said, "when the little cock do crow
For here they will not let me stay.
Oh but if I had my wish, oh my dearest dear," she said,
"This night should never, ever be day."

"Oh pretty little cock, oh you handsome little cock,
I pray you do not crow before the day.
And your wings shall be made of the very beaten gold
And your comb of the silver so grey."
But oh this little cock, this handsome little cock,
He crew out a warning too soon.
"It's time I should depart, oh my dearest dear," she said,
"For it's now the going down of the moon."

"And where is your bed, my dearest dear," he said,
"And where are your white Holland sheets?
And where are your serving maids, my dearest dear," he said,
"That wait upon you while you are asleep?"
"Clay is my bed, my dearest dear," she said,
"The shroud is my white Holland sheet.
The worms and the creeping things are my servants, dear,
To wait upon me while I am asleep."
(Traditional)

The Lover's Ghost is still revered in Wexford so
many years after its first wondrous rendering. There
was stillness in the Parish Hall when the last notes faded
off. Then a roar from the crowd that signaled to the
judges that they might as well head for the pub – there
was no need to judge a winner.

And what of The Southern Folk Four? We were
disqualified. In our efforts to balance out all four
members' tastes, we had inadvertently included a well
known English folk song and were acidly reminded by
the judges that this was "an Irish ballad competition."
Perhaps it was just as well, for in every possible aspect
we, like every other competitor, had been outclassed by
Emmet-Spiceland. Our group dissolved. Denny,
perhaps taking our defeat as a message from the gods,
retired from the stage. Claire moved to Manchester and
performed there on the Irish scene with her husband,
Jerry McGuire. I would love to have gathered her
impressions of that magical night for she had a keen
intellect and memory; alas, I never heard from her again,
and she passed away some years back.

I don't know if Deckie was introduced to Donal
Lunny that night but their paths have continued to

intertwine down the years in such bands as Moving
Hearts and many incarnations of Christy Moore's live
and recorded performances.   I must have asked Donal Lunny for his phone
number backstage although it's hard for me to imagine
now that I had the nerve. Nonetheless, my next solo
venture was to form a Wexford Folk Club. To raise
money for this venture I decided to run a benefit concert,
and who better to top the bill than Emmet-Spiceland. I
rang Donal from White's Hotel where I had already
assured the management that I could deliver the band
on a particular night. To my amazement, Donal
answered and was seemingly thrilled with my offer of
100 pounds. His last words to me - would I be
supplying "pints and biddies?"
   I assured him there'd be oceans of beer on hand
and the flower of Wexford womanhood would be in
attendance. With that we concluded the deal, and a
couple of months later Emmet-Spiceland once again
knocked the socks off Wexford. Apart from making
enough money to guarantee a couple more top-of-the-
line concerts for this newly minted folk club, I was able
to play a set of my own songs as opening act and had no
bottles thrown at me – a singular achievement, I felt.
   Within a couple of months Emmet-Spiceland
were top of the Irish charts with a lovely arrangement of
Mary From Dungloe. They caused a sensation in Ireland
for they introduced youthful sex appeal into Traditional
Irish music. For the first time, girls were screaming at a
folk-group. Andy Irvine, then a member of Sweeney's
Men, who would later form Planxty with Donal Lunny
told me recently, "We all hated Emmet-Spiceland – they
got all the girls"
   It was the age of The Mamas and Papas and other
harmony groups; Emmet-Spiceland's genius was to

combine that aesthetic with romantic Irish songs. Hard core purists disdained them but they opened up Traditional music to an audience that had heretofore disdained it. Their follow up, *Bunclody*, is one of my favorite Irish ballads; it's probably no coincidence that it's about a beautiful small town in North County Wexford on the banks of the Slaney River that I have many connections with.

Bunclody

Oh were I at the moss house, where the birds do increase,
At the foot of Mount Leinster or some silent place,
By the streams of Bunclody where all pleasures do meet,
And all I would ask is one kiss from thee sweet.

'Tis why my love slights me, as you might understand,
For she has a freehold and I have no land,
She has fine store of riches in silver and gold,
And everything fitting a house to uphold.

Oh, were I a clerk and could write with good hand
I would write my love a letter that she might understand
For I am a poor fellow who is wounded in love
Once I lived in Bunclody but now must remove

So fare the well, father, my mother, adieu
My sisters and brothers farewell unto you,
I am bound for Americay my fortune to try,
When I think on Bunclody, I am ready to die.

(Traditional)

Who knows why Emmet-Spiceland didn't make it internationally; they had all the ingredients, but the music business is strange and there's little accounting for its ups and downs. Brian Bolger left the group early on and moved to France. They continued to be a huge draw but Donal Lunny, the backbone, seemed to tire of the pop celebrity life that had engulfed the group. Like his comrade in the original Emmet Folk, Mick Moloney, he wished to plough deeper into traditional Irish music and expand it from the core rather than from the frilly outside.

The recordings of Emmet-Spiceland don't do the band justice. A saccharine 1960's string arrangement sits astride most of the songs and makes them far less than they were live. Still, if you can get beyond the treacle, you'll experience those lovely harmonies and hear echoes of the cool beauty of their music. Onstage, they were much less polished, more driven, the guitars were gnarly and up-front, and most importantly, they stood tall with all that blessed exuberance of those who know they're doing something that no one else has attempted before.

CHAPTER NINE

Let's leave Donal Lunny for a while – never an easy task when dealing with Irish music – but I want to backtrack and deal with someone who's rarely considered a Celtic artist yet is fundamental to any understanding of modern Ireland and the music that has sprung from it. He was born in Ballyshannon in County Donegal but moved to Cork City in his early years. He may have been the most thrilling guitarist I've ever seen – he was definitely the most consistent and passionate. His name was Rory Gallagher.

Rory

Hey Rory, you're off to London
Playin' the blues with a band called Taste
Gonna hit the big time?
You better - you're the best
On your night you could even leave
Hendrix in the dust

> *I want to thank you for what you did*
> *No more messin' with the Kid*
>
> *Hero came back to Dublin*
> *The only one sober we're all out of our heads*
> *Long hair flyin'*
> *Blue denims drippin with sweat*
> *Volts of lightnin' in your fingers*
> *Pride of bein' the best*
> (Larry Kirwan)

Does that song seem bittersweet with a whole dollop of regret, and not a little sorrow wrapped around it? Well, that's how I feel about Rory when I recall the love and energy he injected into each of his shows. Most of the time, though, when I hear his recordings I just get swept up in the excitement and pride we Irish felt in this force of nature - "old son," as we fondly called him. When he'd walk offstage dripping in sweat, his long hair streaming down his denim jacket, we'd begin to bawl out to the rafters:

> *Nice one, Rory, nice one, son*
> *Nice one, Rory, let's have another one*

Of course, we knew he'd be back on stage within minutes playing a number of encores and even upping the ante on the drive, creativity and showmanship that he'd already have doled out over an explosive couple of hours. But there was always the chance that some dumb-ass promoter might not want to pay overtime to his staff and bring the house lights up. If that happened we'd know full well that our hero would never play

there again, for Rory Gallagher never allowed anyone to
get in the way of the three-way bond between himself,
his music and his audience.

Rory was another showband alumnus – his was
The Fontana, Van's The Monarchs; though showbands
provided a great grounding in music, the key was to
jump ship before you became stuck in their inevitably
soul destroying, imitative groove.

My friend, the musicologist Jack O'Leary, once a
sailor on British Rail Ferries between Ireland and the
UK, recalls Rory and Taste departing Cork for London in
1968 to take a shot at the big time. The young band was
pretty much unknown in Ireland. I was already a fan
though I'd never heard Taste – my closest association
was gazing in awe at a signed picture of the band in a
Cork City chipper.

It didn't take long for Taste to get noticed in
guitar-crazy London where the big three were Clapton,
Beck and Page. Initially what made Rory stand out was
his work ethic. The man just loved to play. He's sold 30
million albums now, but stick to his live CDs; I don't
believe he was ever really captured at his best in the
studio – that puts him in the revered company of
Marley, Springsteen, and many other great performers.
Apparently, while recording he was self-doubting, over-
meticulous and a second-guesser non-paralleled. But on
stage, he was a force of nature, living totally in the
moment and, to my mind anyway, volts of lightning did
flow through his fingers. It was as if he was fighting for
his life the minute he strode across that stage and tuned
up.

Then again, I was such a fan, his tuning up
sounded good to me! But his voice too set him apart
from the big three. Rory could sing the hell out of
anything – particularly if the tune had some connection

to the Blues. His singing was raucous, pleading, passionate and strident, and yet there was tenderness behind it, a link to his own self-doubt, perhaps. Like all the really great performers he was touched either by some divine spirit or something fierce and feral within himself. It would have been hard not to get swept up in the torrent of inspired notes and cries that he unleashed from the stage. Talk about breaking down the fourth wall – Rory vaporized it. I brought many people to see him over the years, some were skeptical on the way in - all were converted and dazed on the way out. Only a supremely ironic and detached individual could resist what that man let loose at audiences. I'm sure there were some such souls, but I never met any.

He once approached me in the Television Club in Dublin. He had won some award that night but yet had no assistant, entourage or anything of the like. It had to be the early 1970's. I was slouching against a wall, shy and unsure of myself in the midst of all the celebration. I thought I might be hallucinating for suddenly he was heading straight towards me in his own shy off-stage manner. He must have mistaken me for some red haired guy from his hometown for he nodded kindly and asked me if he could cadge a lift back to Cork. I was so dumbfounded I didn't know what to say. Whereupon he apologized and said, "Ah, you're probably not going home, right?"

"No," said I, "I'm not," as he turned away, though I felt like running outside, hijacking a car, and driving him to the city on the Lee, just to give a little something back for all the joy he'd given me.

You see Rory was our first homegrown international star. He was like one of the lads – you could never accuse Van of that. Besides, Mr. Morrison was from Northern Ireland. Many people from the

Republic were beginning to learn a lot more about the
North than they wished. Van hadn't a sectarian bone in
his body but, though undoubtedly Irish, he had grown
up in a very different culture. Rory was one of us, and
we took enormous pride in him. We didn't have a
whole lot else; our national soccer team was a joke and
the rest of the world didn't play hurling, but now we
had a guitarist/vocalist who could take on the best: "On
your night you could even leave Hendrix in the dust."

We did have Joyce and Yeats, but they'd both
been dead a long time; meanwhile up the highway the
North was careening from one atrocity to the next. The
very centre had caved in big time, and old Willie Yeats'
blood-dimmed tide had well and truly broken its banks.
Years of British refusal to deal with overt sectarianism
had come home with the chickens to roost. Rory was the
one beacon that lifted us above all that, and every
Christmas, no matter how bad the political situation, he
did a tour of the country that included Belfast. To top it
all, everyone turned out; people who wouldn't walk
down the same side of the street together had to rub
shoulders as they rushed towards the stage to be closer
to the action.

He must have known what was going on – must
have sensed the danger he was exposing himself to, a
lone figure out front of stage soaking up the spotlight.
He could scarcely have ignored the British army ringing
the Ulster Hall to make sure there were no riots entering
or leaving. But Rory was above all that. Music was his
god. With the lightning coursing through his fingertips,
once he hit that stage he didn't give a goddamn; he was
a man possessed and everyone had to suck it up, put
aside their politics, preconceptions, hurts, and
aspirations. And we did because we wanted to share in
the god-given magic that had been bestowed on this

slight figure; life was stark enough, who wanted to ruin
the few sparks of light that gave us hope in those dark
and dangerous days.

Rory looked like us too – he didn't go in for
Hendrix gypsy-vagabond scarves, nor Beck's velvet or
Page's spandex. No, he wore denim jackets and jeans,
plaid shirts and sneakers or work boots in the winter.
And, man, did that guy sweat? His very Stratocaster
was streaked permanently with the buckets of
perspiration that poured off him. And when he sang
Blind Boy Fuller's *Pistol Slapper Blues*:

> *You didn't say you didn't love me*
> *When you were stretched out on my bed*
> *Drinking moonshine whiskey*
> *And talkin' all out of your head...*

Those were the type of women we had in mind for
ourselves when we'd finally get to some Mississippi of
the soul that we'd always promised ourselves.

Rory seemed to be the only one not out of his
head on booze during those shows. The drinking would
come later. His brother, Donal, once told me that Rory
would have been better off if he'd started young like the
rest of us – would have learned to deal with the
condition earlier. There was one show at the National
Boxing Stadium in Dublin when our collective alcohol
fumes could have made a small nation tipsy – no booze
was sold inside the hall so you had to fortify yourself for
two plus hours of abstention before entering. I can't
remember the name of the song, but one audience
member was so moved he shimmied up a pole onto a
narrow beam and began to edge his way unsteadily over
to the stage.

Rory was in the midst of a long solo and was the only person in the hall unaware of this lunatic escapade. The bouncers looked on in amazement – for once none of them willing to follow the perpetrator and kick the shit out of him. Eventually, when the aerialist realized he stood a better chance of joining Rory by rushing the stage, he shimmied on back down another pole and was positively dumbfounded to be turfed out on his arse. That was the effect this Cork guitar slinger had on his audience.

Although Rory was known more for his Stratocaster playing, he was a stunning acoustic guitarist and mandolin player. The Blues with its basic honesty of expression was Rory's foundation, yet you could feel him edging towards Irish traditional music. He often spoke of his interest in the genre in interviews and he became good friends with Ronnie Drew of the Dubliners. There are videos of his last European tour in 1994 when he plays a riveting version of *She Moves Through The Fair*. You can tell he had a great appreciation for the playing of Bert Jansch and Davey Graham. Perhaps even more revealing is his rendition of the old tune *Dan O'Hara* as you feel him meld the Irish Trad influence with a Lead Belly swing.

It makes you wonder where Rory would have ended up musically. It's not outside the bounds of possibility that he would have tackled some of the compositions of another Cork blow-in, Sean Ó'Riada, and worked his considerable magic on them. Regardless of all his rock and blues influences, I've always considered Rory a Celtic musician – even a Celtic warrior in ways, for he took all the passion and melancholy of the Irish psyche and wove it into his music, and left behind a testament of what one man with a huge soul can achieve with a guitar.

Rory's sudden death was like a kick in the head. I had heard rumors about his drinking and it was obvious that he had gained a lot of weight. I suppose all this makes sense now; overmedication and an ease of access to prescription drugs are a large part of our culture (if you don't believe me, take a look in your medicine cabinet). All that aside, it just didn't make sense to me – Rory was always the clean one while the rest of us were out of our skulls. It just didn't seem fair. I had also missed his last show in New York. I was on the road with Black 47. I had never missed a local one before. Now there would be no more shows – no more moments when I'd soar to the sweat-stained strings of Rory's guitar. It was like a curtain closing behind me.

Like many, I was outraged by the showbiz banality of the obituaries in the American press. Their main point seemed to be that Rory had missed his chance – The Rolling Stones had considered him as a replacement for Mick Taylor, but Rory had either turned down the gig or hadn't passed Mick's muster. You gotta be kidding me! The Stones missed Rory way more than he ever missed them. He would never have allowed them to turn into a self-referential tribute band, and don't get me wrong, I love the Stones and pretty much every song in their pre-1979 back catalogue. But what a difference Rory would have made to this great band. He could have single-handedly revived their creative spark. Imagine Keef trying to keep up with this bluesy dynamo? What a power duo they would have made. Talk about intertwining rhythm and lead lines – they were born for each other.

And think of the effect he would have had on Jagger – they could have reinvented the Blues together. But Rory knew better than to join. He wasn't the type to be nailed to the floor in someone else's tradition. Nah, he was on a different mission. He knew what he was after and those of us who were lucky enough to be uplifted by his presence at one of his thousands of gigs count ourselves blessed. How often do you get to see streaks of lightning shooting out of someone's fingertips? In the end, it was like losing a real close friend: you're left with the memories and the ultimate question, what if?

> *What the hell happened, head?*
> *Where did the lightnin' go?*
> *Did it burn right through your fingers*
> *To the cockles of your soul?*
> *Leavin' you stranded*
> *A million miles away from the rest of us....*

> *I want to thank you for what you did*
> *No more messin' with the Kid*
> *So long, old son, that's it*
> *No more messin' with the kid*

(Larry Kirwan)

CHAPTER TEN

I moved to Dublin in 1968. Much as I loved Wexford, it was definitely time to go. Miss Codd had retired and Uncle Paddy was more truculent by the day; my grandfather appeared distracted, more in a world of his own, but although he had slowed down physically he was still a presence down in the yard – a man of stone indeed. I would later look back on those adolescent years and encapsulate them in a play, *Poetry of Stone*. But I had a need to stretch my wings, as did Black Eyes.

I guess I had forgotten to mention her in all this talk about music and politics, but after I left secondary school, I became an articled clerk to a firm of Chartered Accountants. In essence this meant that, for the privilege of working forty hours a week for five years for a pittance and passing five difficult exams, you too could pull the same racket on four teenage clerks when you became a shattered accountant. A pretty dismal deal, I suppose, but it didn't trouble me that much for it

119

was the 1960's - I was out playing in bands or ballad groups most night and besides there was Black Eyes smoldering across the desk when I'd arrive for work exhausted most mornings. I didn't much care for accounting, but I must have been decent at it for early on I got second place in Ireland in one of the exams; probably the worst thing that could have happened from a professional point of view because from then on I did practically no study relying on my wits to get me through all subsequent tests.

I didn't have a whole lot of time with Black Eyes around. It was a tumultuous affair.

Oh he meets a girl but she is not so nice
She wear micro-dresses has stormy black eyes
He no longer has time for the County Library
Learning about life in the back of a Mini...

It caused quite a stir in our accountancy office. Johnny Wyley, our very benevolent boss, sat stone-faced when we informed him that we were leaving. I had noticed an odd bylaw in my articles of serfdom where one could take a six-months sabbatical for an office job in a large commercial concern. Player-Wills, the tobacco firm, took me into their fold; not only that - they paid me a decent salary. It was an odd choice in retrospect since I didn't smoke cigarettes. Whatever, it set me free, so Black Eyes and I departed for Dublin. Young couples didn't move in together in those days – landlords fingering their rosary beads wouldn't have allowed it. Just as well given our tempestuous relationship. I saw her most weekends and that seemed to work out well for both of us. She did her thing and I did mine... she got an apartment near Merrion Square while I moved out to the coldwater culchie flatlands of Rathmines.

Dublin was a delight. It pulsed with music and drinking; no one had much money and few gave a damn. One night I walked into the Coffee Kitchen, a folk club on Molesworth Street; I had played a short set there the previous week and been well received. It was a cellar type room jammed with a hundred or so people; the ceiling was low, condensation streamed down the walls. It was somewhat purist, but microphones were hardly needed anyway as complete silence was demanded for each performer – and received. You signed up for your slot and then repaired to the watering hole of your choice – or, as many did, you got there early for a good seat and took in the bad with the good.

However, there was a surprisingly high standard, for this was no open mike night – you needed an invitation to perform. There was no pay even though some artists definitely drew; well-known acts dropped by to try out new songs or pick up a folkie lady or two. There was an air of structured anarchy to the scene but no one was allowed to perform more than three songs, no matter their fame. Marxism was in the air while the sweet smell of Lebanese Blonde and Afghan Brown melded with the acrid clouds of cigarette smoke. Leo O'Kelly, who had replaced Donal Lunny in Emmet-Spiceland, was a big favorite, as was Sonny Condell. They began to perform together around this time under the name *Tír na nÓg*, then traveled to London, gained a recording deal and opened for Jethro Tull on a US tour – a feat almost beyond belief in the damp, cramped bedsitters of Dublin.

Certain snippets of songs that I heard at the Coffee Kitchen and in the sister club, The Universal up in Parnell Square, are still lodged in my mind, and when I hum them, I can summon up the sweat-stained walls, smell the dampness of the coats on rainy nights, hear the chiming sounds of Yamahas and the occasional, much coveted Martin. On one such night a murmur spread through the room that "a friend of Donal's" was about to play; but then Donal Lunny had a legion of friends – I even considered myself one although I'm not sure that he would have known me from Paddy Delaney's donkey. Still, along with everyone else, my ears perked up, for Mr. Lunny was folk royalty and any friend of his was worth a listen.

This one looked different though. He definitely wouldn't have made the cut for Emmet-Spiceland. Much more of a man, muscular and bulky, with a full beard and a stony expression, he favored us all with the hairy eyeball before plopping down on the performance stool and closing his eyes. He held that pose for a moment longer than was usual, gaining our complete attention. You could tell he was used to playing in places where silence might not be guaranteed and one might have to assert one's will upon a crowd of rowdy drinkers. He left us in no doubt that if by chance we did cough, sneeze or otherwise upset the expected silence, we might pay dearly.

He began to pick the strings confidently, though he was no flashy guitar slinger. No, his playing was more a setting in which to situate his voice. I knew the song from the Wexford Ballad Competition but I had never heard it sung with such honesty. His voice was strong and very rich but his delivery was unlike any I'd heard before. It took me a verse or two until I realized why – he was singing the way Irish people spoke. He had put neither an American twang on it nor your generic *Sean Nós* adenoidal whine; instead he employed his natural Kildare accent with no embellishments. I could feel some of the cognoscenti in that packed room stiffen, this wasn't what they'd come to see, for even in those nascent folk days a certain style and mode of delivery had been adopted and was for the most part adhered to. Before the second verse had ended I was questioning my own delivery – as I have done many times since. Back then I definitely didn't sing in a Wexford accent – I had been too conditioned by years of listening to everything and its mother on Luxembourg and the BBC. But Christy Moore had already found his voice.

His brow was furrowed in concentration, his eyes closed as he sang *The Curragh of Kildare* – and why shouldn't he, being born and bred in that county. And then he began to sweat but, though the room was hot and close, I could tell it didn't come from heat but absorption in the song. There was no bantering or verbal communication with the audience – barely a nod to acknowledge the applause. He has since become one of the world's great communicators on stage – when he's in the mood – and a genuinely funny person when he lets it flow.

On that night he obviously had nothing to say; perhaps he sensed the silent disapproval of a minority of the audience. I can't remember his second song but he finished with *Spancil Hill*. I had never liked the song, probably because I'd always heard it played as an uninspired dowdy waltz by showbands where the words were mere ornamentals to the strictness of a 3/4 time. But that night I got the full meaning of the piece from Christy and straight in the face for good measure; I also gained a new appreciation for the fact that if you burrow deep enough into the spine of a song you can sweep off the dust and allow the original intent to become crystal clear again. As Christy sang, I could feel the pain of that young man, Michael Considine, writing

to his sweetheart Mary MacNamara from worlds away
in far-off Gold Rush California, knowing he'll never see
her again or return to his home in East County Clare.

Spancil Hill

Last night as I lay dreaming, of the pleasant days gone by,
My mind being bent on rambling to Erin's Isle I did fly.
I stepped on board a vision and sailed out with a will,
'Till I gladly came to anchor at the Cross of Spancil Hill.

Enchanted by the novelty, delighted with the scenes,
Where in my early childhood, I often times have been.
I thought I heard a murmur, I think I hear it still,
'Tis that little stream of water at the Cross of Spancil Hill.

And to amuse my fancy, I lay upon the ground,
Where all my school companions, in crowds assembled 'round.
Some have grown to manhood, while more their graves did fill,
Oh I thought we were all young again, at the Cross of Spancil
Hill.

I went into my old home, as every stone can tell,
The old boreen was just the same, and the apple tree over the
well,
I miss my sister Ellen, my brothers Pat and Bill,
Sure I only met strange faces at my home in Spancil Hill.

I called to see my neighbors, to hear what they might say,
The old were getting feeble, and the young ones turning grey.
I met with tailor Quigley, he's as brave as ever still,
Sure he always made my breeches when I lived in Spancil Hill.

I paid a flying visit, to my first and only love,
She's pure as any lily, and as gentle as a dove.
She threw her arms around me, saying Mike I love you still,
She is Mack the Ranger's daughter, the Pride of Spancil Hill.

I thought I stooped to kiss her, as I did in days of yore,
Says she Mike you're only joking, as you often were before,
The cock crew on the roost again, he crew both loud and shrill,
And I awoke in California, far far from Spancilhill.
                                    (Michael Considine)

The applause grew as the singer stood up from the stool.
Many of us had been moved but some others considered
the song to be old fashioned and the wrong side of cool.
The great are rarely cool – what touches the heart and
soul often has a problem with the jaded or fashion-
conscious mind. Christy Moore has always been
somewhere in that bag, a consummate artist with a
common touch who speaks for and to a great number of
Irish people, but is considered too odd and homegrown
for others.
        He gave a curt nod to the audience, packed his
guitar and strode out the door without a glance behind.
He didn't stop to glad-hand anyone or make the
requisite small talk with the club organizers, just up the
steps into the mist and away with him into the thick of
the Dublin night. I made a mental note of the man. I
had a feeling I'd be hearing more about him, and I
wasn't far off the mark. A year or two later he recorded
a live album at a pub in Prosperous in his native Co.
Kildare that would change the face – and sound – of
Irish music. Inevitably, the ubiquitous Donal Lunny, a
childhood friend, would play a major role. He was
joined by Andy Irvine who we've already met with

Sweeney's Men, and one of the great Irish uilleann pipers, Liam Óg O'Flynn.

The sound was different. It wasn't that we hadn't heard the pipes before; Paddy Moloney, among others, had broken recorded ground with them. But there was something about the way they settled in the lee of Christy's commanding voice that snared an echo of another time. Add to that the trebly intertwining of Donal's bouzouki with Andy's mandolin over the singer's stately guitar; this innovation had already happened with Sweeney's Men, but there was a confidence – or perhaps a couldn't care less - about it now a couple of years down the line. With all the elements mixed together exceedingly well by Bill Leader, it was a sound that caught your attention.

The uilleann pipes really stood out, particularly on *Cliffs of Dooneen*. The pipes originated as a solo instrument, rarely used in an ensemble. They're a curse and a blessing beyond compare, as I know from my years dealing with them as a lead instrument in Black 47. They're designed to be played in the temperate cool and damp climate of Ireland and can flatten or sharpen with the slightest change in weather conditions – forget about the extremes of American air-conditioning or the summer's sweltering heat on an outdoor stage! All of this meant little to the pipers of old; for with no rhythm instrument snapping at their heels who was counting which side of A440 they began a set of reels upon - a far different matter in a Rock 'n' Roll band when the player is seeking to keep this bizarre looking instrument (Dave Letterman famously called ours "a stick in a carpet") within an ass's roar of a sax and trombone not to mention a whammy-barred Stratocaster.

But Liam Óg is a master technician as well as a sweet soloist who has never stopped growing in both art

and technique (take a listen to his stunning work with
Seamus Heaney on 2003's *The Poet & The Piper*). Still on
a long ago night in Prosperous he found that sweet spot
where the pipes can curl around the lyrics and turn
them inside out, and in so doing vividly display those
cliffs to people who have no notion of what they might
look like and may never set real eyes on them. How
lucky we are that those moments in time were captured.

Cliffs of Dooneen

*You may travel far far from your own native home
Far away o'er the mountains far away o'er the foam
But of all the fine places that I've ever seen,
There's none to compare with the Cliffs of Dooneen*

*Take a view o'er the water fine sights you'll see there
You'll see the high rocky slopes on the West coast of Clare
The towns of Kilrush and Kilkee can be seen
From the high rocky slopes at the Cliffs of Dooneen*

*It's a nice place to be on a fine Summer's day
Watching all the wild flowers that ne'er do decay
The hare and lofty pheasant are plain to be seen
Making homes for their young round the Cliffs of Dooneen*

*Fare thee well to Dooneen fare thee well for a while
And to all the fine people I'm leaving behind
To the streams and the meadows where late I have been
And the high rocky slopes of the Cliffs of Dooneen*
(Jack McAuliffe)

Donal, Christy, Andy and Liam Óg so enjoyed
each other's company and musical chops they decided
to keep the unit going and named it Planxty. *Cliffs of*

Dooneen had been picked up by RTE Radio and soon became one of the most popular Irish songs. I was living in New York by then and was somewhat unaware of the stir being caused by the band, but on my first visit back I was struck by the ubiquity of the song and the almost air of reverence that would descend upon any group of people when the tune began. Apart from its lovely melody and Christy's wistfully direct delivery, the song spoke to Irish people of their unique heritage and the serene but passionate beauty of their countryside. It also highlighted for them the notion that they had inherited this priceless possession but would only retain it for a short span of time so it would behoove them to cherish it and pass it on in good shape.

At the time, I had been living the wild life on the streets of the Lower East Side, had experimented much with many things and was trying to fit back into Irish life if only for a month or two. The song was a gateway back to many of the things that I had grown up with, and was even a way to relate to family and friends again. It enabled me to set my feet back on the ground and come to terms with the country I loved, even though I knew I'd be leaving soon again and would probably never return permanently. This latter thought was a big revelation and caused a lot of bittersweet reflection late at night and at many tearful Shannon Airport farewells, not too far from the mythical cliffs themselves.

For some reason the song brought me back to a summer afternoon while studying Irish in Ballingeary (*Béal Átha'n Ghaorthaidh*) in West Cork. Along with some of my Wexford CBS school friends, I walked to lovely *Gougane Barra*. There on the side of a hill we came upon a farmer staring down at the beautiful valley. He seemed lost in thought and put no pass on our bantering adolescent approach.

We paused next to him as he leaned against an old fence and followed his gaze. He refused to tear his eyes away but did silently acknowledge our presence. The view was indeed breathtaking: the land below a water-colored mosaic of small green fields and golden hay patches, and scattered throughout, some tiny lakes of sparkling water – all held together by a shimmering haze of heat. The sun beat down on us and the sky was clear and blue as it rarely is in West Cork. The old man turned to us and said, "I've lived here nearly every day of my life, but sometimes the sight of it still takes my breath away."

I think that's the effect that the recording of *Cliffs of Dooneen* had on so many Irish people – including me.

CHAPTER ELEVEN

When talking about Irish music from the late 60's onwards, it's important to take into account the "national question," and in particular the events transpiring in the North of Ireland during that period. It's true there were many musicians who had no interest whatsoever or who actively sought to distance themselves from the carnage that was occurring in the British controlled Six Northern Counties; even so, their songs were still cast in relief by the news reports that bookended many music programs.

Most rock musicians had little time for the Troubles – with the exception of Northern bands like Stiff Little Fingers and The Undertones; and that stands to reason, their musical influences were from the UK and US and so, in general, they tended to look beyond Ireland and what was, at best, a very intractable situation in the North. This often seemed like a waste to me, as there was such lyrical grist for the mill in what was going on scarcely one hundred miles up the pike from Dublin. It would be so interesting to hear how Rory Gallagher, Phil Lynott and others might have incorporated the scalding scenarios and riveting

characters into their songs. Dolores Riordan of The
Cranberries did write *Zombie*, a scathing song about the
Northern situation that is one of the highlights of her
repertoire, but I'd love to have heard her take on the
feminist civil rights activist, Bernadette Devlin
McAliskey.

Traditional musicians sometimes tended to be
more politically aware. Perhaps that's because of the
roots and nature of their music; still, many also were
apolitical or just plain uninterested. Christy Moore was
not one of these. Thus, although Planxty made few
overt political statements in their songs, you could feel
the band's solidarity with certain Northern nationalist
elements along with a general independent point of
view that emanated from the group. Beside which,
Christy has always exuded a moody, "don't mess with
me" quality and made little bones about his heightened
political awareness. Although he is often seen as an
Irish everyman, he has always maintained a certain
distance from the state and its trappings.

This disassociation was heightened by the
election of a coalition government in 1973. Previous
coalition governments formed by the conservative Fine
Gael party, the more liberal Labor Party and other fringe
parties, led to a loosening of the belt, as it were, in Irish
life. But this new administration took power at a
particularly troubled time in the Northern conflict when
it seemed as though the whole mess might spill over into
the Republic.

Oddly enough one of the most liberal (up until
then) members of the coalition, Conor Cruise O'Brien,
was the chief belt-tightener. He would have a huge
effect on Irish political and cultural life. Although his
parents had deep nationalist sympathies and
connections to the iconic 1916 Uprising, O'Brien was

outraged by purported republican leanings in the state run Raidió Telefís Éireann (RTE). As Minister for Posts and Telegraphs, under Section 31 of the Broadcasting Authority Act, he strengthened restrictions against members of the ultra-nationalist Sinn Fein Party being heard or interviewed on RTE. Likewise, he enforced a ban on all songs that might suggest republican leanings – these included many traditional rebel anthems and indeed any piece of music that encouraged pro-nationalist sentiment.

This was to have an unforeseen consequence in that a generation of Irish children would grow up relatively unaware of songs that up until then had been part of the DNA of Irish culture. Because of their sensitivity to the ban, broadcasters tended to lump in many traditional songs that might have only had glancing allusions to rebellion or lack of respect for our English neighbors. Luckily Thin Lizzy had recorded *Whiskey in the Jar* some short years before the righteous Dr. O'Brien went on his cultural Jihad.

Whiskey in the Jar

As I was going over the Cork and Kerry mountains
I met with Captain Farrell and his money he was counting
I first produced me pistol, I then produced me rapier
Sayin' "stand and deliver for you are a bould deceiver"

Musha ring dum a do dum a da.
Whack fol the daddy-o,
Whack fol the daddy-o
There's whiskey in the jar

I counted out his money and it made a pretty penny.
I put it in me pocket and I took it home to Jenny
She sighed and she swore that she never more would leave me
But the devil take the women for they never can be easy

I went up to me chamber all ready for me slumber
I dreamt of gold and jewels and sure it 'twas no
wonder
Jenny took me charges, she filled them up with water
Sent for Captain Farrell to make ready for the
slaughter

Now some take delight in the carriages a'rollin'
Others take delight in the huntin' and the sportin'
I take delight in the juice of the barley
And courtin' married women in the mornin' bright
and early
(Traditional)

I wonder if Phil Lynott and The Cruiser (as Dr.
Cruise-O'Brien was called) ever ran into each other.
Dublin was a much smaller town in the 70's and both
were of an artistic bent. Perhaps they met at The Bailey
on Duke Street, a literary watering hole owned by
mutual friend, John Ryan. I'm sure the good doctor was
aware of Phil. It was hard to ignore him. He was like a
force of nature breezing through the Dublin streets,
often times a bunch of inner-city kids trailing and
flailing behind him as though he was a reincarnated
pied piper – and this was long before he gained
international fame and fortune as the lead singer of Thin
Lizzy.

There's a statue to him in Dublin now and Phil must be smiling down on it – though, as statues go, it doesn't really do him justice. In many ways, he replaced the old literary guard of Brendan Behan, Patrick Kavanagh and Myles na gCopaleen (Brian O'Nolan), and he wasn't unaware of the fact. From an early age he frequented The Bailey, one of the best pubs I've ever had the good fortune to raise an elbow in – though now not even a shadow of its former self. Proprietor John Ryan was a raffish gentleman and a confirmed patron of the arts who had much time for anyone who might add to the artistic life of Dublin. It was in The Bailey, for instance, that Patrick Kavanagh first handed Luke Kelly the words of *Raglan Road* and bade him sing them to the tune of *The Dawning of the Day*. Phil fancied himself as a bit of a poet too, and he was way more than that, but before he had gained even a modicum of local recognition you just knew that he was destined to become a major international rock star.

It wasn't only because Phil was black that he stood out in a Dublin that was then very homogenous; no, he was just larger than life, and in the nicest possible way. Although outgoing and open, he was no braggart, and he seemed to leave an air of kindness and concern in his wake. Perhaps one of his most endearing traits was that he had a very thick Dublin accent. Now I don't know whether he cultivated this but it was quite stunning for an ignoramus like me up from the bogs of Wexford to hear a black man give forth in a Crumlin accent; and this was before I ever heard him sing.

He was extremely handsome in a devil-may-care way and the most charismatic person I ever encountered. You only had to be in his presence to feel the room light up; and if he flashed you a smile or nodded in your direction, your day was made. The jig was up if he actually spoke to you – and he smiled and bade "howya" to everyone as he strode purposefully around the city, though truth be told I rarely saw him enter a building; I guess he liked the great outdoors.

I swear to God that as he swaggered up O'Connell Street, there would be a line of people craning their necks backwards to get a better look at what had just sailed by. It wasn't just the modern celebrity thing either, where you stop to gawk at some less than impressive figure from the tabloids just because there are cameras pointing and beefy security guards pouting. No, Phil Lynott was the real deal, and it seemed like the very stones of Dublin city were entranced by him. Some people even prayed for him and it's hardly exaggeration to say we all felt better about ourselves after we had been touched by this very special person.

His mother, Philomena Lynott, quite a character herself, had emigrated to Birmingham after World War II. There she had a relationship with an Afro-Guyanese man, Cecil Parris; although he offered to marry her when Phil was conceived, she declined. Thus Phil was illegitimate at a time when such a state was socially frowned upon, to put it mildly; add Phil's color to the mix and one can see the difficulties the young woman confronted. Philomena sent him home to be raised by his grandmother while she worked on in the UK to provide money for his upkeep. He had no father figure but much love in his granny's house. By sheer force of character he blunted the racism and social stigma that one might expect in a tough working class environment of the 1950's and he soon became the most popular boy in his school.

But Phil was always bent on musical expression and achieving rock stardom. By the time I first saw him he already had considerable flair and a well-developed eye for the camera. Tall, thin, black, with a stylish Afro, and a bandana or two streaming behind him for good measure, he looked not unlike an Irish Hendrix. We lesser beings from the arse-hole of wherever were totally tuned in to both the Dublin Beat and Folk scenes by our slavish devotion to a magazine called *Spotlight* (later *New Spotlight*). While this weekly bible mostly featured articles on showbands, Pat Egan – now a top Dublin promoter - minutely chronicled the comings and goings of the Beat scene. Hipsters who might know fewer than 3 chords on an imitation Stratocaster were figures of wonder and awe to cool culchies the length and breadth of Ireland because of a couple of mentions in Pat's terse, but informative, column. Shay Healy - who would later write a Eurovision winner and direct *Green Cop Rocker,* a television feature, on my Black 47 partner Chris Byrne – did much the same for the Folk scene.

Both Pat and Shay had plenty to write about for Dublin was crawling with talent back then. Much of this had to do with the general social and sexual revolution that had hit Ireland in the mid '60's. In other words, if you had the least thought of spreading your wings or getting the hell out of your conservative village, town or cow-pasture, you hotfooted it to Dublin where the booze was cheap, the women had retired their rosary beads, and all virgins, blessed and otherwise, were in a mood for experimentation. Once there, should you have the least inkling of talent, you were likely to run into kindred souls with whom you might start a band, group, theatre company, or just hold forth on such matters in the many pubs that dotted the city.

Artistic social life tended to center on a mile or so of storied real estate. Were you to take a walk from St. Stephen's Green down Grafton Street, around Trinity College onto O'Connell Bridge and up that crowded

boulevard to Parnell Square, you would be a very
unlucky person if you weren't forced to skip around the
like of Luke Kelly, Gay Byrne, Charles Haughey, Phil
Lynott, Gary Moore or Brendan "Brush" Shields.
Brush was one of the more interesting characters
in Dublin. He was already a bass-playing legend by the
time I patrolled those streets, penniless but thrilled at
my good fortune at just being allowed to add my small
dash of color to this cosmopolitan scene. Brush had
recently formed Skid Row with Phil as lead singer.
Although he cut a distinctive figure by dint of his
personality, clothes weren't really Brush's thing. Even
then you could feel that he didn't trust "the scene" and
intrinsically recognized that fashion would wax and
wane.

He was already married and used to potter
around Dublin with his young wife who pushed a pram,
often with a scarf-covered head in the style of much
older Irish women. Since everyone else was preening
like so many electric peacocks, this made Brush stand
out even more. He was forever cordial and polite to
anyone who wished to engage him in conversation on
his walks up O'Connell Street; nor did his wife seem to
bat an eyelash - this was his job after all - she would wait
patiently no matter what the weather. That was in his
down time, but the minute Brush hit the stage, he was
all business and intensity. I had never heard a louder
bass player; add to the fact that he could play a mile a
minute and favored many notes on his bottom E and A
strings, let's just say no one had need of their morning
prune juice after a rip-roaring bluesy set from Skid Row.
At this time there arrived in Dublin from Belfast a
16 year-old guitar prodigy by name of Gary Moore.
Gary too was often seen trudging around the damp
streets and was equally unmistakable for he had the

longest hair of anyone I had ever seen, man or woman. He too caused consternation in his strolls for he was slim and good looking, and attracted many whistles from those assuming he was a particularly fine-looking young lady. This seemed to cause him no problem, probably because he was silently auditing some fantastic guitar figure that would pulverize us as soon as he hit the stage later that night. I understood, though I could rarely get my fingers around Rory Gallagher's runs, but Gary's blistering solos mystified me. If the humor was on him, he could play the Blues like an old hand from Biloxi, Mississippi, but it was his technotronics, for want of a better word, that astounded me.

And it wasn't that he was like some Hendrix clone either, for Jimi's divine creativity was usually based on the Blues and Soul. The squalls of notes that Gary produced in his early live playing with Skid Row seemed to be coming from some other dimension. I wasn't even sure how much I liked it, but I was careful not to offer that philistine opinion, for every musician in Dublin was howling to the heavens that Gary was the biggest thing since the sinking of the Titanic. As he matured his style became more melodic and practical – though still virtuosic – and there's little record of those early live Skid Row gigs, but that longhaired Belfast boy wonder most definitely knocked the socks off everyone in those blissful, distant Dublin days.

Noel Bridgeman, a wonderful drummer who sported a red Afro, with a no-prisoners-taken flailing style not unlike Ginger Baker, added to the wonderful noise that was Skid Row, the band for whom Phil Lynott sang. But not for long! At some point it was deemed within the group that Phil's vocal pitch was suspect and that they'd do better as a power trio. So, while Phil was away getting his tonsils extracted (which did apparently improve his tunefulness) he was, as they say, given the pink slip. This move caused pandemonium in the uber-cool world of the Dublin Beat scene. I too was flabbergasted and felt very badly for Phil, particularly on his eternal walks around the city, now that everyone who was anyone had heard about his demotion.

But whatever his inner feelings, he never seemed to blink an eye – I suppose that's a further testament to his single-minded devotion to becoming a rock star. In fact, as a consolation prize, Brush gave him bass lessons and before we knew it, Phil was hammering away on that four-stringer as if he had emerged straight from the womb holding it. Better still, after a detour into a fine band, Orphanage, he formed Thin Lizzy with Eric Bell, and a boyhood friend, Brian Downey, on drums.

Although many great guitar slingers would do time in Thin Lizzy down the years – including the amazing Mr. Moore - Eric Bell for me is the unsung hero. He too was from Belfast and cut his teeth in a late edition of Them; heading south of the border, he cut no less of a figure around Dublin with his mass of curly red hair, although I think he may have given it a blonde rinse from time to time. Whatever about hair, he sported a long, rugged, green army coat that shielded him from the damp Dublin winters. His guitar solo on *Whiskey in the Jar* still causes shivers; with its exquisite, slightly overdriven rawness, it's a sound I've often tried to emulate. It seemed to weave sinuously around Phil's hoarse Hendrix/Dylanesque vocals on that track and provided the perfect modern counterpoint to the tale of a betrayed 18th Century Highwayman.

Phil and Eric were inseparable in those early Lizzy Dublin days. Although they hadn't achieved any particular success except with the cool Beat Scene aficionados, they were cloaked by a shimmering

ebullience, a feeling that something was just about to
happen that would put them over the top.

One night Pierce Turner and I were having our
weekly dinner out at the Luna, a Chinese Restaurant
that perched on a second floor over O'Connell Street,
just across from the GPO; lo and behold, who sat down
at the table next to us but Phil and Eric! After
exchanging cursory greetings, we returned to our food
but kept our ears cocked for any pearls of wisdom that
might drop from the mouths of these demigods. The
gist of the conversation was that Lynott felt they had to
move to London, but Bell was reluctant. Phil did most
of the talking, insisting that they'd never make it "if they
got stuck in Ireland." The phrase stayed with me as I
was feeling much the same myself. I can't remember
Eric's reasons for not going, except a general reluctance
to leave what they were undoubtedly building in Dublin
for the bleakness of London. He'd apparently had some
painful experience while over there with Them. In any
event, nothing was decided - over that particular
Chinese dinner anyhow.

Of course, they did go but only after electrifying
us with their version of *Whiskey in the Jar*. I can't
emphasize just what an impact this recording had on the
youth of Ireland. We were well used to Horslips by then
and many of us loved them, but there was a certain
universality to *Whiskey in the Jar*. It exploded out of
mono car speakers in much the same way that a Kanye
rant does nowadays – distorted and with way too much
wattage for anemic speakers but immediate and
personal nonetheless - everyone played it at full volume,
an anthem of self-affirmation. A very popular
traditional song already, it had been recorded by The
Dubliners, among others, and was considered a
standard.

Yet, it was like we were hearing it for the first
time. Phil's voice seemed to probe the song's very soul
and revealed new angles and meanings that had never
occurred to us before. Eric's guitar was a revelation. It
was akin to Rory digging into the Blues, yet the Blues
was someone else's music. The man from Belfast was
stoking and amplifying part of our birthright. This was
our music and it was rawer, more revelatory and funkier
than anything else on the radio that year and for many
the year to come.

Pierce and I left Ireland soon after to pursue our
own creative dream. We performed *Whiskey in the Jar*
many times in Irish pubs around America but it always
seemed weak and flimsy to me in comparison to the real
deal. In the end I stopped singing it – what was the
point in battling Lizzy's perfection?

I didn't see Thin Lizzy again until October 1977.
Eric was long gone by then. He quit in the middle of a
New Year's Eve concert, throwing his guitar into the air
and pushing his amps into the front rows of the
audience. The constant touring, drug and alcohol abuse
finally took their toll. There were persistent rumors
about such doings in the band, yet the few times I met
Phil in the US he seemed as clean as a whistle – and I
could tell because I wasn't. Such was the case at the
Palladium on 14th Street when Lizzy topped the bill with
Graham Parker & The Rumour opening. I went along
for sentimental reasons but, in truth, I was more
interested in Parker and the new sound he represented
that was coming out of London. Many in the audience
must have felt the same for a significant portion left
during the changeover.

At first Lizzy seemed jaded: the rock-star lights
and smoke machines dated them. Punk had changed
our perception; after all, it had been born only blocks

141

away on The Bowery. The twin lead guitars sounded overplayed and bombastic. I'm sure the band could see the host of empty seats and the scarcity of dandruffed heads bobbing to their Pop-Metal. And then Phil took control. I'm not sure what he said to his band-mates but it was vitriolic and spat from the teeth. The house might not be full, perhaps Graham Parker had scored some sort of critical victory, but this was Thin Lizzy from Crumlin, the boys were back in town, tonight there was going to be a jailbreak, and suddenly the band jelled, kicked arse, took names, and it was Dublin all over again with everything to play for and no prisoners taken until after the final sweaty encore.

Up in the crowded dressing room, Phil was his usual courteous, friendly self. He said he remembered me; of course, he didn't, but he inquired what type of music Pierce and I were playing and showed interest in our take on things. But I could see he was disassociated from everything that was happening in that champagne room; nor did he take a drink, just stood with his back to the wall and watched the usual shenanigans that are played out in a headliner's dressing room. No one mentioned Graham Parker but I could tell he was on Phil's mind. The black rebel from Crumlin was now the establishment and the punk barbarians were at the gates. Was it my imagination or was Phil wishing he was down the hall in the opener's dressing room plotting world dominion?

I don't think Thin Lizzy ever came back to New York although they did tour relentlessly around the world. There was always a new album to support, and once you got trapped on that stardom treadmill, it was never easy to get off. I'd heard rumors of heroin/cocaine use and excessive drinking, but like many others, I was deeply shocked when the news broke on a bitter 1986 January morning that Phil had passed away. I won't say it was the end of innocence – far from it. For I had tasted many things myself by then – but it was the end of something; perhaps, the Rock 'n' Roll dream. I was sad for days and then I filed it away with all the other train wrecks I've witnessed in this rockers' world. In the end, you have your own life to live, you get on with that and, callous though it may seem, you thank your lucky stars it wasn't you.

I find it really hard to look at Phil's statue in Dublin; I usually give it a curt nod and stroll on. The intention is well meant, but to me it looks like a parody of the man who strolled those streets, the very life force exploding out of him. Nah, instead I stop every time I hear him electrify that old chestnut, *Whiskey in the Jar*, and I crack a smile – and occasionally a bottle – for the black Crumlin rebel who gave light and hope to so many of us who set off on our own Rock 'n' Roll journeys.

CHAPTER TWELVE

In the early 1970's, Ireland was changing rapidly, but within the bubble of everyday life that wasn't as yet quite obvious. True, the sexual revolution had hit a conservative country like a hammer in the late 60's, while the urban and rural guerilla warfare being waged by the Provisional IRA in the North was beginning to break down the long entrenched Unionist stranglehold, sending shock waves across the border; still and all, the Catholic Church had managed to hold on to much of its power and the parish priest was still the focal center of life, at least in the rural areas. On the entertainment side, showbands still ruled although their revenue was curtailed by the closure of ballrooms and clubs in the North due to the sectarian violence. Notwithstanding this, the ubiquitous showband van, Ford Transit and Volkswagen, could still be seen speeding through the countryside as Ireland entered the European Economic Community (EEC) on January 1ˢᵗ, 1973. This union led to a great infusion of cash into the country and an immediate rise in the standard of living as the infrastructure of the country was updated to match European codes.

Increased drinking was to have a huge effect on the social mores of the country and in particular on the dominance of the showbands. Contrary to general assumption, Ireland was not always a rip-roaring haven of alcoholic consumption – mostly because of a dearth of money. Until the mid-1960's, pubs were dank affairs; people did not drink at home, and if a woman did occasionally enter a public house, she would imbibe quietly in a snug – a small partitioned room out of the public view. This began to change when tourism became more important to the economy. Hotels sprang up around the country and most included a comfortable bar where residents might gather after dinner. Pub owners soon caught on that if they added a lounge where ladies might socialize without fear of social ostracism, they could essentially double their income.

Up until then young people had made the acquaintance of the opposite sex in dancehalls overseen by the local parish priest. Remember that the sexes received separate education – boys in schools controlled by priests and brothers, girls in convents run by nuns. Boys from my generation had little contact with girls until thrown together at dances around the age of eighteen; even then this innocent introduction often proved brutal because of the awful social convention that encouraged girls to refuse any number of prospective dance partners until the man of her dreams approached. Oh, the number of hearts and egos that were bruised and even permanently damaged on an average night in any Irish ballroom.

Dancehalls had one other huge drawback – alcohol was not served. Having had a taste of freedom in the newly popular, and much less socially stratified lounges, many began to chafe at the rules and restrictions of parish ballrooms. The end wasn't long in coming, and you can still see the hulks of these huge "ballrooms of romance," usually surrounded by a large weed-infested parking lots. This didn't happen overnight, yet the rate of closures was inexorable once the rot set in.

But Irish people like live music, and the newly built lounges took care to provide it. However, because of their size, they could only fit small combos. Many showbands began to scale back. The first players to be discarded were the brass sections, and gradually there was a paring down to two, three or four musicians more concerned with getting the audience to sing along than dance on the small rectangle of floor between the tables and the bandstand.

And then there was the day the music died in Ireland. Unlike the saga of Buddy Holly, Ritchie Valens and The Big Bopper, it didn't come courtesy of a plane crash. No, the Troubles in the North put one of the final nails in the coffin of the showbands. On the night of July 31, 1975, while returning from a gig in the Castle Ballroom in Banbridge, Co. Down, The Miami Showband was attacked seven miles outside Newry. Three band members, singer/keyboardist Fran O'Toole, trumpeter Brian McCoy and guitarist, Tony Geraghty were killed, while bassist, Stephen Travers and saxophonist Des McAlea were seriously injured. Two members of the Loyalist UVF (Ulster Volunteer Force) were killed while planting a bomb in the band's van. There has been much speculation - backed up by the survivors - that a British Army officer was in command of the attack.

While all members of the band were popular, Fran O'Toole was a particularly revered figure. He had been a member of The Chosen Few, a Dublin beat group. Although barely older than us, he also had a kind word for many aspiring musicians, including yours truly, when I opened for The Miami at a number of Co. Wexford ballrooms. Fran's murder changed everything. Nothing seemed sacred from that point on; showbands not only hesitated to cross the border, they steered clear of many of the border counties on the Southern side. Live music didn't die instantly, but hotel discos had already taken root and received a major boost after this horrible event.

The Night The Showbands Died

Tell me Julie are you still alive
Do you take the 15 out to Rathmines
Is your bed still warm do you listen to my music?
"Hey, kid, use it or lose it," You said
I still think of you and the showband scene
Hooking up down in Slattery's
Strolling up to the Club Television
Monday nights when all the heads were on exhibition

Nothing left between us now
Might not even know your face
Three thousand miles between us
And so many more days
Still I know you cried, Julie
The night the showbands died

Hey, hey Julie what's goin' on
Do you see the heads from any of the bands?
Did you end up marrying that bass guitarist
The one who became the famous artist?

> *Silicon suits, ballroom romance*
> *Belfast on fire, would you care to dance?*
> *All mixed up no rhyme nor reason*
> *Don't cross the border in the middle of marching season*

> *Another band headin' home*
> *Down the A1 Newry town*
> *British Roadblock up ahead,*

> *"Goodnight lads, what's the craic*
> *Step out of the van, just a wee check"*

> *"Careful with that guitar there, man*
> *What are you puttin' in the back of the van*
> *Jesus, no need for violence!*
> *UDR, UVF, British accent*
> *What's goin' on?"*
>
> *(Larry Kirwan)*

Something else was happening too. Traditional
Music was in the process of getting a first class shot of
Rock 'n' Roll from many quarters. In the UK, Fairport
Convention and Steeleye Span had already laid the
groundwork, and East of Eden had an unlikely Top Ten
hit with *Jig-A-Jig*, but Horslips, to my mind, were the
legitimate fathers of Celtic Rock, a genre still prospering
in the US. Oddly enough, that ubiquitous Irish music
catalyst, Donal Lunny, had little to do with this twining.
However, his oft-times collaborator, and my old
Wexford friend and bandmate, Declan Sinnott would be
Horslips first guitarist.

Eamonn Carr, Barry Devlin and Charles
O'Connor had a background in graphics – this would
later show in their very original album cover and stage
designs – while Jim Lockhart was a keyboard player

with designs on combining Sean Ó'Riada with Rock and
Jazz influences. Declan Sinnott had played with
Eamonn Carr in Tara Telephone, a poetry / music project
with Beatnik influences. I remember inquiring from him
what Horslips sounded like before I saw the band. He
flashed me his enigmatic smile and shrugged, "We
basically play what we like, stick a good beat behind it,
and if that's not going down too well, we finish off with
Street Fighting Man – keep everyone happy."

Declan was apparently not smiling the night he
either left or was dismissed from the band; the story
goes that he took a swipe with his guitar case at the
Horslips van as it was pulling off without him.
Whatever the veracity of this tale, it makes for a good
story. Johnny Fean replaced him and solidified the
Horslips lineup. The band caused a sensation around
Ireland, for they took Irish traditional tunes and put the
power of god into them courtesy of a revved up rhythm
section and Johnny's rip-roaring guitar. They looked
cool too, their long hair flying, although Barry now
blushes at the memory of his oft-worn fur coat that I, for
one, never let him forget.

Because they had become such a draw, Horslips
was able to take the battle right into the "enemy's"
backyard – the country ballroom, long ruled by
showbands. Their stories of these escapades are
priceless and curried by a self-deprecating humor. I
once almost crashed a hired car on a summer vacation in
Ireland when I heard Jim and Barry in a radio interview
relate the sad saga of The Zulus Showband who opened
for them in some ballroom or other. Concurrent with
Horslips success was the rise of The Indians Showband.
These veterans had been members of the very respected
Casino Showband – fine musicians who were going
nowhere. Their manager persuaded them to change

their name, and adopt Native American costumes and headgear – or at least the Irish version of it. The Indians overnight became one of the big national draws and inspired a flurry of other bands seeking to change their fortunes by morphing into some ethnic or tribal group.

The manager of the Royal Earls apparently persuaded his charges to change their name to The Zulus and paint themselves black. All went to plan: the local punters gave them a rousing reception before Horslips took to the stage. Upon finishing their show, Horslips found the Zulus in total consternation in the dressing room. It had been discovered that the paint supplied by the enterprising manager could not be washed off. Thus, the next day they would be forced to attend to their jobs and chores around the small town of Abbeyleix, blacker than any inhabitant of Harlem or Dorchester.

Horslips' first album, *Happy To Meet, Sorry To Part*, caused quite a stir due to its concertina-shaped design but I was blown away by a number of the tracks, in particular, *Paddy's Green Shamrock Shore* which featured a long and lovely organ intro by Jim and a wistful vocal by Barry. *An Bratach Bán* lifted me out of my chair. Here to a Ska beat Jim Lockhart added a defiant Gaelic chant from the Island of Barra.

An Bratach Bán

Mhic Iarla na bratach bána
Chona mí to long thar sáile
Chona mí to long thar sáile
Stiúir óir is dhá sheol airgid

Stiúir óir is dhá sheol airgid
Is cupla chon de ór na Spáinne
Cupla chon de ór na Spáinne
Chona mí to long thar sáile

Son of the earl of the White Flag
I saw your ship over the sea
I saw your ship over the sea
A rudder of gold and two sails of silver

A rudder of gold and two sails of silver
And couplings of Spanish gold
And couplings of Spanish gold
I saw your ship over the sea
(Lyrics used by kind permission of Horslips/Crashed Music)

I guess it was the unapologetic nature of the rendering that appealed to me most. Although I could only catch a couple of the words (my Irish is rudimentary at best and this was also sung in Scottish Gaelic), I had a feeling that it had something to do with the Celtic tradition of the *aisling* – some great nobleman or lovely woman would arrive from over the seas and liberate the Celts from English oppression. Even all these years later the song still occasionally rattles around in the back of my head.

But Horslips real importance may have been that they made Irish traditional music cool to many people who might have up until then dismissed it as "Diddely Di" or "auld Irish." One had only to see a ballroom full of heads who might normally have been digging Zeppelin or Rory surrendering to the frenzy of instrumentals like *The High Reel* or *King of the Fairies* to know that Horslips had moved traditional Irish music

151

out of a dowdy staidness and put it full center in the spectrum of modern life.

Their best work for me was when they took a mythological Irish story *Táin Bó Cúailnge* (*The Cattle Raid of Cooley*), and adapted it to the world of rock without losing the tale's innate depth and complexity. *The Táin* deals with the war between Cúchulainn of Ulster and Queen Maeve of Connaught over a prize bull. The subtext is one that I often feel has homoerotic shadings, as Cúchulainn is forced to fight and kill his dear friend, Ferdia, Maeve's champion – but then, maybe I've lived in New York City too long. Again the artwork of *The Táin* was arresting – a mailed fist in stark shades of black & white.

Dearg Doom, the standout track captures the essence of the full work. It begins with one of my favorite rock count-ins by drummer, Eamonn Carr, and is followed by Johnny Fean ripping out a riff from the traditional tune *O'Neill's March*. A little of Jimmy Page added to a whole lot of Sean Ó'Riada leads to a powerful concoction. The song echoes the Celtic Warrior ideal: better to die young and fulfilled on the battlefield rather than old, decrepit, and racked with memory in some lonely bed.

Dearg Doom

My love is colder than black marble by the sea.
My heart is older than the cold oak tree.
I am the flash of silver in the sun.
When you see me coming you had better
Run, run, run
From Dearg Doom.

You speak in whispers of the devils I have slain
By the fire of my silver Devil's Blade,
And still you dare to flaunt yourself at me.
I don't want you, I don't need you,
I don't love you, can't you see
I'm Dearg Doom.

And when the stars go out
You can hear me shout
"Two heads are better than none,
One hundred heads are so much better than one".

I'm a boy who was born blind to pain
And, like a hawk, I'll swoop and swoop again.
I am the flash of Hawkeye in the sun.
When you see me coming you had better
Run, run, run
From Dearg Doom.
(Lyrics used by kind permission of Horslips/Crashed Music)

Again one has to put a band like Horslips in the context of the turmoil that was ripping apart the North of Ireland. On the face of it, you could say that their music was pro-nationalist, they were singing in Gaelic at times and playing songs that would seem to be more appreciated in Catholic areas. And yet they weren't considered partisan. It's to their credit that they played all through the awful 1970's in the North. This took considerable courage. Remember that bands like Rory, Lizzy and Horslips did not receive police or army protection when traveling back to Dublin from Belfast.

This could be hair-raising, especially in light of what happened to the Miami Showband.

In 1981 during the Bobby Sands Hunger Strike, I did a tour of Ireland with Major Thinkers, a New York based New Wave (for want of a better word) quartet. Talk about good timing and expert planning! Every gig in the North was cancelled; however, we had been invited to appear on the Gloria Hunningford UTV show, very popular back then, and drove up for the occasion.

Belfast was on pins and needles, but with plenty of Guinness aboard and the flashing of American accents and dollars, we breezed through the many sectarian symbols and army checkpoints. Alas, our hired van had battery problems and began to labor up the many hills on the deserted darkened road back to Dublin. At one point, we were forced to disembark and push the bloody thing to the top of a hill, so that we could get a running start on it and hopefully re-engage the battery. Amazingly, although we were unaware of it at the time, we were within miles of the Miami massacre. Dave, our unflappable driver, switched off the lights at the top of the hill to spare the battery while we huffed and puffed, got the van rolling and then hopped in.

We were still some yards from the bottom of the hill when a vehicle pulled directly in front of us from the darkness. Dave slammed on the brakes and we flew around like so many rag dolls. Suddenly blackened faces appeared at the windows and guns were thrust in. There was much yelling of commands from outside, but that scarcely matched the level of panicky screaming from within. Five seconds of consternation ensued as visions of another band massacre flashed through my mind. After a minute or so, order was restored though the guns still pointed at our heads. It was established that we had "aggressively and unsafely" approached a

regular army checkpoint that had come under IRA attack in the past – the Provos, apparently, were not beyond adding explosives to a high-jacked vehicle before sending it careening down the hill. When we suspiciously turned off the lights and pushed our van over the crest of the hill, it appeared as though we were the wily RA up to our old tricks again. T
he youth and fearfulness of the British Army patrol left me with little doubt that one of them could easily have panicked, thereby setting off a chain reaction to another slaughter. We were lucky and got off with a severe dressing down by a young sergeant. But it goes to show the risk that Horslips willingly took all through those bloody 1970's in making sure the citizens of Northern Ireland got to hear their thrilling music.

I went to see Horslips at their last gig in New York City at the Palladium in 1978. Amazingly, Van Halen was opening. It was not a happy night, although, like Lizzy with Graham Parker, the band played well. But you had a feeling their time was drawing to an end – less because of Van Halen than the emergence of the Punk explosion in the UK. No matter how good you are, if you're fighting a trend, rock music can provide a lonely, unsettling canvas upon which to practice your art.

Once more I found myself back in the headliner's dressing room, again with Pierce Turner. Barry, the front man, was doing his pump-it-up routine to make the best of a bad experience. But everyone knew the score – Van Halen was not an easy band to follow; the whole Horslips entourage wished to get the hell out of there post-haste and party somewhere else. Still and all, the record company had sent over a case of champagne. Turner and I were hitting the bottle hard and trying to keep the party going – free booze can be a great incentive.

Eventually, however, only a couple of jaded groupies and some of the tech crew remained. We took a bottle of champagne each – after all, no point in letting a party go to waste – and sat on the Palladium's back door steps. It was a lovely New York spring night. We finished our bottles and headed back to the East Village. My last memory of the night was the two of us leaning over some garden wall and throwing up to beat the band.

When I told Barry this at an interview in SiriusXM some years back, after he had laughed to his heart's delight, he sighed contentedly, "Well, at least something good came of that bloody night."

CHAPTER THIRTEEN

Do You Love An Apple

Do you love an apple? Do you love a pear?
Do you love a laddie with bonnie brown hair?

But still I love him, I can't deny him
I'll be with him wherever he goes

Before I got married I wore a black shawl
But since I got married I wear sweet bugger all

He stood at the corner, a fag in his mouth
Two hands in his pockets, he whistled me out

He works at the pier for nine bob a week
Come Saturday night, he comes rolling home drunk

Before I got married I'd sport and I'd play
But now, the cradle, it gets in me way
                                    (Traditional)

Larry Kirwan

Traditional Irish music was doing fine on its own in the 1970's, thank you very much. In fact it may have been basking in its salad days. Planxty was lighting up the country, The Chieftains were becoming international stars, and many people's favorite traditional band was just about to unleash its magic on the world; it probably comes as no surprise that Mr. Donal Lunny was to have a large hand in The Bothy Band's inception and shaping.

My introduction to the roots of The Bothies began at the Leinster Cricket Club in Rathmines, of all places, sometime in the early part of that decade. Now I knew the club well – not for the alien game of cricket – but for the attempted seduction of young suburban Dublin ladies. A "hop" was held at the club's pavilion every Saturday, and around the time I hit Dublin the rules of attendance had been relaxed allowing bogmen the like of myself to be admitted. I don't remember much in the way of romantic success, but the club was a short walk over from The Hill, a rough and ready pub where my brother, Jemmy, and his classmates from Atlantic College Radio Officer School did much of their carousing. I daresay I got wind of the nascent Folk Club at one of our dancing/romance expeditions.

In any event, I showed up one night with the hope that I might be invited up on stage, all the better to pulverize the audience with some of the most depressing original songs in the Dublin of those days – and that was saying something! But instead a trio had gained a residency and did not solicit guest artists. This band was comprised of two fine acoustic guitarists along with a young woman plonked in the middle playing a clavinet. They had absolutely no rapport with the audience, in fact, they didn't appear to notice that they

158

were playing in a public forum, rather it was as if they had set up in the kitchen back home and were exchanging riffs. Now and then one of the guitarists or the keyboardist would sing and the others might break into harmonies, all done sotto voce. Nor did the audience feel any requirement to pay attention; instead, they chatted amiably about whatever subjects one touches upon at a radical folk event in a conservative cricket club.

In fact, I wasn't even aware that the singers were giving forth *as Gaeilge* until I approached the dimly lit stage to get a better gander at them. I can't say that *Scara Brae* made a huge impression on me at the time; still and all, I have never forgotten them. The singers were Mícheál Ó'Domhnaill and Tríona Ní Dhomhnaill, with Dáithí Sproule, who later went on to play with Altan, the other guitarist. I have since learned that Maighread Ní Dhomhnaill was an integral part of the group but, unless she was hitting the bar or the bathroom for an extended period, she did not make an appearance on that particular night.

I had never heard anyone harmonizing on songs *as Gaeilge* before. It would become commonplace enough in the years to come with the formation of Clannad. Oddly enough, two of my drinking and dancing companions from Atlantic College, the somewhat taciturn Duggan brothers as we knew them then - now Noel and Pádraig Ó'Dúgáin - would soon form Clannad with their nieces and nephews, the Brennans. Like my brother Jemmy they decided to forgo a life at sea tapping away at their Morse code; then again 1971 was not a great year for graduation in general – the prevailing sentiment in that nihilistic time was that the best thing to do in college was burn the joint down.

The mood in the country had been set on edge that August by a British Army initiative in the North with the rather classical name of Operation Demetrius - a sectarian sweep-up of 342 suspected IRA members. This ham-fisted action sparked four days of intense rioting in Catholic areas during which 24 people were killed and thousands fled their homes, many to the South. The fact that a large proportion of the 342 had little or no IRA connections did not endear the British to the nationalist population. To compound matters, the following January, 1972, 26 unarmed civil rights marchers were shot by the British Army in Derry, 13 of them fatally; as a consequence the British Embassy in Dublin was set on fire, and from that point on battle lines were firmly drawn.

The Bothy Band was not formed until late 1974, but the intervening years had not been particularly happy either side of the border. In the failing state of Northern Ireland rural areas like South Armagh and East Tyrone were in open revolt while teams of bombers kept urban areas always on panicky tenterhooks. All of this was curried by a settling of festering scores and sectarian tit-for-tats. From the Loyalist perspective the suspension of their Stormont Parliament in 1972 and the introduction of direct rule from London was a giant slap in the face. Stormont stood for "a Protestant parliament and a Protestant state," according to their first Prime Minister, James Craig.

Although the British intention, no doubt, was that once this recalcitrant, gerrymandered governing body was abolished, real and non-sectarian law and order could be introduced. It had the opposite effect of unleashing the dogs of war on the Unionist side, with widespread attacks on isolated Catholics, leading to an even greater divide between the two communities.

Down in the Republic the worst fears of many were realized as the war spilled over and came home with a vengeance. Although no side took responsibility for a spate of bombings that began in 1972, it was suspected that the first one at the Film Centre Cinema in Dublin was set off by Republican elements protesting against the introduction of the Offences Against the State Act. There seems little doubt now that the rest of the carnage that peaked with horrific twin bombings in Dublin and Monaghan in 1974 was caused by the UVF.

There was strong suspicion that British security forces were working in cahoots with the UVF with the intention of provoking the Irish government to bring in even more draconian measures against the IRA. The deaths of 33 people with 300 more badly wounded in the twin bombings only added to the feeling that life was teetering out of control and Dublin, which up until then had seemed a particularly carefree city, now shuffled about looking over its shoulder.

It was under these inauspicious circumstances that Donal Lunny, tired of the constant touring and seeking new outlets for his musical vision, eased out of Planxty in 1973. The word was that he had thoughts of forming his own record label. His exit was surprising to many as Planxty seemed to be going from strength to strength both musically and professionally. But Donal has always had a streak of restlessness and, being a veteran of many bands myself, I can testify that there are often unseen elements of unease percolating when you put a number of highly talented and opinionated people together under stressful conditions.

It's not unusual to have a number of highly virtuosic players in Irish Traditional groups, water, after all, tends to find its own level, and the system of Feiseanna and Fleadh Cheoil competitions tends to throw great players together, sometimes at a very early age. And yet there is something special about The Bothy Band both for the caliber of its members and the unique chemistry they unleashed - all under Lunny's watchful and encouraging eye. Donal always had a lust for life, an appreciation for latent talent and a general friendliness that tended to bring out the best in anyone.

I witnessed this first hand under extreme circumstances. At the end of that mostly aborted Major Thinkers tour of Ireland in 1981 we set up a session in a Dublin studio with Donal producing. We had a very liquidy farewell gig in Wexford the night before that stretched on until the morning. On the wrong side of hungover, I elected to dose myself with some suspect Brewer's Yeast, with the notion of fortifying myself with organic B vitamins. Unfortunately, the yeast appeared to have sat on a shelf of the local health food store since the Normans hit the town in 1169. This led to some violent bouts of nausea on the road to Dublin.

To cap it all, we crashed into a shop awning on the narrow main thoroughfare of Arklow town, whereupon the windshield collapsed. It was a raw January afternoon and the rain swept in on us the whole way to the Dublin studio. The idea was to record and mix from 8pm, then leave with a finished product for the early flight to Kennedy Airport. This was the hardest session I ever had in a studio, my voice ragged, exhausted from many trips to the bathroom, and yet, Mr. Lunny ,with his off-handed encouragement and casual demeanor, pulled a decent performance from us that still sounds interesting, even if it never propelled the band to the Olympian heights we considered our due.

The Bothy Band, on the other hand, always sparked in some form or another. I guess it was down to

162

individual talent. Paddy Keenan is a stunning piper. I once had a live cassette of him performing solo. He was playing so fast I was certain the tape must be speeding, and yet when I checked the key, he was as close to A440 as a piper ever is. With the Bothies he was all about feeling, and gelling with Matt Molloy on flute and Kevin Burke on fiddle. Paddy often played with his head down, no doubt concentrating while coaxing the tonal wildness of the pipes into unison with the more easily tuned fiddle and flute. He often continued to stare down when the tune had ended thus adding to his innate mysteriousness and charisma.

Matt Molloy has been a mainstay of the Chieftains for many years now. Apart from his obvious dexterity, the tone of his flute is a thing of wonder – not to mention that he is the proprietor of Molloy's of Westport, one of the finest pubs in Ireland. I first met Kevin Burke when he played some tunes with Turner & Kirwan of Wexford in a Brooklyn saloon. He was at that time doing a short stint with Arlo Guthrie's band. English born but very Irish in manner, he off-handedly remarked that he had played violin on either *I Am The Walrus* or some such psychedelic Beatles classic. I couldn't tell if he was joking, boasting, or just relating a fact, but recently he did confirm that he did play on a couple of Beatles tracks but wasn't quite sure if the session had been used.

There was a blistering depth to his fiddling with The Bothy Band and if you watched closely enough you could occasionally see him share a smile with Matt and Paddy at the precious balance they were creating. Then one of them, with barely a flicker of the eyebrow, would suddenly up the ante and off they'd charge in unison or split away into harmonies and counterpoint that still ring in my ears all these years later.

Larry Kirwan

Still and all, I think the musical key to the Bothies success was Tríona. Though a very retiring and self-effacing personality, her sense of chording and structure on the clavinet, along with the rhythmical trust she shared with her brother, Mícheál, powered the band. Take a listen to the live version of *The Morning Star* (from *After Hours*) and note her flawless entry in counterpoint to the tune. I often use it in the first set of songs on Celtic Crush; there's a remarkably uplifting element to the arrangement that sets the style for an early morning radio show. You can almost see that dawn star as it flickers in its fading brilliance before being sent on its way by the rising sun.

Tríona was a fine singer and I probably listened to her version of *Do You Love An Apple* a hundred times in my East Village apartment. I must confess I never cared much for this old music hall chestnut until I heard her version. Now I love the song no matter who attempts it. But it's brother Mícheál's voice that really haunts me. There's a richness and restrained majesty to it; and though I never had the good fortune to meet him, one can sense that he had a beautiful soul. Sadly, he passed away in 2006 with little recognition of his genius outside the cloistered world of Irish Traditional music circles. Take a listen to *Calum Sgaire* when he sings in Scottish Gaelic about Malcolm Macaulay, a fisherman, and Margaret Macleod, star-crossed lovers who can't find each other on a misty peninsula the night they were supposed to elope and save Margaret from marriage to a rich older man.

Although, like me, you probably won't understand more than a couple of words, the melody will stay with you forever, and every time you dig it out of your consciousness you'll be transported back to that foggy desolate night on the Isle of Lewis. There's a dignity to Mícheál's delivery and a power of softness to his voice as it meshes intimately with the cool, understated brilliance of his guitar work.

What a boon to be able to delve back into the band courtesy of YouTube. This medium allows you to appreciate the propulsive nature of Donal's bouzouki playing, but even more, you can sense his ability to listen to the other five performers, see where they're going and encourage them to take the daring leaps that made The Bothy Band the greatest traditional live group. And oh, the clothes, the hair, the times, the knowledge that the world may be falling apart outside, but with the Bothies playing, there's a center holding that you can almost touch and grasp onto.

Was it the times that made them so great – the sense of abandonment that ignites their playing? Irish Traditional music can be as formal as its classical cousin – there's a perceived way to perform it and, in attempting to reach a certain conservative plateau, players often hold back and not let the sparks fly as one is encouraged to do in jazz or rock. What still sets The Bothy Band apart is that they went beyond where mere tradition might have taken them. The band's era didn't last long. By 1979 they had broken up and gone their separate ways, each of them marked by their experience; they and everyone else in their field would be forever compared with their younger Bothy selves when the times and their collective inspiration set them apart.

Like all great bands, they sounded better live. Listen to *After Hours* – particularly the *Live in London* section where they're playing in front of a crowd of homesick Paddies who are hanging on every note. You can actually feel the excitement simmering in the room. There's a low murmur of anticipation that explodes when the audience senses a familiar tune. They don't want to just listen; they want to be a part of the process. And, oh my god, they are! The players recognize the crowd's feral hunger for the band's music and are sparked by it. Each one performs as if hearing and playing the tunes for the first time. Along with Bob Marley's *Live in London*, and Rory Gallagher's *Live in Europe*, it's one of my favorite live discs.

Many Trad ensembles have been influenced by The Bothy Band - it's a tough row to hoe, not unlike guitarists following in the footsteps of Hendrix. To my way of thinking, there was a moment back in the mid-1970's when a rare craziness was in the air and some musicians had the luck or imagination to grab onto it. Hopefully, a new Irish Traditional band will take the Bothy experience, turn it upside down, inside out, then discard it and come up with something new and even more brilliant. Until then we have those six special players who sparked a magic that they wove around each other thereby gifting us a body of work that still inspires today.

CHAPTER FOURTEEN

Inishowen Peninsula

On the Inishowen Peninsula
There is a man
Who doesn't know who I am
Or how I came here on my honeymoon
With the sun of June
And Paudie's collie doggie
Who we normally called Moon
Will come soon will come thatchers
In from the pastures
On a sunny kind of winter's day

I saw him stroll across the bog
Separating fog
And calling out the name of his dog
Who must be soggy and so wet
Where have our souls met
On a sunny kind of winter's day

> *Birds sing in the treetops*
> *On a sunny kind of winter's day*
> *And life was so priceless*
> *Before he went away*
>
> *He fell off the edge of Ireland*
> *Someone saw a something*
> *Floating out to sea*
> *Or could he be he in Culdaff*
> *Who'll have the last laugh*
> *On a sunny kind of winter's day*
>
> *Birds sing in the treetops*
> *On a sunny kind of winter's day*
> *And life was so priceless*
> *Before he went away*
>   *(Pierce Turner & Larry Kirwan)*

O
n certain sunny kind of winter's days, I sometimes flash back to the first frigid months Pierce Turner and I spent in New York City – full of hope and wonderment as we explored the teeming concrete canyons. I had spent five months of the previous summer and fall in the city and the Poconos, but that had been more of an exploratory expedition, getting the lay of the land, all the while dipping my toe in the American mix, checking out the prospects of sinking or swimming. Still, at the very worst, on that trip I had a ticket home. Now it was for real – a one-way fare, if things went wrong, look out!

We had plunged into Bob Dylan's New York with little but the army jackets on our backs and a couple of acoustic guitars. We were determined to see if we could "make it," whatever the hell that meant. We'd combined our money and bought Pierce out of The Arrows Showband. By then he was making the princely sum of twenty-five pounds for six gigs a week, and all the miles that called for buzzing around the back roads of Ireland.

However, he still owed money on the amp and organ that the band's management helped him purchase. They were far from keen on him leaving – after all, they'd "invested heavily in him." He was in all the band's photos and publicity, and in general one didn't leave a well-known showband; you were either fired or retired. Besides, he would not be that easy to replace; although not one of the stars, he was a fine keyboard player and a great harmony singer.

But Pierce had seen the light – he could be doing the same thing in another five or ten years – knocking out carbon copies of whatever pop masterpiece graced the Top Twenty, with nary a thought of the band even listening to one of his original songs, let alone adding it to the repertoire. I had decided to return to the US anyway. I'd caught the New York bug and didn't see a lot of future in Ireland. So, Pierce took the jump and we left on a cheap one-way flight from London.

We'd been a team for some years already. Beginning in Wexford we'd played in bands together and dreamed of being different. We'd shared an apartment in Dublin, ran a record company, wrote songs till the cows came home. But nothing seemed to click for us. We'd got a singles contract with Jackie Hayden at Polydor Records and released a jaw-dropping mournful opus about the Bangladesh flood called *We Have No More Babies Left*. With Pierce on harmonium and me on a West African drum that my father had brought back from his travels, we were lucky we weren't arrested for further depressing a country that was already sliding into national disaster up North.

In typical Turner & Kirwan fashion, we were a little ahead of the curve. We beat George Harrison and his Bangladesh Live Madison Square Garden album by well over six months. For all the good that did us! However, the B Side, *Neck & Neck* had caught the ear of a Manhattan music industry insider, Neil Kempfer-Stocker, who invited us to drop by his 57th Street office should we ever be in the neighborhood. To top it all, we had failed to even make the early heats for a national TV talent show, *Reach For The Stars*, that Fran O'Toole of the Miami eventually won singing James Taylor's *Fire and Rain*. We sang *Inishowen Peninsula* above. The producer/talent spotter was not unsympathetic. He encouraged us to come back with some song the like of *Fire and Rain* and he'd give us another shot. That was the writing on the wall, as far as I was concerned; it was definitely time to go. Whatever impact we were going to make on Irish music, it would have to be an ocean's breadth away.

As ever though, faraway fields, be they concrete or grass, are never as green as one imagines. It turned out Neil Kempfer-Stocker was even more broke than we were and was crashing overnight on the 57th Street office couch, unbeknown to his boss. When Pierce and I finally got an apartment, "Stocker," having dropped his double-barreled name, spent much time on our couch. That was New York in those days - everyone hustling and, for the most part, getting by because the living, besides being easy, was cheap. Neil actually secured us a fine apartment on First Avenue from Grover Kemble, a one-time member of Sha Na Na, who needed to bump town in a hurry – no questions asked.

The East Village was like that back then –
between eras. The 60's had burned out, but some of the
revolutionaries and hippies stayed on – stuck in time
and habits. Most streets were very markedly Ukrainian,
Polish, or Puerto Rican, with little or no social
interaction between them; there was also a smattering of
Italian, Russian, Dominican, African-American - there
were no Irish. You basically moved to the Far East
Village if you wanted to be left alone, to live your own
particular lifestyle, or had no money to speak of.

We fit right in. There were few bars over there
then except some very segregated and sullen, kick-arse
Ukranian joints, and a scattering of Spanish-speaking
cantinas where you could end up with a dagger in your
ribs if you were stupid enough to ogle a senorita. You
learned manners quickly along with respect for your
neighbor, no matter what you thought of him – or her.
Later I was to realize that such luminaries as Patti Smith,
Tom Verlaine, Richard Hell and Johnny Thunders lived
in the neighborhood when I recognized them onstage as
locals who shopped the same bodegas and hardware
stores, but I had no idea where they hung out except for
an odd sighting at poetry readings in St. Mark's Church.
Then again, heroin was everywhere and the streets
could be dangerous enough at nights with junkies, and
those who prey on them, on the prowl.

Pierce and I lived schizophrenic lives –
rearranging Irish ballads and knocking off pitch-perfect
Simon and Garfunkel imitations for Manhattan lounges
or rowdy pubs and dancehalls out in Bay Ridge, in the
depths of Queens, or up the Bronx. We played our own
music wherever anyone allowed us – and often when
they didn't. We soon began to develop a style, although
it was so out there and quirky we could never quite put

a name on it. I think it was the Daily News who described it as *Irish Acid Rock.*

We didn't care for the description but, in retrospect, it wasn't too far off the mark, particularly in the substance department – it was a free and easy time, the gentle haze of pot hung over most performances – even in Irish bars, so conservative back then that most owners thought our clientele smoked "them fancy-smelling European fags." When we eventually began to attract a larger audience, we were given much rein to stretch the envelope musically, and boy, did we do so with relish. We had every intention of returning to Ireland triumphantly that Christmas but were warned by our immigration lawyer not to leave the country until our papers were settled. It took us three illegal years before we finally made it home. By then it was too late – we had pushed too far from the center and didn't really fit anymore. The country had moved into its first EEC phase and we had a surfeit of New York fire in our blood.

By then we'd also found the Bells of Hell. We stumbled in off 13ᵗʰ Street one day, met Malachy McCourt, the owner, told him we were going to be the next big thing - that Simon & Garfunkel had no idea what was about to hit them. Malachy showed us his vacant back room and suggested we start that evening, if by chance Madison Square Garden could spare us for the night. There was only one rule in the Bells – *Thou shalt not bore thy neighbor!* We had few problems on that score. Over the next five years we packed that place with the greatest collection of freaks, revolutionaries, druggies, perverts, pimps, saints, defrocked Christian Brothers, radical nuns, politicians, whores, writers and rock critics.

It was a Mecca for the unhinged and those who had no place else to go. In one corner might be Lester Bangs, Billy Altman, Nick Tosches, in another assorted Hamills, Breslins and various British journalists; across the counter a Clancy Brother or two might be holding forth amidst various members of any number of wings of the Irish Republican movement, and tossed into the general gumbo, for good measure: nymphomaniac nurses and psychiatrists, proper young ladies from the Evangeline residence some doors up the street, and Hilly Crystal and his wife, Karen, bemoaning the failure of his new club CBGB's across the street – yeah, CB's actually began its storied existence among the ivied brownstones of 13th Street between 6th and 7th Avenues.

By this time Pierce was playing a clavinet, and perched atop it, a moog synthesizer that we had hooked up to that old showband standby, the Echoplex. He also played a high-hat with his left foot. I played a super-affected Ovation guitar through a Fender Amp and kicked the bejaysus out of a kick drum with my right foot. We had need of the percussion because in those days most people liked to take to the floor and express their inner feelings through the medium of dance.

What a scene! And it was only added to by the arrival of many of my friends from the *Starseed* group – a pagan-hermetic outfit led by Simon The Mage, the authority on Aleister Crowley in those days, and the Wiccan high priestess, Judith McNally, who moonlighted as Norman Mailer's right hand person. Norman occasionally took in the show and shook a mean leg when the humor was on him. Judith, with a distinct interest in my welfare, got me the very unlikely job of helping Norman maintain his very temperamental Porsche; I used to take it to a drug dealing mechanic acquaintance on Avenue C who worked wonders on its stalling engine. This elevated me in the great writer's estimation and for a while I was his general fixer – one of my triumphs was "rewiring" his mother's ancient air conditioner (hungover beyond belief, I had sunk to the floor of her sitting room and discovered that the AC had been unplugged).

My main task for Norman though was working out the odds on a college football betting system that he had spent years fantasizing about. His hunch did prove to be correct but only 53% of time – far from enough of a spread to bet the farm upon. Ah, indeed, heady times!

But the music was everything to Pierce and me. We had no thoughts of commerciality – selling out was the only cardinal sin. Thus, as I have already stated, we adapted Ewan MacColl's *Travelling People* into a synthesized ode that knocked the socks off Emerson, Lake & Palmer any old day of the week, in our minds at least. Not to mention our 15 minute deconstruction of *The Foggy Dew* that I sliced up with an extended bottleneck solo and Pierce stitched back together with his magnificent Moog assault – did I mention that in the midst of this Pierce would stick a piece of cardboard between the Moog keys sending the synthesizer into a startling echoing loop, whereupon he would do a Yogic headstand against the back wall, while Neil Kempfer-Stocker, manipulating the tones from his soundboard, would hammer his Moog Taurus foot-pedals. Talk about taking Irish music to extremes; and yet if you had the right amount of booze or other substances aboard, it all made eminent sense.

We released an album called *Absolutely and Completely* and it received extensive radio play nationally on progressive FM stations – remember them? One of the songs, *Girl Next Door*, was particularly radio friendly. I wrote it at the end of a chaste fling with my favorite East Village bartender. Although I could tell she was very fond of me, nothing seemed to click – I discovered exactly why when I saw her marching in the annual Greenwich Village Gay Pride Parade. It was the first Lesbian themed ditty to get major exposure in the US and garnered us a sizeable radical sisterhood following that added muscle and commitment to our already diverse audience.

The song got but one play on Irish radio. Pierce and I had sent the album to John Woods, the head of Polygram in Ireland. He signed us up instantly and rushed the album out. John was a lovely man but of the strictest Catholic scruples. His friend, Val Joyce, played the track on his radio show and then called John to congratulate him on its originality and to inquire if he'd actually listened to the words. Whereupon John did, four minutes and some seconds later he recalled whatever copies he could and deposited the rest in the Polygram dumpster. Thus ended our association with this prestigious label, but lo and behold, some enterprising Dublin huckster raided the dumpster, and for years after, copies of the LP with mutilated covers turned up all over Ireland and even made it across the sea to the UK and mainland Europe.

The Girl Next Door

Your bedroom blackmail has worked real good
You've gone and left home like you said you would
The note you scribbled on the kitchen wall
Said, "so long, stupid!" and that was all
I suppose that I should be relieved
Even act just a little pleased
But since you gone life has been such a bore
Why did you leave me for the girl next door?

175

My barroom buddies think it's rather strange
They laugh at me and call you funny names
My mother said she knew all along
Always said that you would do me wrong
Still I wish you would consider, dear,
Leaving her and returning here
'Cause since you gone life has been such a bore
Why did you leave me for the girl next door?

Wish that I could be like Bogie
Hey, I'd sweep you off your feet
But now you tell me that she can give you
Everything you need

You've wrecked my head I really must confess
You've left me in the most dreadful mess
I always thought you were so super straight
But I found out about you too late
I suppose that I should be relieved
Even act just a little pleased
But since you gone, life has been such a bore
Why did you leave me for the girl next door?
(Turner & Kirwan of Wexford)

But CBGB's had already changed New York City
and it changed us too. When Hilly found his cavern
over on the Bowery, oddly enough, Turner & Kirwan of
Wexford may well have been the first band to play there.
Man, it was one dangerous place – this was even before
Punk was invented on the premises. The building
housed a men's shelter upstairs, and on opening night –
attended by many of the Bell's clientele - someone threw
a knife down at the gathering crowd outside. This did

little for the club's reputation. But Hilly was nothing if not resolute. He hired Turner & Kirwan to play Monday and Tuesday nights. However, our fan-base failed to follow us across the Bowery despite all our cajoling. Eventually, we were forced to tell Hilly that we were leaving for Ireland for an extended Christmas vacation and that he should not count on us for Mondays and Tuesdays in the new year.

When we finally arrived back, Patti Smith and Tom Verlaine had discovered the place and turned it into something quite different. Thus, not for the first or last time, Turner & Kirwan of Wexford happened to be in the right place at the wrong time, or something to that effect. Eventually we did work our way back to the Punk cathedral on the Bowery and I had the distinction of being the only person ever barred from CB's – according to Hilly anyway. Before singing *Rose*, our ode to Aleister Crowley's wife, I performed a banishing ritual replete with Judith McNally's sacred *athame* (ceremonial dagger); as luck would have it, Hilly had been on one of his rare binges and arrived in to witness this calling down of the spirits (all nice ones, I assure you). After our set, this oft-celebrated champion of free expression informed me that I was "too demonic" for his clean-cut club, and from that moment on I would no longer be welcome. I believe my astonished retort was "You gotta be kiddin' me, man!" And I guess he was for I graced his stage many times later with Major Thinkers and Copernicus – but never again with the scabrous, demonic Turner & Kirwan of Wexford.

I did attend closing night. I hadn't been in CBs for some years. Hilly's cancer had taken a firm hold, but as ever, he was still quietly full of dreams. It was like a class reunion. People that I hadn't liked 25 years previously smiled at me and I at them – many times I racked my brains that night trying to remember just what grudge, real or imaginary, I had been holding. But there was an air of sadness abroad. The bathroom walls – always a treasure trove of great graffiti – were so full they seemed to pulse in shades of psychedelia. And as I zipped up the last time, I almost shed a tear to think I'd never pee in those urinals again. Back upstairs I rejoined Hilly. I'm sure I was the only one present who had frequented his first CB's incarnation on 13ᵗʰ Street and helped him drown his financial sorrows in late nights at the Bells. Whatever, we fit easily, no words were necessary – he looked much the same, a little thinner because of his illness, but not bad considering.

I wondered how I looked to him. I knew it wouldn't arise for Hilly wasn't big on either introspection or that type of observation. As we stood there watching Patti Smith, he finally turned to me, a quizzical look on his leathery face, "Why did I ban you all those years ago, man?"

Patti was in full flight at that moment and Lenny Kaye was strumming up a storm. A 747 landing on the bar wouldn't have made such a din. For the first time, Hilly seemed frail as he leaned his ear towards my mouth for an explanation. For once, I couldn't find the words and just said, "It was nothing, Hilly, I'll tell you another day." He just nodded, same as he always did and turned back to keep a weather eye on Patti.

Truth was though that Punk changed everything. By the time it hit national attention, Turner & Kirwan of Wexford was at its creative peak. We were performing *Adoramus*, our best work; it consisted of a novel, a musical, and a show that had people like Mailer flocking to the Bells, and David Bowie to Hurrah uptown, to see what the fuss was about. But again, we were in the right place but the wrong time; the world had changed.

Hilly's Cavern on The Bowery was sending shock waves
around the world. Television was reinventing guitar
rock, Talking Heads was, well, turning heads, Blondie
was Marilynizing pop music, and The Ramones were
spreading the glad word that anyone who had three
chords, a sense of fun, and a love for Rock 'n' Roll could
reinvent themselves and the fatigued format.

I was there the first night The Ramones played
CB's. It was pretty empty. When they hit the stage, I
wasn't quite sure if they were real or a parody of a
cartoon act, but did they look cool in James Dean black
leather jackets, white t-shirts and blue jeans! After about
15 minutes and nearly as many songs, they careened to a
halt and appeared to be arguing about what they might
play next. The bartender, an opinionated Brit, turned to
me and hissed, "Nothin' but a bunch of bloody fascists,
mate!" When I inquired why, he just kept repeating,
"bloody fascists" like a mantra. I tried to make the point
that some of them seemed Jewish to me. He wouldn't
have any of it, "I don't care what religion they are -
they're still a crowd of bloody fascists!"

CB's in the early days was a quirky place peopled
by many people with odd takes on life. But then New
York back then was hardly a hotbed of logic either.
Perhaps, in the oddest of ways that Brit bartender was
right. For The Ramones did turn his world upside down
in promoting their new order. I saw them a couple of
years later in The Bottom Line opening for his favorite
band, Dr. Feelgood. It wasn't that The Ramones were
better, for Dr. Feelgood was a great outfit and still one of
my favorite live acts. They just didn't seem relevant
after Blitzkrieg Bopped.

The Ramones turned my own world every which
way too. For one thing, neither Pierce nor I wanted to sit
down anymore. And so we chucked in seven years of

experimentation with Turner & Kirwan of Wexford. We became Major Thinkers, recruited Pierce's girlfriend, Mary Ellen Strom and Cindy Lee (later a Yoga teaching powerhouse) to dance with us, scored a record deal with CBS, hit the radio, got dropped, and went our amiable separate ways. Pierce had never quite left his love of Ireland behind; he splits his time between our old apartment on First Avenue and Wexford – not far from his Wicklow Hills. Whenever I think of him – which is often – I hear one of his best songs that we played so many times together.

Wicklow Hills

Spring still paints fire escapes with Hopper shades
Radios rap and screech like trains
A figure's floating through the sewing set
Some guy walks by suspended by the sky
Takes more imagination
When every thing's remote control
For me it's just a case of what's on the other side of clothes

Tell everybody I'm gone away for ten years
I'm gone to wander among the Wicklow Hills

New Jersey white kid in his Sunday jeans
Stuck to the corner of the street
Fat gypsy lady smacks the windowpane
Some guy walks by suspended by the sky
Takes more imagination

When every thing's remote control
For me it's just a case of what's on the other side of clothes

Tell everybody I'm gone away for ten years
I'm gone to wander among the Wicklow Hills
(Pierce Turner)

In due course, The Ramones, Television and all the Bowery Punk bands spread their wings to London and turned that city on its ear, influencing a whole generation of British musicians, including an ex-pat who would change the way Irish people listened to music.

CHAPTER FIFTEEN

To many people Irish emigration is synonymous with moving to North America. While that may be partly true for those living in the western counties of Ireland, it is far from the case for those on the eastern seaboard. England is closer, more accessible, and there's less long-term commitment needed. In Wexford one could go drinking on a Saturday afternoon, run into some of the lads heading back to London that evening, go home, pack a bag, kiss the Mammy goodbye, buy a ticket, board the boat train and, before you know it, you're disembarking at Paddington Station the following morning. With the proper connections, the Wexford mafia would get you "the shtart," and you'd be on some building site mixing cement on Monday morning.

America was a different kettle of fish; it took planning, saving, and a whole other level of heartbreak – the thought that you might never come back. Though the loneliness could be acute and the indifference of the English chilling, yet the UK was still somewhat of an extension of home – you ate the same food, drank the same beer, watched the same television, followed the same soccer clubs, and listened to the same music on the radio.

Even in the black famine days of 1845 to 1850, most Irish emigrants to the US and Canada traveled to Liverpool first to catch the big ocean-going sailing ships heading for New York, Boston, Toronto, Baltimore, Savannah and New Orleans. The little "coffin ship" sailing out of Galway, Sligo or Limerick was a much less common means of transatlantic crossing. One of three things happened when the emigrant reached Liverpool: they caught their connection and ultimately reached America, they were too sick and poor to travel on – for one had to bring enough food and drink for the journey - or they took jobs in the cotton mills and factories spawned by the new industrial revolution that was changing the face of Lancashire. Many of this latter group also feared the challenges of the new world, the overpowering and stormy ocean, and the sheer heart-scald of bidding farewell forever – for few returned from the new world.

The Irish were not welcome in England – but they had a certain value in that they would gladly undertake the most menial of tasks to earn their crust of bread. Still, British politicians had long painted them as an indolent race of idolatrous dependents who would erode the standards and aesthetics of good Protestant hardworking citizens, the backbone of the empire. So, Irish immigrants stuck together, moving en masse into, and often downgrading, British neighborhoods as Mexicans and Central Americans are now accused of doing in the US; the Irish built their own churches, drank in their own pubs and clubs, and for the most part, accepted their lot.

From the famine years on, wave after wave of
emigrants took the boat to the UK; it was only a matter
of time until some of the brighter, more prosperous
graduates of UK Catholic secondary schools entered
universities, broke away from their Paddy
environments, and assimilated. This process accelerated
after World War II when the new Labour Government
introduced free university education. Still there was a
sense of separateness, and many parents encouraged
their children to take up traditional Irish music or
dancing, and if that failed to attend the dancehalls and
pubs where visiting showbands and ballad groups
entertained.

Some emigrants kept a foot in both camps – they
sent their children home for long summer holidays,
often to get them off the streets and keep them out of
trouble. It was common enough in Wexford to have
cousins and friends from London and Birmingham be
part of your summer gang but return back to "the big
smoke" in late August. Others tried returning home on
a permanent basis – this tended to cause all sorts of re-
acclimatizing problems for themselves, and even more
so for their children. Gerry Diver of The Popes told me
that he considered himself totally Irish when growing
up in England, but when his family relocated to Ireland,
his Irish friends and schoolmates thought of him as
English.

It's interesting too just how many of Irish descent
strut the boards as members of British rock royalty: the
Gallagher Brothers of Oasis, Johnny (Rotten) Lydon of
the Sex Pistols, Steven Patrick Morrissey and John
Patrick (Marr) Maher of The Smiths, to mention but a
few. Lydon, in particular, writes acerbically about his
lack of acceptance in British society because of his Irish
emigrant background. One wonders how spiky and

confrontational the original British Punk movement
would have been if the teenage Johnny Rotten wasn't
possessed of such a burning hatred for the British
establishment on account of the discrimination he
suffered as a boy.

It's often the case that those with roots outside
their adopted country can view their new environment
and society with greater clarity and more minute detail
than their peers. I've often felt that Joni Mitchell, Neil
Young, Van Morrison and Robbie Robertson can cast the
US in greater relief than most of their native born US
musical contemporaries. In much the same way, Shane
MacGowan of The Pogues seems to intrinsically
understand Ireland and the Irish spirit much better than
many native born and reared Irish artists.

MacGowan is a master songwriter and a
charismatic front man and singer, but I feel that his
recognition and grasp of a particular Irish zeitgeist is
what sets him apart. He stands dead square in the
center of so many competing aspects of Irish life; nor has
he ever shied away from their socially unacceptable
elements but rather pulls together emigrant, poet,
boozer, revolutionary, iconoclast, pilgrim, atheist,
seanchaí, self-promoter, self-destructor, scholar, reveler,
rebel, conservative, radical, and eternal roustabout.

In my opinion he took two strands of the Irish
creative DNA, James Clarence Mangan and Brendan
Behan, married the former's stream of opiated
consciousness with the hardnosed, patriotic street poetry
of the latter. If he had stopped there, he'd be just
another footnote in Irish music history but, no, he
seasoned that combustible union with many other
competing opposites – the country-city divide of
Puckane, County Tipperary and London, the British
Public schoolboy who worked a series of dead end

proletarian jobs, the Traditional Irish music lover who
wanted to out-clash the Clash and out-whip the Pistols,
the rebel who craved attention but detested the
manufactured adolescent stupidity of rock stardom.

Regardless of what any of us may think of him,
he has created an enduring genre and style by tapping
into the deep conservative reservoir of Irish music
sensibility and melding it with a dry-eyed, hard-edged
punk sensibility. How often have you walked into a pub
and heard a crowd bellowing a multi-million selling U2
standard? And yet which of us hasn't come upon a
group aping Shane's diction and rhythm on *Dirty Old
Town*. Even though he has written some of the finest
songs in the Irish tradition, perhaps even more a tribute
to the man, he only has to touch something and it
becomes his; who knows, or cares, that Ewan MacColl
wrote *Dirty Old Town* and Phil Chevron composed
Thousands Are Sailing – Mr. MacGowan irrevocably
nailed them! Besides all that, he kicked White Christmas
into the middle of the broad majestic Shannon and gave
us our own Yuletide anthem, *Fairytale of New York*,
which will outlast us all - fan and critic alike.

John B. Keane once told me that the people in
certain parts of rural Kerry still spoke like Elizabethans.
I don't know what era the residents of Carney/Puckane
in Northern Tipperary echo; suffice it to say that while
Shane was spending large parts of his boyhood locally,
the area had sweet damn all to do with faraway Dublin 4
or the modern world that so many Irish longed to be a
part of. No, like the South Wexford of my youth, it was
rural, with long memories of old glories, and more than
content to live within the bounds of its own tried and
true mores and customs. The news came in by radio and
when people watched the new Irish television station, it
was to chortle and shake their heads at "the goings on

that do be happening up in Dublin." It wasn't that they rejected modernity; they just accepted it on their own terms. And those terms meant that old stories and songs were still more important than Gay Byrne's new-fangled *Late Late Show* certainties.

That's probably all changed around there now; it definitely has in Wexford, but luckily for us, Shane ingested the tail end of that oral era, and when he finally made his way back to London he took those priceless stories and songs with him. There he let them filter through his own poetic sensibility and allowed them to slosh around with the uncompromising sounds of bands like the New York Dolls visiting from the Lower East Side.

You've got to picture those pre-Punk days of 1974-75. It's not that the music was bad; it had become just too complicated. King Crimson, Pink Floyd and Genesis might seem somewhat of a joke now, but with the right amount of smoke in your head, you could have a rare evening listening to them. The real problem, however, was that you couldn't dance to these bands and unless you were some kind of prodigy or took a degree at Juilliard, you couldn't handle their arrangements. There was, indeed, Reggae, as it emerged from Ska and Rock-Steady, but that was generally marginalized within the Island communities.

Something had to break – and it did – on the Bowery and in London, courtesy of the New York Dolls, an unlikely bunch of dropouts who dressed like transvestites and attacked their instruments with a primal fury. Oddly enough, very few New Yorkers ever saw them. I happened to stroll in on the tail end of one of their few gigs at the Mercer Arts Center while attending a political meeting. I was in the company of Brian Herron, James Connolly's grandson; we weren't at all sure we hadn't stumbled into a belated Halloween costume party. The building itself collapsed some months later, no doubt aided by the sonic shock of the Dolls.

Shane, sick of the musical status quo, threw in with new Dolls influenced rebels like The Sex Pistols and Clash. He formed his own band – The Nipple Erectors, later to be slashed to The Nips. But like any hard drinking musician, his heart was in the pubs while his head was full of the songs and stories he'd heard back in his beloved Puckane days. He'd also heard The Dubliners, Sweeney's Men and the many other popular Irish bands that blared from pub jukeboxes all over North London. He'd seen the showbands pass through Tipperary and be treated like heroes on their visits to the dancehalls of London. Ripping up t-shirts and tying the shreds together with safety pins was all very well, but even the straights had adopted this punk protest and turned it into trendy fashion. As a contrast, why not throw on a dark suit, white shirt and tie – it added dichotomy to revved up Irish ballads, and if it worked for the mighty showbands, then why not for a bunch of revved-up Irish boozers in London.

It took a lot of pints and wandering about in the punk and pub rock netherworld before Pogue Mahone (Kiss My Arse) played their first gig in 1982 with a line up of Shane, Jem Finer, Spider Stacy and James Fearnley, later to be joined by Cait O'Riordan and Andrew Ranken. Right from the start the Sweeney's Men hit, Waxie's Dargle, became one of their big numbers. A video was made of it, and apart from the spirited arrangement, the fact that Spider smashed himself on the head with a beer tray on the chorus showed that this band of tuneful, raucous drunks could not easily be categorized.

Waxie's Dargle

Says my aul' wan to your aul' wan
"Will ye go to the waxies dargle? "
Says your aul' wan to my aul' wan,
"I haven't got a farthing."
I went up to Monto town
To see Uncle McCardle
But he wouldn't give me a half a crown
For to go to the waxies dargle."

What will ya have?
I'll have a pint!
I'll have a pint with you, sir!
And if one of ya' doesn't order soon
We'll be thrown out of the boozer!

Says my aul' wan to your aul' wan
"Will ye go to the Galway races? "
Says your aul' wan to my aul' wan,
"I'll hawk me aul' man's braces."
I went up to Capel street
To the Jew man moneylenders
But he wouldn't give me a couple of bob
For the aul' man's red suspenders."

What will ya have?
I'll have a pint!
I'll have a pint with you, sir!
And if one of ya' doesn't order soon
We'll be thrown out of the boozer!
                    (Traditional)

Though I'd seen The Pogues at their first NYC gig at Danceteria in 1986 I wasn't influenced by them when we formed Black 47 in late 1989. Even more pertinent, I've always been very aware of not indulging in Shaneitis! I had a lot of the same influences: Luke Kelly, Ewan MacColl, showbands, emigration, along with a love of history and stories. In a way it didn't present that big of a problem as I had chucked in rock music on St. Patrick's Day 1985 with the intention of becoming a playwright. Even attending Danceteria that night was unusual. I had been out drinking with the poet, Copernicus. We happened to be passing by the club, saw the crowd and on an impulse went in. It was a fantastic gig. The place was jammed and, for once, I was really able to enjoy a band without comparing it to what I was doing myself. It was also a great social occasion, with many Irish musicians, and those who swing in their orbit, present.

The energy level was tremendous. Danceteria could be a poseur's palace with everyone seeking to out-chill everyone else. The Smiths had made their debut there and it remained their home base in New York – odd, isn't it, two Irish descended bands and yet so different. The Pogues turned the joint into a great big pub – relaxed, boozy, friendly, the dance floor convulsed in a tumult of moshing. Meanwhile, the heavy drinkers were laying siege to the bar – the normally ice-cool barmen, scurrying around like field-mice, fearful of the sarcasm of thirsty construction workers, and yet prepared to break a sweat knowing that this was going to be the best tip night of their lives.

Shane still controlled the band back then. He's always been the central figure, but over the years he appears to have become more withdrawn from his bandmates. His singing and delivery were so on the

money – he was the center, and the center was rock
steady on that particular night anyway. There was a
glamour to him, the smoke rising from his ever-present
cigarette; he was drinking, as one might imagine, but he
wasn't being cheered every time he raised a glass or
bottle to his lips, as became the creepy norm over the
years. And, oh, those songs! It hadn't been long since
he'd discovered his voice and he was reveling in it. As
Miles Davis said, "Once you find your voice everything
else falls into place." All the pieces were coming
together for Shane and the rest of the Pogues on the
stage of Danceteria.

Two other things come to mind – James
Fearnley's playing and theatrics. He made that most un-
cool of axes, the piano accordion, the hottest instrument
in the house, ripping off great riffs even as he charged to
the lip of the stage to meld with the surging crowd. And
Cait O'Riordan looked so effortlessly attractive: how
interesting to have a woman in a band that seemed as
much a bunch of the lads off to see Arsenal take on
Manchester United. I met her years after she left The
Pogues to marry Elvis Costello, and could tell that
shyness and a natural reserve were very much a part of
her psyche. But on that wonderful night in New York
City, there were very few Paddies in the crowd who
didn't fall head over heels in love with her.

It seems odd in retrospect that I, or any of the
other New York Irish musicians present, didn't start
some kind of similar band the next day. I understood
intrinsically what The Pogues were doing and could
have knocked off a first class Irish-American imitation
without breaking a sweat. But I suppose that would
have been too simple. And anyway, I was sick to the
teeth of my musical self and was just about to have a bit
of success with my first play, *Liverpool Fantasy*.

191

This was not the case four years later when Black 47 opened for The Pogues at The Palladium on 14th Street. I was back in the game full time, for better or worse. I was also just beginning to find my own voice and thrilled to be invited on the bill. The infamous Frank "Galigula" Gallagher, who had been Talking Heads soundman and had terrorized Major Thinkers in the same role, had returned to London and was working with Frank Murray, The Pogues manager. On Galigula's prompting, Frank signed Black 47 to a deal with his new record company and was about to release a four-song cassette EP for us. We were instantly accepted as part of The Pogues family.

And what a family! Spider, a lovely man, arrived in our dressing room and made himself at home. I knew both Terry Woods and Phil Chevron vaguely and they dropped by too. Then Shane arrived. He stood with his back to the closed door, his eyes slightly glazed. It struck me at that point that perhaps his fabled drunkenness was a way of keeping people at a distance. For he was constantly under assault – every drunk who ever showed up at a gig felt a kinship and was not shy about letting MacGowan know. I had to wonder if our dressing room was a calm port in a storm; his band mates barely acknowledged him while Black 47 members care little for celebrity. He took in the conversation but didn't add anything and then shuffled off without a word.

On that night in March 1990, The Pogues were one of the best bands I'd ever heard. It wasn't that any of them were virtuosos but they connected in such a kinetic manner that they could have blown an army regiment off the stage. Although I missed some of the theatrics of Andrew Ranken, who had stood behind his drum kit at Danceteria and Cait's ineffable coolness, they were now more of a rock band and the equal of any on the planet. Terry and Phil had thickened and colored the sound adding a new glow to Shane's songs. Even back then, however, the man from Puckane seemed just a shade removed. No one in the audience seemed to notice but you could feel it in the body language of the band onstage.

I noticed it even more nine months later when we opened their Christmas show at The Brixton Academy in London. That may have been one of the most magical nights of music I've ever experienced. Perhaps, there was an added special element for me as I hadn't been back to Wexford for Christmas in six years – still haven't been for that matter. We were doused in a baptism of fire even before we arrived on stage with the crowd chanting, "Get Off – We Want Shane" at the mere mention of our name. Hardened by a year of playing to Bronx Paddies, this rather churlish welcome was sorted out pretty quickly by turning up my amp to 10, my distortion pedal to the max, and hitting a big open E chord. I still meet people who claim they lost some of their hearing at that show. That sonic assault introduced some measure of manners to that unruly crowd and by the end of our short set we had made at least a grudging impression.

I'd had a couple of drinks with Joe Strummer before The Pogues went on so was in good form when I went back upstairs to watch their show. I think I may have cried watching Shane and Kristy MacColl perform *Fairy Tale of New York*; it made me realize that I'd probably never feel totally at home anywhere again at Christmas. I would have shed more copious tears if I'd known that the vivacious and kind Kristy would be dead at such a young age some years later. Although most people associate that song with New York, for me it will always be part and parcel of that magical night in London.

I had many more encounters with Shane and The Pogues at various festivals down the years. I even saw the band when Strummer was front man – great as Joe was, The Pogues always seemed a shell of themselves without Shane. Stands to reason, I suppose. I also shared bills with The Popes when Shane led that redoubtable combo; although they got off to a great start, after a while you could almost feel Shane asking himself what the hell he was doing. But then, most bandleaders go through that at one point or another. Given all the tabloid ups and downs, Shane is an amazingly resilient person. One night in Chicago, he seemed so ill before going on stage I actually said "goodbye" for I didn't think I'd ever see him again. How wrong I was - the next tour he looked his normal disheveled self – the man must have an iron constitution and the genes of a Hercules besides being the finest songwriter of his generation.

The strangest, and most poignant, interaction I ever had with him was at an *Irish Voice* benefit in Terry Dunne's club, Tramps, on 18th Street in 1992. It was before Black 47 had signed a record deal – yet we were doing well at the time, playing four or five nights a week, so in many ways it was just another gig to us – at first. We had done our sound check when the late Gerry Conlon, a comrade and Guilford Four member, asked me if Black 47 would back Shane for five or six songs. I immediately declined, as none of the band, including myself, were really familiar with the Pogues' repertoire. This was a big gig for Shane, I emphasized, his first since leaving The Pogues, and I didn't want to be responsible for messing it up. Shane was an icon in New York, to my mind, and he deserved something better than a band that didn't have a clue about his oeuvre. Besides, who wanted to be ripped apart by Shane's fans in the Irish media for sabotaging his comeback?

Gerry, on the other hand, having spent 12 years in British prisons on a false charge, was nothing if not a resolute negotiator. He was also a great friend and persuaded me that the least I could do was come down the street where Shane was drinking and have "a chat with the man." Terry George, then Irish Voice Music Editor, later director of *Hotel Rwanda*, was there along with Joey Cashman, Shane's manager, and Victoria Clarke, Shane's partner. Shane himself was very quiet. I remember thinking, "Jesus, this guy hasn't made any arrangements for a backing band." I also recalled various kindnesses that The Pogues family had shown to Black 47, but still I could see a disaster in the making. Gerry again asked me - this time in front of Shane - if I'd help. I replied that the only Pogues song I knew the chords for was *Dirty Old Town*.

Shane stared long and hard as if trying to bring me into focus before declaring in his broad London accent, "Don't want to do any fucking Pogues' songs."

This caused much consternation at the table, but Shane was adamant and didn't appear to give a fiddler's fart one way or the other. But I instantly saw a way forward. "How about if we do five or six Irish ballads that we both know."

"Fucking great," he exclaimed as if I'd just come up with a very succinct and plausible explanation for the Theory of Relativity. Thereupon, we sketched out songs of the ilk of *Black Velvet Band*, *The Wild Rover*, *The Irish Rover* and any other kind of fucking rover that we were both aware of.

"What key do you want to do them in?" I inquired. This notion seemed very inconsequential to

Shane who mumbled something to the effect of "how the fuck would I know?" Then he returned to the conversation at the table, apparently rejuvenated now that another of life's small problems had been resolved, whereupon I concluded that our interview had been terminated.

Gerry had already told me he had Seamus Egan on banjo and Mary Courtney on vocals lined up. I rushed back to Tramps and recruited Black 47 members Chris Byrne on pipes, David Conrad on bass and Thomas Hamlin on drums, all of whom felt that at the worst this would be an adventure. I played one of The Pogues songs on the jukebox, then figured out what key I'd sing it in. When that was established, I transposed the proposed set of Irish ballads to keys that would be comfortable for Shane, and gave a list of the familiar ballads and keys to the very capable musicians. Shane arrived from his soiree at the bar down the street and we lashed into his sound check. To my amazement, the whole thing sounded great. The band swung, and Shane was in top form. Talk about exuding a sigh of relief!

It was a long night as happens at benefits. Lots of bands, many speeches and then Black 47 to play a long set. Shane would close out the night. In the adrenaline of performing with Black 47, I had almost forgotten that we had this last "little" gig to do. The crowd hadn't! Shane's fans had traveled from all over to witness his first Pogueless gig. You could cut a knife through the excitement. Backstage I gave him a set list such as it was, but he motioned it away.

"Just call it," he mumbled, and for the first time I could tell that this thing was spiraling out of control. Shane had thought he was just coming out to do a couple of songs – no big deal – but everyone else saw it in far more dramatic terms. Terry George was onstage rattling off a litany of Shane's accomplishments that likened what was about to unfold as up there with the Second Coming and, in the bargain, driving the crowd to a frenzy. The rest of the band had sussed out the vibe and was quiet and fidgety, apprehension masking their normally devil-may-care faces. When Terry finished, the crowd roared in anticipation and there was nothing for it. Shane was nowhere to be seen, and we hesitated – much like the Christians must have done before meeting the lions in the Coliseum. Employing more acting chops than actual confidence, "Fuck this," says I, "We're pros. Let's do it." And we did.

To my surprise the stage was already occupied by a number of musicians, some of whom I was familiar with, others I didn't know from a hole in the wall. One of them had even appropriated my microphone. I pushed him the fuck out of the way. The crowd was howling so much it was impossible to communicate with the new arrivals. Then all of a sudden, Shane was standing behind me, cigarette in hand, shades so dark I couldn't tell if he could even see the ground beneath his feet, let alone the chaos that he was inspiring. I caught the eyes of the sound check band – now that they were onstage all apprehension had fled and they looked as if they could have subbed for the orchestra on the Titanic. And then, with a count of four, we were off and into *The Black Velvet Band*. The crowd roared its approval and we were away in a canter. About half way through I could tell there was something wrong – one of the new guitarists was playing in D rather than G – he looked at me in amazement when I somewhat graphically suggested that he change his tune, or failing that, get the fuck off the stage.

Shane was beginning to feel a bit of wear and tear himself as the lead vocal monitor waxed and waned, probably because the soundman was trying to come to terms with some of the feedback being caused by the instruments of the uninvited musicians. There was also the problem of keeping pitch with the backing guitars streaming through the side fill monitors in varying keys. As far as the crowd was concerned, however, we could have been playing in some Mongolian micro-tonality – they were there to see their hero and whatever his backing musicians played was hardly of great moment.

Around the fourth song, however, it became obvious that there would be no Pogues' classics. This set off a ripple of discontent but, to my mind, we were in the back stretch of this race; a couple more tunes, no major mishaps, and we'd be in sight of the winning post. The heat was almost intolerable what with the crowd surging over the lip of the stage and the number of players jostling around on it. Before the fifth song we hit a dip. I couldn't find my set list, more players had materialized onstage, along with a chorus of back up singers who wouldn't have known a harmony if it had bit them in the arse. I was running out of breath myself, what with the long Black 47 set, and trying to add high harmonies to Shane on every chorus. I felt a little faint and knew a shot of whiskey was my only savior. However, there wasn't a drink to be had what with the new arrivals all striving to emulate Shane, who actually wasn't imbibing. For some reason he had removed his shades.

I felt a little shaky, the sound of the crowd faded away, I recognized that I was dehydrated, and for a second I thought I might faint. Then the roar of the crowd returned with a vengeance. I looked at Shane and could see through the sweat that he was experiencing some kind of discomfort himself – either with me, the world in general, the heat, but more than likely, the thought that this charade had gone on long enough. There was a slight panic in his eyes that I'd never seen before. I had been calling the shots with count-ins and finishes, and the eyes of the sound check band were on me but, for the life of me, I couldn't think of any other songs. Luckily, Seamus Egan, one of the greatest Irish musicians and someone well used to stage crises was close by, nonchalantly gazing out at the crowd. His hands were poised above his banjo and he seemed to be in perfect control of himself, if not the situation. I edged over to him and inquired, "What's next, man?" He looked up at me, smiled, cocked an eyebrow, and muttered derisively, "The fucking Irish Rover."

It was hardly one of my favorites either but the crowd ate it up. This was the Pogues/Dubliners hit, and they were back on sacred ground. I don't even remember what we finished with. It could have been *Mursheen Durkin* or some song of that ilk. I didn't care either. The job was done. So was Shane. He was already off the stage as the audience ripped into the customary *Ole Ole Ole Ole…* to signal that they would be expecting the great man to return. I experienced a rush of happiness and not a little relief. We'd pulled off a big one. The crowd loved it – now Terry Dunne would fete us with top shelf drink, and I for one was ready - I could have drained a bloody ocean.

It was quite a long way down to the cellar dressing rooms and the further from the stage we moved the cooler it got. I could still hear the roar of the crowd and even more the stamping of their feet overhead, but as far as I was concerned it was over. Shane was leaning back against a whitewashed wall surrounded by well-wishers – his shades were back on. I winked at him as I passed; his answering nod seemed infused with the relief of one who has been in the lion's den and had no intention of making a return visit. Not so, his entourage and an ebullient Terry Dunne – none of whom seemed to have ever heard of the "Leave 'em wanting more," maxim.

I was on my second drink in the midst of my brothers and sister from the sound check band when Terry Dunne shouted at me, "For Jaysus sake, head, you have to do an encore or they'll wreck me fuckin' club!" He did appear to have a point as some of the plaster was now coming off the ceiling from the stamping going on above. Dubious at first, Shane reluctantly appeared to agree with him. I couldn't believe it! Then again there was no way out of the club without braving the crowd. But my mind was a blank. I couldn't think of any more Irish ballads though I must be on speaking terms with three or four hundred of them.

From out of nowhere, the beautiful Victoria – the very one Shane had proclaimed had left him for "the fat man who wrote Gloria" - bounded over to me, poised, collected and, in her mind anyway, logical and declared, "You'll have to do Sally MacLennane!"

I vaguely recognized that it was the title of a Pogues' song but it could just as well have been a Verdi aria. "I don't know it," says I.

"You don't know it?" Victoria looked at me as though such a thing were beyond the bounds of belief.

"How does it go?" I inquired.

She had still not recovered from my admission of ignorance when Shane spared me any further shame by interjecting sullenly, "Not doing any fucking Pogues songs!"

So, we were back to square one but the plot was thickening for now actual clumps of plaster were descending from the weakening ceiling. I racked my brains for any bloody come-all-ye but nothing came. Amazingly, no one was making any suggestions. Finally, Terry Dunne threw out to no one in particular, "What's the first fucking song you ever learned?"

"The Wild Colonial Boy," I shot back on autopilot.

"It'll have to fucking do!" Terry muttered, obviously far from a fan of this chestnut. Victoria didn't seem too pleased either. I didn't care, Australia, America, the moon, it was a song we all recognized, and I even remembered that I had learned it in the key of D. Shane didn't appear to care one way or the other but he did intimate that he had a passing acquaintance with the words.

Lucky for all of us the Times, News or Post didn't review the gig, but the following Wednesday the Irish Voice proclaimed that MacGowan was brilliant and might have reached stratospheric heights had it not been for the quality of the band that had sadly been incapable of going where the maestro went. You can't win, as they say. But thanks for the memory, Shane, it was a blast!

CHAPTER SIXTEEN

There is a truism in Irish life that when things are bad economically, music and the arts in general tend to flourish. The 1980's stand out as a particularly bad period in the economic and political life of the country, but a vivid one for theatre, film and music. The decade began with the tragedy of the Hunger Strikes in the North of Ireland, and in many ways, those terrible events were to color the following years. Either directly or indirectly, they definitely had an effect on the music of the period.

Two bands stand out. One reflected a desire to look outwards and not be overly tainted by the often nihilistic politics swirling around them - a political statement in itself. The other, while embracing the jazz of the US and the progressive rock of the UK, burrowed even deeper into Irish Traditional music and the ethos of the political struggle. Hardly surprising the latter group, Moving Hearts, had as its prime movers and shakers, Donal Lunny and Christy Moore, with a cameo appearance by my old band mate, Declan Sinnott. The other group, U2, is the most successful commercial musical act ever to emerge from Ireland.

It's almost hard to imagine an Ireland without U2, so emblematic have they become, and yet it's difficult to nail down exactly what they mean to Irish consciousness or the national psyche. I heard founding member of Black 47, Chris Byrne, once remark, "They might as well have come from New Haven as Dublin." And there's a truth to that, for in ways U2 are more universal than Irish, and yet only the depressed Dublin of their youth could have spawned this socially conscious, creative colossus. Without Punk would there have even been a U2? It's hard to say. Bono once declared that they had only "three chords and the truth." While many might question their possession of the latter, they sure as hell knew the magical major fingerings necessary to belt out basic Rock 'n' Roll - and few would deny they put them to a mighty use. They soon added the extra minors necessary to struggle through Peter Frampton covers, and before any Dublin begrudgery could stop them, they had broken out of the stable door and were on their dizzying ascent to the top.

Jim Sheridan, then the artistic director of the Project Arts Centre in Dublin, told me that U2 were the worst band he ever heard when they first played his theatre but within months the best. They were then performing *2-4-6-8 Motorway* by Tom Robinson and *Anarchy in the UK* by The Sex Pistols; within a year they were playing songs from their first album, *Boy*. To my mind, what set U2 apart was a quality they shared with James Joyce and Roy Keane: a refusal to be anything but the best. Both iconic writer and towering soccer player shook off an Irish culture riddled with self-doubt, and in so doing refused to be saddled with the standard national inferiority complex. Ireland has always been deeply influenced, and often stymied, by the social and political web cast by the UK; yet, as the country became aware of itself in the 1970's and its place in both the EEC and the world, someone was bound to assert a new cultural independence. Alone among his peers, Bono had the balls, smarts, charisma, talent and universal appeal to seize that moment and propel U2 to international superstardom

There are those who would argue that U2 never totally came to grips with the complexity of the situation in the North of Ireland. The band's defenders would counter that the situation had long spiraled out of control before U2 had sufficient influence to effect any change. Besides, how could mere musicians change a history and culture built on a foundation of "much hatred, little room," as WB Yeats described it. And yet there were oppressors and victims – Catholics were discriminated against for almost 50 years with the tacit acceptance and even compliance of the British government. When the Northern Ireland Civil Rights Association (NICRA) marched peacefully, its members were brutally attacked by police and Loyalists. Internment and trial without jury were commonplace throughout the conflict, and the death from shooting of 13 people in Derry in 1972 led to the revival of the historical slogan "Sunday Bloody Sunday" - first used in 1920 after the slaughter of spectators by British forces at a Dublin sporting event.

Hence there was a lot of charged symbolism employed by U2 in the use of this song title. John Lennon's song about the massacre is not one of his greatest but still graphically captures the actual event in Derry: *Well it was Sunday bloody Sunday when they shot the people there, the cries of thirteen martyrs filled the free Derry air.*

U2's song tends to sweep aside the actual events and goes more for a *cri de coeur*: *How long must we sing this song... 'cause tonight we can be as one."* They're both valid points of view – one agit-prop, the other inspirational - one replete with details, the other exhortations, or as was once put to me by an activist – platitudes. I don't think Lennon's song was ever a big favorite in the North of Ireland, but it sounds more like Derry on that awful day. On the other hand, U2's song may have achieved more in the long run by becoming a Rock 'n' Roll anthem, thus causing more people to learn about the massacre and perhaps become more politically aware. This point of view, however, did not score many points with residents of the many Northern areas that were under siege from British soldiers and Loyalist terror gangs during the length of the conflict.

And yet U2 always sought to highlight the damage done to individual dreams by sectarian hatred and violence. Recently while speaking about the song *Raised By Wolves* from the band's latest CD, *Songs of Innocence*, Bono remembers the Dublin bombings of 1974. "The bombs were set to go off at the same time on a Friday evening, at 5.30pm. At that time on Fridays in 1974 I would have been at the Golden Discs shop in Marlborough Street, just around the corner from where the bombs exploded. But that day I had cycled to school so didn't get the bus into town afterwards as usual."

I wonder would U2 have been a different band had Bono transmuted that close call into a song for the first *Boy* album? Then again, neither Rory Gallagher nor Phil Lynott introduced the events or characters of the Troubles into their songwriting back in those desperate days either. I wonder why? One late night in the Bells of Hell, I put a similar question to the rock critic Lester Bangs. He looked at me with all the regard one might bestow on the incestuous third cousin of the village idiot before declaiming, "What's that got to do with Rock 'n'

Roll! You don't expect The Ramones to be out there saving the world, do you?"

I saw U2 at The Ritz in New York City on their first American date in 1980. They were one of three bands in a somewhat sparsely attended show. Though they had just released *Boy*, there was already a huge hype about them (oddly enough, *The Hype* had been one of the band's early names). Instead of coming on with a flourish, Bono strode up to the microphone, peered out into the shadowy club and advised us that we should forget anything we'd heard about the band and judge them on what we were about to hear. The supporters of the other two bands scratched their heads at this somewhat imperious request and then the band kicked in.

The most interesting thing initially was The Edge's guitar sound with its emphasis on delay and chorus effects. The sound pealed throughout the large club; oddly enough, the tone reminded me of Jerry Garcia's, though in a more stuttering and rhythmic manner, with much use of open fifths; passionate and overdriven as it sounded, there was a studied coolness, literally and figuratively, to his playing that remains to this day. His style has been much copied in the succeeding years and has sent many guitarists back to the drawing board to figure out just how he could get so much sound out of seemingly so little playing.

After a confident but not particularly illuminating start, Bono began to take over. And could that guy sing! But again, it wasn't the singing that seduced the audience but the sheer magnetism of the man-boy prancing that well-worn stage and treating it as if it was some parish hall back home. Within a couple of songs I was quite certain that this band would be one of the biggest in the years to come. They didn't on that night

quite have the material for world dominance but they had something more important – a talented, committed dynamo who would walk through walls to "make it."
      And make it he, and they, did. I didn't find them pointedly political or even particularly socially aware, even though they were already gaining a name for being so; but they did have a yearning for a vague universal redemption and freedom from oppression. In the hands of another lead singer their pleas might seem naive but Bono exudes a commitment that when combined with the power of an excellent band can spark an audience in a way few others have ever done. Look at the faces of the audience at a U2 show and especially as they wend their way out of some huge stadium – uplifted and ready to face the new day, as if they had just emerged from some fist-in-the-air religious revival gathering. And to think it all began with three punk chords, that oh so ever-elusive truth, and a refusal to be second best.
      U2's recent marketing coup of adding their CD, *Songs of Innocence*, to everyone's iTunes account has brought out the Bono haters in full force. Many consider it "legal spamming." It definitely borders on the intrusive, particularly as it does not appear to be one of their best albums – again that's all subjective; and in some people's eyes U2 would be objectionable if they had written the *1812 Overture* - perhaps a tribute in itself.
      My beef with them comes from a much more utilitarian point of view. Musicians are already on the ropes from illegal downloading and the expectation among many that artistic content be available free of charge. By giving away an album that they put years of work into, U2 only add to that expectation. My question would be – is a marketing ploy, no matter how brilliant, worth the risk of hammering one of the final nails in the coffin of artistic independence. For if musicians cannot

support themselves and pay for their recordings from sales, then ultimately they come under the influence of whomever foots those bills. It's a big question and one I hope that the U2 brains trust has given serious thought to. I wouldn't like to think that the idea sprang from the dwindling (comparatively speaking) sales of their more recent CDs. But that's a churlish thought more suitable for a Bono hater – and I'm emphatically not. I have great respect for the man, his songs, voice, comportment and the great good he has done in his philanthropic pursuits.

My favorite U2 song, by the way, is *One*, which combines for me all the band's great qualities and never fails to move and inspire me. To capture a measure of the song's universality, take a listen to Johnny Cash's austere and almost spectral version.

Somewhere at the other end of the spectrum, Moving Hearts were intrinsically political – at least while Christy Moore was their lead singer. How interesting too that it's nigh impossible to pick up a copy of their first eponymous album or its successor, *Dark End of the Street*. For some reason that tends to happen with political records, especially if they're on major labels – Black 47's *Home of the Brave* (EMI) and *Green Suede Shoes* (Mercury) CDs have also been deleted notwithstanding decent sales, and only recently became available on iTunes. Both have songs that speak about the Troubles, as do the Moving Hearts albums – all coincidental one would imagine and hardly grounds for a conspiracy theory; but while Black 47 was safely ensconced in New York, apart from the occasional tour of Ireland, Moving Hearts was in the thick of the conflict.

The Hearts formed in 1980 just as the North was heading into one of its great crises. Although the carnage had continued relatively unabated since 1968, in the detention camps of Long Kesh and Armagh

Women's Prison, a certain modus operandi had been established – both Loyalist and Republican prisoners were allowed right of association with their own members and use of their own clothing. This changed in the Republican prison camps in 1976. Detainees were required to wear prison uniforms, which meant that they would now be treated like regular criminals. Over a period of years this led to "the blanket" protests initiated when prisoners' clothes were taken away and replaced by prison uniforms. When the prisoners refused to don the uniforms, blankets were given in their place. Eventually because of provocation, prisoners refused to leave their cells and defecated within.

This led to a stalemate of some years, but after a 53 day hunger strike that ended in October, 1980, it appeared that the British had conceded to the essence of the prisoner's five demands: the right to wear their own clothes, not participate in prison work, freely associate, receive one visit, letter and parcel per week, and regain full restoration of remission lost through the protest. However, the authorities did not keep their word and on March 1, 1981, Bobby Sands led two other comrades on the legendary Hunger Strike.

To judge from their songs, U2 seemed oddly unmoved by this event up the road – however, in fairness to them, they were not alone; few rock musicians in Dublin or anywhere else raised their voices either, and at least U2 have been firmly behind many other humanitarian causes worldwide. The conundrum U2 and many people in the Republic of Ireland faced was that if you supported a revolutionary like Sands, did that mean you were supporting the Provisional IRA too?

Christy Moore and, one imagines, some of his colleagues in Moving Hearts felt no such qualms.

Christy, coming of age in the folk world of the mid-1960's had long held strong left-wing beliefs. Familiar with the situation in Northern Ireland from playing so many gigs up there, he was not unaware of the discrimination against Catholics. It was hardly a big step for him to vault from the nationalist stridency of *Follow Me Up To Carlow* to *90 Miles From Dublin*, his stinging denunciation of the apathy of his fellow Irishmen in the South and a declaration of his own sympathies with the plight of IRA prisoners in the H Blocks.

Moving Hearts were a revelation right from their first residency in Dublin's Baggot Inn – they began with a Monday night that soon burgeoned to a Monday/Tuesday/Wednesday residency - and according to regulars, they got better with each performance. The Hearts boasted a cross-section of musicians including alto-sax player Keith Donald of the Greenbeats Showband. Declan Sinnott - who stood next to me admiring Keith's chops at dances in Wexford Parish Hall – was their first guitarist. Davy Spillane contributed his usual wizardry on the uilleann pipes, while Eoghan O'Neill on bass and Brian Calnan on drums were a crack rhythm section as fluent in jazz and world music as rock. Rounding them out and guiding the arrangements was the ubiquitous Donal Lunny on bouzouki and, as often as not, Prophet synthesizer.

Christy Moore, angry and even disgusted by the disassociation of his fellow citizens with the events in Northern Ireland, was the focal point. Moore had always exuded a rare moral authority from the stage. Now he really came into his own. The genius of the Hearts, and perhaps saving grace, was that intermingled with the band's concern for the destruction of civil rights in the North were sprinklings of outrage over nuclear proliferation, imperialism, housing rights, the macabre side of organized religion, and other skullduggery. Up until then many Irish musicians had political leanings, now for the first time onstage was a band much of whose raison d'etre was political involvement. This was a heady concept and Moving Hearts began to draw an audience that was not only wowed by technical and innovative musical fluency but one that identified strongly with various social and political messages. At a time when most politicians seemed ineffective at best and morally craven at worst, the band filled a void and assumed a stature that few groups of musicians attain. As events in the North spiraled even further out of control, Moving Hearts was a band for an increasingly disaffected generation of Irish to hang its hat on.

Within weeks of their first gigs at The Baggot Inn, Bobby Sands began his hunger strike on March 1ˢᵗ, 1981. Those very words, "Hunger Strike," summon up darkness, anguish, and blighted hope. Time has tempered some of the roughest edges, yet many of the events of that year are still etched in my mind. There was always a feeling that sense might prevail, but when you measured that fragile hope against the tin-eared obstinacy of Mrs. Thatcher and her associates, your worst fears and doubts tended to prevail.

On the one hand there was the unblinking belief of Sands and his comrades that they would sooner die than back down from their five demands, and on the other, Thatcher's determination to withhold Special Category Status, treat the prisoners as common criminals, and in so doing, break the back of the IRA in a very public confrontation. Was ever a woman less suited to come up with a compromise that would save face on both sides? As far as the IRA command structure inside Long Kesh was concerned, they had already compromised when ending the previous October's strike; now they considered the conflict much the same as an armed battle, this would be to the death. As Kieran Nugent, the first person to be confronted with the demand that he wear a prison uniform, stated – "The only way they'll get me to wear that is if they nail it to my back."

As the months dragged on, the tension rose in Belfast, Derry, London, New York, and especially at Moving Hearts' shows. Gardai often patrolled outside pubs and clubs that the Hearts played at, and confrontations with exhilarated audiences were common as they trooped out from defiant gigs. Then there was the amazing moment when we held our breath on two continents: Bobby Sands from his hospital bed won an amazing electoral victory in the Fermanagh and South Tyrone by-election. Surely the Iron Lady would not let him die. But hope soon dissolved and Bobby Sands MP passed away on May 5, 1981.

Although we'd all been awaiting this moment, the most common first reaction was shock, soon to be followed by rage. Even the most apolitical Irish person caught some echo of it. This should not have been allowed to happen. Bobby Sands was employing an ancient Celtic rite – when wronged by your stronger enemy, go sit at his door and starve yourself until he makes amends. Mrs. Thatcher swept such trivialities aside. Sands' funeral attracted up to 100,000 people and radicalized many Irish both at home and abroad.

To compound matters, three more hunger strikers who had set out on their mission shortly after Sands were now approaching critical juncture and three others had followed them. Ten young men would die before the families of the final batch insisted on medical intervention. Some days later, the new British Secretary of State, James Prior granted prisoners the right to wear their own clothes, and by 1983, all five demands had been attained. Mrs. Thatcher had won a rather pyrrhic victory.

This was the background Moving Hearts played against. I don't doubt that it had something to do with the band's short life. Interestingly enough, the Hearts also formed on a cooperative basis with the seven band members and three of a crew sharing profits and costs – always a tough road to travel. Within two years Christy Moore left the band to pursue his solo career. Mick Hanly who had written *On The Blanket* replaced him as lead singer. Major Thinkers opened for this incarnation in New York City in 1983. While the Hearts had moments of brilliance at that show, there seemed to be a feeling of unease onstage. In certain ways there had always been a tension between a folkie lead singer and a rhythm heavy, jazz-inspired bunch of musicians. Christy had enough righteous anger and charisma to harness that tension and even knock sparks out of it; Mick, for all his strengths, seemed to me to be somewhat a fish out of water. It did not surprise me when he took his leave; nor did his replacement Flo McSweeney, despite spirited renditions, seem to have a handle on the band either.

But, oh my God, their first instrumental album, *The Storm,* recorded in 1985, was a revelation. Fluid and insightful, it seemed to meld the ancient world of the pipes to the modern domain of jazz. But it's hard to keep a big musical group together; I can only imagine that financial pressures and lack of record company support must have led to a gradual disbanding. For there they pretty much left it - with an occasional reunion, mostly to pay down the debt incurred by the commune in their four years on the road.

In 2008 they got together again. You often fear such reunions. In trying to recreate old glories, bands can get bogged down in detail and become caricatures of themselves. The players were no longer the young studs of the Dublin musical scene – battles had been fought, some won, some lost; it was rumored that sobriety had whipped some drinking problems. I, for one, wondered how it would all sound. For once a happy ending! The idea had been to revisit what they'd done instrumentally and see what almost a quarter century of varied experience would add. The results were magnificent and are captured on a CD/DVD *Live in Dublin*. The sound is richer, more assured, with a new maturity tossed in that adds to the delight; it's the crown jewel in their recording career.

There are moments you feel like hearing Christy weigh in but the man was there when he was needed; some things are better off left unsaid the second time round – let the music do the talking. The songs, and particularly their lyrics, were about a particular period in Irish history, painful and troubling to the soul. They're an important part of our culture and it's odious that the corporate music business saw fit to delete them. But these suits, bean counters and blandies can never take away the fact that one band made a stand back in an awful time, and in combining music, politics and the weight of history, refused to be silenced. For that we owe Moving Hearts a huge debt of gratitude.

No Time For Love (If They Come In The Morning)

No time for love if they come in the morning
No time to show fear or for tears in the morning
No time for goodbyes no time to ask why
And the wail of the siren is the cry of the morning

They call it the law - apartheid, internment, conscription,
partition and silence
It's the law that they made to keep you and me where they
think we belong
They live behind steel and bullet-proof glass, machine guns
and spies
And tell us who suffer the tear gas and torture that we're in
the wrong

The trade union leaders, the writers, the rebels, the fighters
and all
And the strikers who fought with the cops at the factory gate
The sons and the daughters of unnumbered heroes who paid
with their lives
And the poor folk whose class or creed or belief was their only
mistake

They took away Sacco, Vanzetti, Connolly and Pearse in their
time
They came for Newton and Seal and the Panthers and some of
their friends
In London, Chicago, Saigon, Santiago, Cape Town and Belfast
And the places that never made headlines, the list never ends

The boys in blue are only a few of the everyday cops on their
beat
The CID, Branch men and spies and informers do their job
well

Larry Kirwan

Behind them the men who tap phones, take pictures and
program computers and file
And the ones who give the orders which tell them when to
come and take you to a cell

So come all you people give to your sisters and brothers the
will to fight on
They say you get used to a war but that doesn't mean the war
isn't on
The fish needs the sea to survive just like your comrades do
And the death squad can only get to them if first they can get
through to you
(Lyrics by kind permission of Jack Warshaw – recorded
by Moving Hearts)

CHAPTER SEVENTEEN

New York, NY 10003

Got into town on a Saturday night
With a Fender guitar and I checked out the sights
Drank my way down to the Lower East Side
'Cause I was nuts about Thunders and Suicide

Formed a band called the Major Thinkers
With a couple of musicians and some heavy drinkers
Went up to Max's and I said
"Hey man, I'm gonna blow your club right off the map"

New York, New York what have you done?
You've wrecked me 'til I have become
Half the man I might have been
Half the hero of my dream

New York, New York it's over now
You beat me still I wish somehow
Just for once I could have proved you wrong
But you knew best all along

Well, I met Sheila down at Blanche's bar
She was dressed all in black but her heart was a scar
She took me back to Avenue C
Hey, we were happy there, her and me

'Til a man from the Black Rock saw the band
And he said, "Hey, you dudes are just sizzling hot
Gonna cut a record, make you all stars
But first things first, sign your soul away here"

So we cut a song about Avenue B
And the boxes boomed it all over the streets
But the record company, ah, they screwed us all up
Sheila went off and joined the Scientology Church

Then Mike stopped a bullet in Staten Island
And my whole world turned ultra violent
But there's one last thing I just gotta see through
There's one last thing I gotta say to you

Sheila, baby, give me one last chance
I've just gone and formed Black 47
I don't care about the money, you can keep the fame
I just wanna beat this city at its own dumb game

(Larry Kirwan)

I played my last gig with Major Thinkers on St. Patrick's Day, 1985, at Irving Plaza. It was a very good show, if I remember correctly, but I was glad the whole thing was over. Musically I'd come to a dead end. I could still turn out good pop songs that people liked but I wasn't sure why I was doing it

anymore. I had definitely turned off the music business
– not that I'd ever imagined it was any kind of altruistic
pursuit, by any means, but the ravenous, commercial
nature of it was not something I wanted to be a part of
anymore.

With that in mind, I took a stroll across the street
to Terry Dunne's original Tramps on 15ᵗʰ Street and took
a hit of ecstasy. With plastic shamrocks winking at me
from the walls, Buster Poindexter saluting me with
Danny Boy, I hung out with Lisa Lowell, Soozie Tyrell,
Thomas Hamlin, and other Rock 'n' Roll denizens of the
night. By the time I made my shaky, euphoric, dawn-lit
way home to Avenue B & 3ʳᵈ Street, I had much on my
mind to confront.

What the hell had I been doing all these years and
what had I to show for it? Not much in the way of
financial resources for sure certain. Having celebrated a
headlining Irving Plaza gig, I probably had less than $20
in my pocket. Whatever check I received from the gig
would go straight to Citibank to pay down my working
overdraft. And yet I felt lighter than the morning star
floating in the East Village sky. It had been a good life
so far – born in a small town in the South East corner of
Ireland, I'd made my way through music to Manhattan.
No matter what had gone wrong, I'd gained a major
record deal, played in some of the great halls of
America, made a legion of friends, and emerged from
the whole thing not only in one piece but alive and
kicking. True, I'd lost my musical voice and that was a
matter of deep regret. I'd burned out, I suppose; but
that was yesterday, now it was time to let the whole kit
and caboodle go, pick up the pieces and start all over
again.

When I awoke in the early afternoon, I was still
euphoric if a little knock-kneed. I stumbled over to my

makeshift desk, turned on my IBM Selectric and added a couple of sentences to *Liverpool Fantasy*, a play that I'd been writing about The Beatles – if they hadn't made it. All of a sudden this idiosyncratic work began to make total sense – before I had been just thinking about the plot and its ramifications, now I was actually living it. I wrote a few more sentences, and then some more; by the time I looked up the light was fading in the evening sky. I had already put the music world behind me. I was now a full-time playwright – whatever the hell that meant!

I pretty much gave up listening to music except for some Jazz, Classical, World Beat, and Irish Traditional. Having devoured popular music all my life, I wasn't rebelling against it – I had just lost interest in the genre. Perhaps it was the advent of MTV and the stranglehold it had achieved on the pop form, but the early 80's, with a few exceptions, seemed like a wasteland with more emphasis on style than content. And I take some responsibility for that – the haircut had become as important as the song. Touring with Cyndi Lauper – and I consider Cyndi one of the great singers of the last 40 years – shone a big light on a world I no longer wanted to be a part of.

The 70's are often derided and written off as the era of bell-bottoms and disco; but that's the official media/TV portrayal. Down the Lower East Side we considered Studio 54 to be an overpriced kip, full to the rafters with buffoons and poseurs. Our world rattled and hummed to Reggae and Punk, Marley and Strummer. We had a lot more than three chords at our disposal, if not much of a lock on the truth. Who'd want the full, unvarnished truth anyway? Doubt and indecision have large and leading parts to play in the creative process.

I wrote every day, lived with the characters of my
plays rollicking around in my skull, learned how to
negotiate with method-obsessed actors, met a fine
director, Monica Gross, and together we produced
Liverpool Fantasy at Charas/El Bohio Culture and
Community Center on the Lower East Side. Within a
year of Major Thinkers' demise, I had a hit of sorts, and
the following year the play received good reviews at the
Dublin Theatre Festival. I had made a vow to myself
that I would incorporate the Punk DIY credo into my
theatrical pursuits. Everything I wrote would receive a
production or, failing that, nothing less than a first class
workshop or staged reading.

It was a frenetic life – even with a play in
production I worked everyday on a new one. I did
whatever it took to make a living: ran a typing service,
worked construction, painted houses, did the occasional
gig in the Bronx, wrote, sang and produced for the poet,
Copernicus, did a tour of Eastern Europe and the Soviet
Union with him, and played improv funky music with
Chill Faction – but just for the hell of it. With all of that,
I managed to pass through the latter half of the 80's
unscathed by popular music. To this day I'm not sure
what songs and bands I missed.

My absence didn't garner much notice and life
pulsed on in the world of Celtic and Irish music – for
Sinéad O'Connor, perhaps Ireland's greatest singer,
emerged in the 80's. When we think of Sinéad, we often
get blindsided by her many public controversies and,
yet, that voice of hers is amazing. But it's not just the
voice: her innate understanding of music and its various
genres brings to mind Joe Strummer. Having a
conversation with Strummer was like taking a master
class in music and its relation to society. I never had a
discussion with Sinéad; I'm not quite sure give and take

is her thing, although I did conduct a memorable (for me anyway) interview with her for Celtic Crush.

It was one of the strangest I've ever participated in, mostly because I had a bad dose of Bronchitis. In fact, I had declined the opportunity of speaking with her, and was home in bed when I was informed that Sinéad was waiting and there was no one else available to conduct an interview. I knew her brother Joe, one of the kindest and most considerate of literary figures; besides I figured that it would be an insult to a great artist if no one showed up. So, I hopped the subway uptown, dizzy, trembling – and slightly late. Sinéad, luckily, had just finished her sound check and there she sat. She did not seem particularly happy, so to be on the safe side, I shamelessly dropped Joe's name – I figured that might gain me a couple of points. It did at least soften her cough – if not mine – for she smiled at the mention. I made sure to sit as far away from her as possible and dug my fingernails into my palms to help resist the ever-present urge to cough my brains out.

Usually, I intersperse questions with songs but because of my late arrival the engineer had already decided that Sinéad would sing the three songs agreed on and then do the interview. I should have arisen and left the recording studio, but I was so weak I figured I might topple over. And so began one of the great and strangest musical experiences of my life, as Sinéad sang three songs directly to me while accompanying herself on acoustic guitar – her keyboard player positioned off in a corner.

Her eyes were incredibly beautiful – mine hooded and brimming over from the illness. At times my ears would fill with white noise, and occasionally my hearing would almost totally fail; at other times it appeared that her voice was coming from behind my head. And, oh, that voice! It was so incredibly communicative and in tune – each note and word made total sense to me, and I wondered what it must be like to possess such a gift. I can't even remember her first two songs. I didn't say a word after either of them – for fear that if I spoke I might explode in a paroxysm of coughing.

However, after the second song, perhaps puzzled by my silence, she shrugged and inquired if there was anything I might wish to hear. I murmured that it would mean a lot to hear her version of *I Don't Know How To Love Him* (she was promoting her album, *Theology*). She appeared to think this was a strange choice – not so if she knew how many times Pierce Turner and I had performed it in Brooklyn bars, or that the best version I had ever heard was a massed male chorus belting it out around the piano in a Christopher Street bar. And then she sang the Lloyd-Webber/Tim Rice standard, quietly but with a currying of religious fervor, and for the first time I experienced just what the song was about.

Then it was time for our chat. She must have thought I was in the realm of zombie-hood, so careful was I not to raise my voice for fear of spewing germs all over her. I could sense her natural combative streak and that she did not suffer fools lightly, nor turn the other cheek to insult, real or imagined, without striking back. My one mistake was over her Curtis Mayfield cover, *We People Who Are Darker Than Blue*.

When I confessed that it was a new one on me, she inquired acidly what rock I might have been sheltering beneath these last 30 years. I'm not sure how I answered because my ears had begun to ring and sweat had broken out on my forehead from the stress caused by this rebuke, combined with the ongoing exertion of holding my breath. I must confess that I briefly toyed with the notion of advising her to go fuck herself, but I just didn't have the energy to make it sound convincing. And so I excused myself. I'd felt I'd done my bit for Irish music and was giving myself a mental pat on the back for not spewing Bronchial whatevers all over Ms. O'Connor's beautiful face.

None of my suffering and restraint seemed to have made any impression on Ms. O'Connor, however, and I had managed to make it to my feet, although holding on like hell to the edge of my chair, when one of my favorite colleagues, Pat McKay, who runs the Reggae Channel, came breezing in the door in her inimitable friendly fashion. She threw her arms up in the air in celebration, then enveloped Sinéad in a sisterly hug, and gushed, "Sinéad, honey, congratulations, you're pregnant again."

Perhaps it was the illness but I hadn't noticed any such change in Ms. O'Connor's general physiognomy; still and all, discretion being the better part of valor, I figured that this was an opportune time to make a break for the door. Before I could yank it open the oxygen appeared to vacate the sterile studio and a freezing second later Sinéad informed her Jamaican sister with a restrained steeliness, "Actually I've already had the baby but am having some trouble losing the weight."

Without missing a beat, Pat exclaimed that time and a little exercise would take care of any such concerns, and was passing on best wishes from Sly & Robbie and other such Reggae royalty as I bounced off walls on my way to the elevator.

There are times when it seems like Sinéad can't catch a break. Partly it's because of her penchant for shooting from the hip. The media loves her – or hates her – depending on your point of view, but whatever, she always makes good copy. Her actions may appear

A History of Irish Music

extreme at times, yet if you look back, she has been on the money with most issues. As regards women's rights around the world, and Ireland in particular, she has been in the forefront of that struggle – and if you haven't already noticed, she is one of the few woman I've written about in this collection, surely an indicator that not all has been equal opportunity on the Irish music scene.

Many have criticized her action on *Saturday Night Live* when she tore up a picture of Pope John Paul II while singing Bob Marley's *War*. However, her reason for doing so was to highlight the ongoing issue of the Catholic Church's cover-up of child abuse. In retrospect, given all that's come out over the last two decades, she was making a very brave and even prescient statement at the time. Let's face it - everyone in Ireland knew or, at least, suspected something about what was going on concerning clerical child abuse, and the cruelty meted out to "fallen women" and their children in various convents, and state and church approved orphanages. Most everyone turned a blind eye or chose to stay silent about these matters and, in so doing, sentenced many children to horrors that could have been prevented decades before the rot was exposed.

Sinéad was one of the few, if abrasive, voices to speak up. Listening to her sing *I Don't Know How To Love Him* left me in no doubt of her deep spirituality; and when the Catholic Church finally modifies its anachronistic rules, then perhaps they'll consider the credentials of this courageous woman who was ordained a priest by the Irish Orthodox Catholic and Apostolic Church over fifteen years ago.

One huge mistake Sinéad made, I believe, was at the *Bob Dylan 30th Anniversary Tribute Concert* in Madison Square Garden some two weeks after the

Saturday Night Live event. Now, it may have sounded a
lot different onstage, but the booing was quite light. No
one reacted one way or the other in my section of the
Garden. In fact, we had to crane our necks to figure out
where the actual booing was coming from. At the same
time there were many cheers for her and not a little
vocal encouragement. In fact, most of the noise I heard
was audience members shouting "shut the fuck up" to
the small minority of Sinéad haters in that audience of
15,000 plus.

Whatever! Is there a performer in Rock 'n' Roll
who hasn't experienced dissent? It's the name of the
game – especially if you lay your own views out hot and
heavy. Neil Young who was playing that night made
the point that his own audience was less than happy
with his dogged performance of synthesizer-based songs
from his *Transformer* CD. Sinéad would have won a
huge victory and redeemed herself to American
audiences by just getting on with the job and singing her
song that night in the Garden. But, perhaps, that was
never the intention.

Regardless, she is one of the most versatile and
chill-inducing singers to emerge from Ireland. We'll
always have her more well-known standards like
Nothing Compares 2 U and the recent sadly overlooked
Old Lady, but she took the Irish folk canon to new places
with her *Sean Nós Nua* album, produced by the
ubiquitous Donal Lunny. Take a listen to *Lord Franklin*
for sheer delicate intensity. Despite all the controversy
she has raised over the years, whenever you have a wish
to be transported to a different time and place, Sinéad is
your woman.

If Ms. O'Connor was wowing the international
music world with her voice, looks, and extensive
knowledge of Pop, Soul, R&B, and Reggae, a musical

renaissance was occurring West of the River Shannon.
The province of Connaught and surrounding areas had
been well known for *Sean Nós*, Irish Traditional, Ceilí
and Country music, often provided by well-rounded
showbands who could put a beat behind just about
anything and whose main function was to get the
punters up and dancing, then send them home sweating.
     Oliver Cromwell immortalized the very name of
the province when he declared that the ousted Irish
landowners of Leinster, Munster and Ulster should go
"to hell or to Connaught." This they did, with many
attendant deaths on their journey; after crossing the
Shannon River, they took what "small stony fields" they
could, many of them harboring a smoldering resentment
against those who had replaced them. After Cromwell's
death and the Restoration, some made it back and
reclaimed their homelands, but most stayed on,
considering themselves to be the "real Irish" and having
scant respect for those from Dublin and the more
English oriented East Coast. The Potato Famine years of
1845-47 killed untold numbers of them while many more
emigrated to the USA, Canada and the UK. Thus, the
"Wesht" as it was often pronounced locally, though
considered backwards by the East, could boast of a quite
liberal cross-cultural pollination from returning
emigrants and their descendants – this manifested itself
quite often in an understanding of American popular
music in general and Country music in particular.
     And yet, perhaps because of the neglect of the
province down through the years of the Irish Free State
and later the Republic, the people of Connaught seemed
to often sport an inferiority complex, or perhaps more
likely a reluctance to blow their own horns. One such
person was Seosamh Ó'Héanaí (Joseph Heaney) from
Connemara in County Galway, a cultural giant. His

227

knowledge of *Sean Nós* and his expertise in delivering it
had a tremendous influence on Luke Kelly, Ronnie
Drew, Andy Irvine and many others in the nascent
Dublin Folk scene of the 1960's. He was a regular in
O'Donoghue's and spent time in London fostering the
British Folk Music scene too. After a triumphant gig at
the Newport Folk Festival he moved to New York and
worked as a doorman on Fifth Avenue.

During a residency at Paddy's Pub, a Connemara
hangout in Brooklyn's Sunset Park, Turner & Kirwan of
Wexford used to play a set of fast Irish ballads that
would culminate in a shit-kicking, double time version
of *The Hills of Connemara*. I noticed that a fairly decrepit
looking man in his 60's would lead the audience in
hand-clapping and singing. One night on a break I
happened to sit next to him. He introduced himself as
Joe Heaney. I remarked that there was a very well
known *Sean Nós* singer of the same name. He gave a
wink and a broad smile, and said, "That's me!" The guy
was world famous and yet he displayed no airs or
graces. Nor was there a trace of musical snobbery about
him – for nothing could be further from the austere
tradition of *Sean Nós* than Turner & Kirwan's frantic
barroom ballad delivery. We never even put any
thought into those songs – our only concern was to get
the punters dancing, get paid, and get the hell back to
the East Village to work on our own original
"masterpieces." But as Joe said to me that night, "I love
anything with a bit of a go to it."

The West might have been content to remain in
isolated and semi-contented stasis had it not been for the
arrival of a catalyst from Edinburgh, Scotland by name
of Mike Scott. His band, The Waterboys, had achieved
some success in the UK and was highly regarded by
critics and punters alike. They were generally lumped

in with the so-called Big Music of U2, Simple Minds and Big Country, but Scott was not the type to be pigeonholed. A marvelous songwriter, he had an interest in the spiritual side of life and combined that with a search for new ways of expression. He arrived in Ireland in the mid-1980's at the invitation of a member of The Waterboys, Dublin born fiddle player, Steve Wickham, still a musical collaborator thirty years later. On his trips to the West Scott fell under the influence of the music, the people and the cultural history. Rather than imposing his own considerable musical knowledge, Scott's way has always been to join in, soak up the atmosphere and become one with the local musical zeitgeist. After some years of such immersion, he moved the band to Spiddal, a *Gaeltacht* area, just outside Galway. He recruited some of the area musicians including a wunderkind young accordionist, Sharon Shannon, and they recorded *Fisherman's Blues*, an album of original songs that sprang from the music and social scene of the West.

It was all there: shades of Irish Traditional, Country two-steps, flecks of *Sean Nós* and American pop in an irresistible cocktail that took Ireland, and what seemed like every Irish person in the UK and US, by storm. I can vouch for this firsthand for when Chris Byrne and I played early Black 47 gigs in the Bronx in late 1989, we were looked down on as, not only, heretics but fucking eejits because we couldn't perform any songs from that album. Although we were dedicated to turning Black 47 into a fully original band in as short a time as possible, neither were we suicidal, so I quickly took a brief detour to learn the title track along with *And A Bang On The Ear* (although we did do the latter at double-time which turned it into a frenzied *Jive*, the Irish form of *The Jitterbug*.)

As talented as Sharon Shannon is – and she swings that accordion masterfully – I doubt if she would have achieved her well-earned success without her apprenticeship in The Waterboys. Though Mike Scott eventually moved on to other forms of rock music until returning somewhat to the fold with the magnificent *Appointment With Mr. Yeats* some years back, Sharon has in many ways kept the flame of The Waterboys burning through the music of her own fine band. She has also stretched the style by the addition of hints of Reggae and Tango, and gone on to resurrect and nourish careers of disparate characters such as old *Ceilí* band head, Dessie O'Halloran and young Roots Rockers like Mundy.

But when you talk about the West, there's one hell of an elephant in the room if you don't mention The Saw Doctors. I've always considered this dynamic band to be the perfect synthesis of showband and punk group. Eyebrows may be lifted at the mention of the oft-despised showband, but I mean it in the best sense. The top showbands were peopled by great musicians who could play in a myriad of styles – all with the intention of "turning the floor black" a.k.a. getting everyone in the hall up from their seats and dancing. I've seen many Saw Doctors' shows over the last 25 years, and it's a rare punter that's not shaking a leg at some point of their performance. And because Black 47 has gone *mano-a-mano* with them at so many Irish festivals down those years, I can attest to the fact that unless you're at the top of your game, these guys will roll all over you. The Punk – take no prisoners - influence probably accounts for that.

Leo Moran and Davy Carton have been the mainstays in The Saw Doctors since their founding in 1986. Carton cut his teeth in the Punk outfit Blaze X, while Moran got his start with a Reggae band, the rather enigmatically titled, Too Much For The White Man! Odd as that name might be, given Leo's less than suntanned complexion, the fascination with Reggae in Ireland has deep cultural roots. The aforementioned Oliver Cromwell, after defeating the Irish in 1649, had many prisoners on his hands. Being a strategic thinker, he sent thousands of these young men and women to the West Indies, especially Barbados and Jamaica, to work as slaves in the sugar cane fields. Many of these Irish cohabited with Africans - the next wave of slaves - and with time their descendants became part of the great island mélange. I think the Irish recognized echoes of their lost people when Ska in the 60's and Reggae in the 70's became popular. Take a listen to the opening guitar line in Bob Marley's *Redemption Song*. The melody has unmistakable Irish roots.

Tuam, home of the Saw Doctors, was once known as the Showband Capital of the World. A small country town, it boasted six top of the line outfits, including the nationally known Johnny Flynn Showband. It wouldn't surprise me if young Leo and Davy watched the Transit vans come and go, and dreamed of some kind of career in music too. Like me, they undoubtedly despaired of showband conformity and identified much more with the cooler groups from the US and UK. And still, there's a friendliness and audience compatibility that oozes off The Saw Doctors onstage, not unlike the showbands in their prime. This would all add up to a hill of beans if the lads hadn't been capable of turning the raw fodder of rural life in Galway and Mayo into compelling pop songs that once embedded in your brain are almost impossible to exorcise.

I remember spending a night in some god-forsaken village in North Galway during the summer of 1990 on a rainy night when you felt that Noah in his Ark

might come floating by. I had made my sloshy and
squelchy way to the only pub for miles around. It was
deserted except for a bunch of pool-playing, cider-
slugging delinquents. No one spoke to me and I'm
always meek as a poorhouse mouse when guys with
booze aboard are wielding cue sticks. They had
commandeered the jukebox and were taking a walk on
the bland side – everything from Abba to Phil Collins. I
was resigned to staring into my pint for the night when
from out of nowhere a recorded voice in a thick Galway
accent proclaimed, "I have fallen for another, she can
make her own way home;" this was followed by an up-
tempo jubilant racket that had me off my seat and over
to the jukebox in seconds flat before *Dancing Queen*
might surface again.

It was The Saw Doctors. I deposited whatever
coins I possessed and played the record another three
times. This caused no little stir with the pool players –
one of whom detached himself from the others and
proceeded to tell me that he was related by marriage to
one of the band. While he was giving me the lowdown
on "the lads," I switched to cider and by the end of the
night I too was wielding a cue stick and pogoing with
the locals to *N17*, another Saw Doc's jukebox favorite.

I Useta Lover

I have fallen for another she can make her own way home
And even if she asked me now I'd let her go alone
I useta see her up the chapel when she went to Sunday mass
And when she'd go to receive, I'd kneel down there
And watch her pass
The glory of her ass

I useta to love her, I useta love her once
A long, long time ago
I useta to love her, I useta love her once
A long long time ago
It's gone, all my lovin' is gone
It's gone, all my lovin' is gone

D'you remember her collecting for Concern on Christmas Eve
She was on a forty-eight hour fast just water and black tea
I walked right up and made an ostentatious contribution
And I winked at her to tell her I'd seduce her in the future
When she's feelin' looser

So now you know the truth of it she's no longer my obsession
Though the thoughts and dreams I had of her would take six
months in confession
See I met this young one Thursday night and she's into free
expression
And her mission is to rid the world of this sinful repression
Then we had a session
It's gone, long, long gone
I have fallen for another and she can make her own way home

(Written by D. Carton/L. Moran
/P. Stevens/P. Cunniffe IMRO)

Mike Scott's presence in Galway helped the Docs in no small way for he legitimized many local musicians in the eyes of the Dublin critical cognoscenti, and in so doing raised the confidence level of the musicians themselves. Having a real live rock star in their midst encouraged locals to dream that they too could be part of a world musical community – that you didn't just have to be from Dublin; real live culchies could top the charts too. Scott also produced their first single, *N17*, and took the Docs on tours of Ireland and the UK.

The hidden member of the band, and in some ways the most important cog in the wheel, is Ollie Jennings. Ollie was a founder of the Galway Arts Festival and became manager of The Saw Doctors soon after they formed in 1986. If the devil is in the details then Ollie is right there looking over Old Nick's malodorous shoulder and offering unsought advice. I've known, or been guided by, some great managers, including Elliot Roberts of Neil Young fame, but I have to say that when it comes to loyalty and being willing to go the extra mile for your band, Ollie tops them all. I've felt his sting on behalf of his charges on occasion – though we've always remained friends – and his temper is not a pretty thing.

In typical Irish show-business begrudgery, I've heard him criticized for not having enough vision – a ridiculous charge, from my conversations and observations of the man. All I can say is that I wish that Black 47 had been lucky enough to have a manager of his caliber behind us. For what most people on the outside don't understand is that holding a band together and creating favorable work conditions is the most important job of any manager – and Ollie has definitely accomplished that and so much more.

I've played before the Docs many times and after them too – neither gig is easy, for there's a fierce anticipation of their arrival onstage, while the single-mindedness of their fans can be daunting. Often times the only way to deal with this is to create some drama of your own onstage that will cause a diversion; with Black 47 we did that by increasing the punk or political quotient, or both.

On our very first gig with them we created a lot
of drama without even meaning to. Black 47 was still
pretty new, albeit with a lot of gigs under our belt, when
my old drinking buddy, Terry Dunne, asked if we'd
play a set before and after the Docs on their first NYC
appearance in his club, Tramps. Having had the cue-
stick revelation of hearing *I Used To Love Her*, I told Terry
we'd only play an opening set – I knew it wouldn't be
good for the soul to be setting up for a second set with
their many fans streaming out the door. Terry agreed
but demanded we do a really long stint and he'd give
me a shout when to get off – and no messing - he needed
to keep the crowd in the room drinking so that a good
payday might be had for all concerned – including Black
47, he winked.

It never occurred to me that Terry wouldn't
inform The Saw Docs management about this
arrangement. All was well – a huge crowd showed up
and was surprisingly receptive to Black 47. The place
was hopping and we were having a ball. I figured Terry
would show up to give the cease and desist signal at
around the hour mark, for no one wants too long a set
before the headliner. Alas, no sign from Terry and I was
in a quandary – we were approaching saturation point
and The Saw Doc's crew was getting fidgety on the side
of the stage, as well they should. On and on it went –
still no Terry – and now the crew were gesturing to us.
Another couple of songs and they were positively
howling with rage. In the end, we did *Funky Ceilí*, the
place danced and we retired to a frigid Galway
reception from the crew.

I went downstairs, not quite sure what to think,
when I ran into a beaming Terry who declared, "Jaysus,
I thought you were going to stay on all night!" He
winked. Ah, club owners! All was well though as The

Saw Doctors got on stage quickly and pulverized the
crowd.

They went from strength to strength on both sides
of the Atlantic and I've always felt proud of them and
their Culchie Rock. They sum up many things for me in
their songs – emigration, a sense of home, Irish
tunefulness, a sly rural sense of humor, and that
ineffable joy of life when you've got a couple of pints
aboard. Though in the midst of a sabbatical right now
there are rumors around Galway that they'll be back
presently for a few more spins down that old N17. And
that's a good thing for the world would be a lesser place
without the combustible joy they produce at their live
shows.

N17

Well I didn't see much future
When I left the Christian brothers school
So I waved it goodbye with a wistful smile
And I left the girls of Tuam
Sometimes when I'm reminiscing
I see the prefabs and my old friends
And I know that they'll be changed or gone
By the time I get home again.

And I wish I was on the N17
Stone walls and the grass is green
And I wish I was on the N17
Stone walls and the grasses green
Travelling with just my thoughts and dreams

Well the ould fella left me to Shannon
Was the last time I traveled that road
And as we turned left at Claregalway
I could feel a lump in my throat
As I pictured the thousands of times
That I traveled that well worn track
And I know that things will be different
If I ever decide to go back.

Now as I tumble down highways
Or on filthy overcrowded trains
There's no one to talk to in transit
So I sit there and daydream in vain
Behind all those muddled up problems
Of living on a foreign soil
I can still see the twists and the turns on the road
From the square to the town of the tribes

And I wish I was on the N17
Stone walls and the grass is green
Yes I wish I was on the N17
Stone walls and the grasses green
Travelling with just my thoughts and dreams
(Leo Moran/Davy Carton IMRO)

Larry Kirwan

CHAPTER EIGHTEEN

The Fields of Athenry

By a lonely prison wall
I heard a young girl calling
Michael, they are taking you away
For you stole Trevelyan's corn
So the young might see the morn
Now a prison ship lies waiting in the bay.

Low lie the Fields of Athenry
Where once we watched the small free birds fly.
Our love was on the wing we had dreams and songs to sing
It's so lonely 'round the Fields of Athenry.

By a lonely prison wall
I heard a young man calling
Nothing matters Mary when you're free,
Against the Famine and the Crown
I rebelled, they ran me down
Now you must raise our child with dignity.

238

By a lonely harbor wall
She watched the last star falling
As that prison ship sailed out against the sky
Sure she'll wait and hope and pray
For her love in Botany Bay
It's so lonely 'round the Fields of Athenry.
(Lyrics used by kind permission of Pete St. John)

One form of music barely touched by modernity is the humble Irish ballad. In many ways it's the closest thing to "real Irish music," if you take that to be the vernacular of the regular person. *Sean Nós* may be purer in origin since the form stemmed from Irish speaking areas, however it had almost vanished from general Irish life by the 1960's. The ballad, on the other hand, has never succumbed to any challenge and continues to exist by sheer dint of the fact that it is supremely adaptable and speaks to the Irish soul. Go to any Irish international soccer game and once you get past the chants from fans of various English Premier League teams, one song sweeps all of them away and unites the various factions – *The Fields of Athenry*. Though everyone seems to know the tune now, it first became successful when Paddy Reilly, perhaps Ireland's greatest balladeer, recorded the hit version back in 1983.

When I first heard *The Fields of Athenry* I assumed it was a traditional song, such is the expertise of Pete St. John, a Dublin songwriter. Then again, that's what a ballad is all about, telling a story, painting indelible images, and ensuring that the melody is memorable and sturdy enough so that even the most musically challenged *amadán* can make a fist of it. That may sound easy enough; in fact, it calls for much skill and fixity of

purpose to write a great ballad. Its closest cousin is the
pop song, but that tends to be narrower in focus for it's
usually aimed at a certain age demographic and
employs a popular rhythm of the time, while the ballad
must have a timeless quality, attract everyone, and
usually swings to a waltz or a simple march.

I first saw Paddy Reilly perform in the city of
Waterford. It was quite a night as he, Emmet Spiceland
and Sweeney's Men opened for a very popular Wexford
ballad group, The Emerald Folk. At the time, in my
culchie coolness, I thought the billing was all wrong, yet
in fact the Emeralds who had little sophistication, but
much regard for themselves and their music, came out
after all these vaunted Dublin performers and basically
wiped the floor with them. This was because their
direct, forthright songs got right to the message, thereby
appealing to the hearts rather than the minds of the
audience.

Paddy Reilly was, if I remember, the first act of
the night. He was at that time a proletarian Dublin folk
singer with what appeared to be left wing leanings,
hardly surprising for he performed some Ewan MacColl
songs and had obviously come under that great master's
influence. But the song that stood out in my mind, the
chorus of which remains there to this day, was a ballad
I'd never heard before.

Oh Cricklewood, oh Cricklewood
You stole my heart away
For I was young and innocent
But you were old and grey
(John B. Keane)

This paean to an unlovely neighborhood of North
London summoned up so many images of emigration,

for what Wexford person was unaware of the notorious Crown Pub in Cricklewood where so many of our people went to drink, sing and smother their homesickness. It was years later, while drinking in Hugh O'Lunney's Pub in Midtown Manhattan with the playwright John B. Keane that I discovered he wrote the song. Such is the power of the well-constructed ballad: it must summon images, often local and parochial, and yet make them universal and recognizable, even if we've never been within an ass's roar of the places mentioned. It must also make us totally identify with the narrator and instantly deposit us in his world, foreign though it may be. The melody should be simple and pleasing but display enough traces of its own singular identity that we not mistake it for another song. All of this takes skill. Phil Coulter has that galore. An accomplished composer and musician (organist on Them's *Here Comes The Night*), he has written many million selling pop hits, and yet in the popular consciousness he'll probably always be remembered for the following ballad.

The Town I Loved So Well

In my memory I will always see
The town that I have loved so well
Where our schools played ball by the gas yard wall
And we laughed through the smoke and the smell
Going home in the rain, running up the dark lane
Past the jail and down behind the Fountain
Those were happy days in so many, many ways
In the town I loved so well

In the early morning the shirt factory horn
Called women from Creggan, the Moor and the Bog
While the men on the dole played a mother's role,

Larry Kirwan

*Fed the children and then walked the dog
And when times got rough there was just about enough
But they saw it through without complaining
For deep inside was a burning pride
In the town I loved so well*

*There was music there in the Derry air
Like a language that we could all understand
I remember the day when I earned my first pay
As I played in a small pick-up band
There I spent my youth and to tell you the truth
I was sad to leave it all behind me
For I'd learned about life and found a wife
In the town I loved so well*

*But when I returned how my eyes were burned
To see how a town could be brought to its knees
By the armoured cars and the bombed out bars
And the gas that hangs on to every breeze
Now the army's installed by that old gas yard wall
And the damned barbed wire gets higher and higher
With their tanks and guns, oh my God, what have they done
To the town I loved so well*

*Now the music's gone but they carry on
For their spirit's been bruised, never broken
Though they'll not forget still their hearts are set
On tomorrow and peace once again
For what's done is done and what's won is won
And what's lost is lost and gone forever
I can only pray for a bright, brand new day
In the town I loved so well*
                    *(Lyrics by kind permission of
                    Phil Coulter/Four Seasons Music)*

I had left Ireland before Paddy Reilly had a huge hit with this song that sums up in a very heartfelt manner the awful changes that the city of Derry in the North of Ireland was forced to go through in the Troubles. But I would hear snatches of Paddy's singing on the radio while on vacation and marvel at the road he had traveled since that first night he caught my attention in Waterford. I had no idea then the firm friend he would become during the Black 47 years and the influence he would have on the band's progress. After our first months in the Bronx, we began a residency in his pub on Second Avenue that was somewhat on the skids at the time (or as I once put it in an interview: "it was doing so badly even the cockroaches were jumping ship").

His partner in the establishment, Steve Duggan, also his booking agent, began getting us dates on the strength of Paddy's reputation at Irish Festivals, and in fact, secured us our first out-of-town gig at Jimmy McGettrick's Beachcomber in Wollaston Beach, Quincy, MA. The crowd was more puzzled than hostile to our punky/funky Irish music for they had come to hear the straightforward ballad singing of Paddy Reilly. Unfortunately for them, Mr. Reilly was nowhere to be seen, so we were forced to play an extra hour before I figured it was time to save their ears and our lives and vacate the stage.

It was then that Jimmy McGettrick informed me that Steve Duggan had called on "an urgent matter" during our set and wished me to get back to him at "my first available opportunity." This was in the days long before cell phones and so we repaired to Jimmy's office down in the cellar. Jimmy looked on worriedly as I called the redoubtable Steve who told me that "Paddy's plane had been delayed and because of the long journey he might well be a little the worse for wear", but was now on his way and could I please make sure that his guitar was in tune – it turned out he played so frequently in the Beachcomber he kept an axe on the premises.

The acoustic guitar, as it turned out, was indeed in need of tuning, not only that but it was missing a G-string. I searched the guitar case high and low but there were no replacements. There was nothing for it but to stick one of my own thin electric strings on and hope for the best. At that moment Paddy made a grand, if belated, entrance, jet lagged and most definitely "a little the worse for the wear" from some liberal shots of fine Scottish malt provided by Aer Lingus to compensate for the delay. I tried to explain about the electric string but Paddy, though exceedingly courteous and grateful for my guitar ministrations, was in a hurry to get on stage as a row was breaking out between two formidable ladies, each of whom seemed to be under the impression that she was the one closest to his heartstrings in that particular neck of the woods.

Though jet lag and Johnny Walker might have been affecting Paddy off stage, the moment he began to sing all such encumbrances faded away. That powerful voice of his rang through the old boards of the Beachcomber where once Louis Armstrong, Loretta Lynn and Tiny Tim had warbled. He must have played and sang for over two hours before vacating the stage. Perhaps his strategy was to wear down the two ladies; if so, he had miscalculated for both were primed for battle and beyond rip-roaring ready to stand by their imagined man. To add fat to the fire, a third had since arrived and now began to aggressively pursue her suit. By then, with the sweat pouring off him, Paddy had reached some emotional and spiritual plateau far beyond the bounds of romantic entanglement, imagined or otherwise. Taking quick stock of the situation, the three suitors were strategically and diplomatically ejected by the suave and ever-smiling Mr. McGettrick, and I seem to remember sitting downstairs in the cellar with Paddy long after Massachusetts closing time, reminiscing about the gig in Waterford and swapping Ewan MacColl songs over much fine whiskey.

Despite all such ups and downs on the road, Paddy is a keen student of music and spends his free nights in New York City at the Metropolitan Opera. He's also a thoughtful man with much concern for his friends. After the shooting tragedy at the Black 47 St. Patrick's Day Show in 1996, he was the second person to call to make sure that all was okay. The first was a tearful Courtney Kennedy, Paul Hill's wife, forever touched by gun violence herself. She was a regular at Paddy Reilly's and encouraged me to write a song for her father after I confided that I felt the world would have been a very different place had he lived. Although set to a very different beat than a traditional ballad, yet I followed many of the genre's other rules when constructing the song.

Bobby Kennedy

Sing you a song about a man long forgotten
Born in Massachusetts in the city of Boston
He grew up, silver spoon in his mouth
Cocky as hell, he knew what he was all about

Larry Kirwan

His brother Jack came home a hero from the Navy
His Daddy said, "Bobby, I think that maybe
If you and me do a whole lot of work
He'll be the first Irish Catholic to make it to the White
House."

His Daddy, he bought the Democratic ticket
Jack walked all over a man called Nixon
Six months later they're sitting in the White House
"Bobby, let's find out what this country is all about

I want you to be my attorney general
Clean up the unions, meet that man called Martin."
Then he got mixed up in the Cuban Crisis
Lee Harvey Oswald blew his head off down in Texas

Don't get mad, just get even
Keep on going though your heart is bleeding
Love your friends, don't turn your back on your enemies
This is the story of a man called Bobby Kennedy

So Bobby, he took a trip down South
Saw his brothers and his sisters living hand to mouth
Deep in the heart of the Mississippi Delta
While up in DC they're blowing billions on weapons

Saw the look of despair in the eyes of the children
The hopelessness of the men and the women
"Something is rotten in these United States
And if you ain't gonna fix it then get out of my way!"

He said, "I gotta do this, gonna run for President
Gotta put my millions where my heart is."
Ran against Hubert and Gene McCarthy
Give the people a voice though it's breaking up the party

Then someone whacked Martin in a state of paranoia
Bobby won the primary in the state of California
But some crazy mother with an illegal weapon
Blew his brains out all over that hotel

So many years since Bobby got offed
Nothing to replace him, no one doing the job
Don't feed the children, they're costing the moon
Weasels in the White House sing a Democratic tune

Then I hear him say, "It don't make any sense."
You can't balance budgets without a conscience
And no one will deliver you from your enemies
If you go ahead and give up on all your dreams."

Don't get mad, just get even
Keep on going though your heart is bleeding
Love your friends, don't turn your back on your enemies
This is the story of a man called Bobby Kennedy

(Larry Kirwan)

To judge by their lyrics, The Wolfe Tones are a
ballad group not unfamiliar with violence. However,
the first song I remember them singing was *Deportees* by
Woody Guthrie. To say that the Tones are political is
indeed an understatement. Many bands play the
occasional political song and wax eloquently on the
issues of the day but the "bhoys" have never been shy of
wearing their Irish Republican colors. This has led to
much loathing in some quarters, while in others they are
regarded as the Second Coming. Only a couple of years
ago I was introduced to John Banville, the iconic Irish

writer in an NPR studio. Though he hails from
Wexford, we had never met. A courteous man, he
inquired what type of music I played. One of the NPR
people hastened to add, that I wasn't just any old pop-
smith but someone who performed "political music."
"As long as it's not like The Wolfe Tones!" Mr. Banville
opined.

Now I never thought Black 47 sounded remotely
like The Wolfe Tones and our world view differs also,
but for once I was about to claim kinship, if only to rattle
his assuredness that everyone should share his political
opinions. Still, that's the kind of reaction that The Wolfe
Tones evoke. And yet, I often think of them as the
quintessential ballad group. They're rousing, rebellious,
can raise a stadium to its feet, and if they don't speak for
the whole of the Irish people, then they do represent a
driven section. They made little secret of the fact that
they were Provisional IRA supporters. This leads me to
think that they have led charmed lives from the late 60's
through the mid-90's with all their travels around
Ireland.

Now it has been suggested to me, and from
people who claim to know these things, that they were
"under protection," but I've heard those types of fatuous
statements in regard to Black 47 also and never paid
them a moment's heed. Guerrilla armies at war with the
might of the British Empire have neither the time nor
inclination to keep an eye out for traveling musicians, no
matter how partisan or inflammatory the group might
be. That The Wolfe Tones never encountered any major
discomfort probably parallels the Rev. Ian Paisley
coming through the conflict unscathed despite his many
sectarian and demagogic outbursts – the Provos weren't
inclined to assassinate him because of the slaughter that
would ensue.

The four members, Derek & Brian Warfield, Noel
Nagle and Tommy Byrne, were all born in Dublin. They
took their name from Theobald Wolfe Tone, a leader of
the 1798 Rebellion. The original Wolfe Tone was a
Protestant - putting paid to any idea that the band might
have sectarian sympathies. In fact, if anything the
members lean towards the urban and, in particular, the
Dublin form of Republicanism which has always been
highly influenced by James Connolly's left-wing take on
things. While Padraig Pearse and Sean MacDiarmada
(MacDermott) might have garnered more esteem in
rural areas, Connolly has always been held in special
reverence on the poverty-stricken streets of inner
Dublin.

These strong Connolly connotations, however,
have not always transferred to their Irish-American
audience that often favors a simple solution to the very
complex problems fostered by the creation of the state of
Northern Ireland. I actually learned a lot from a small
section of an uncharacteristic Wolfe Tones' audience in
the early days of Black 47. It was on a brutally hot day
during a festival at Yonkers Racetrack when the Tones
were headlining. The stage was set up in the stands, this
meant that we were surrounded on three sides by the
audience with those in front practically able to lean over
us from their seats.

All very well and good until we got onstage, then
there was no escape, which wouldn't have presented a
problem under most circumstances. You're there until
you finish – no big deal. However, in those days, Kevin
Jenkins, an African-American, played bass for us. We
were scheduled to play a short set and there were many
Black 47 supporters in the crowd raising a racket. With
the general din, the odd PA set-up, and the fact that at
such shows we usually string together three or four

songs to begin, I didn't at first catch what was happening. But I did feel tension on stage. It wasn't until we finished the first set of songs that I heard the chant - it had to do with the color of Kevin's skin.

At first I couldn't believe my ears – such things did not happen at Black 47 gigs, nor I'm sure at Wolfe Tones concerts either. Basically, it was just a small group of bad apples screaming for us to get off so that the Tones might take the stage. I looked around at Kevin who, for all intents and purposes, was trapped. He's a big guy – I know his bulk well from the time he ended up sitting on my neck in a very scary van crash – and though he was handling things in his usual professional manner, yet I could tell he was terrified. It was as if he was awakening to the nightmare he had always dreaded. I could have made an issue of it but it was a hot day, much drink had been taken, and emotions were obviously already aroused. Still, I've never forgotten the occasion, and after that, I toned down some of my own onstage exhortations for you never know, in raising passions on behalf of your own cause, you may incite some tangential issue about which you have no interest in – or control over.

That show made me fully aware of the effect alcohol can have on an already fiery gig. Up until then, I'd always been able to use it as a tool to drive a crowd. Now I saw the other side of the coin, the ugliness it can inspire. Alcohol and music have always gone hand in hand in my professional life, but with our way of escape blocked off I now had to defuse the atmosphere. There was no way of rationally dealing with this overt racism, however, for it was deeply ingrained - perhaps some folk memory that had been twisted and distorted. Was it just unfamiliarity – the unexpected sight of Kevin?

Who knows? But it was a lesson learned in a cauldron on a hot day and one I've never forgotten.

The Wolfe Tones were victims of Section 31 of the Broadcasting Authority Act that banned them from Irish radio for so many years; I doubt if they have ever been rehabilitated. But during their years in the wireless wilderness, they provided a valuable cultural service by keeping many of the old songs alive at a time when the tradition might have been lost. This shunning made bands like the Tones even more popular for they were seen as living embodiments of the credo: "When freedom is outlawed, only outlaws can be free." And in a stunning upset, when one would have imagined that some Beatles or Queen song would have triumphed, The Wolfe Tones version of *A Nation Once Again* won a 2002 BBC poll for The Most Popular Song Ever. Now, granted, many voted for it as a way of embarrassing the British establishment, but the song had already amassed a large number of legitimate votes. You can be sure the four members of this fine band enjoyed a good laugh at the expense of all the people and institutions that had censored them down the years.

A Nation Once Again

When boyhood's fire was in my blood
I read of ancient freemen,
For Greece and Rome who bravely stood,
Three hundred men and three men;
And then I prayed I yet might see
Our fetters rent in twain,
And Ireland, long a province, be
A Nation once again!

A Nation once again,
A Nation once again,
And Ireland, long a province, be
A Nation once again!

And from that time, through wildest woe,
That hope has shone a far light,
Nor could love's brightest summer glow
Outshine that solemn starlight.
It seemed to watch above my head
In forum, field and fane,
Its angel voice sang round my bed,
A Nation once again!

So, as I grew from boy to man,
I bent me to that bidding
My spirit of each selfish plan
And cruel passion ridding;
For, thus I hoped some day to aid,
Oh, can such hope be vain?
When my dear country shall be made
A Nation once again!

(Thomas Davis)

CHAPTER NINETEEN

Paddy's Got A Brand New Reel

*So Paddy got a brand new bag
What's the big deal?
Up in the Bronx, Mary gettin' drunk
Paddy got a brand new reel*

*Workin' like a dog out in Queens
7 or 8 days a week
Goin' to confession is your granny's obsession
Paddy got a brand new reel*

*I don't give a damn about you
'Cause you don't care about me
Hey Charlie Haughey, I'm sick of your party
Paddy got a brand new reel*

> *And when I go back home*
> *As I eventually will*
> *Hey politician, better get a mortician*
> *Paddy got a brand new reel*
> *(Larry Kirwan)*

If Black 47 seemed somewhat assured on those first nights in the Bronx, you can chalk a good part of that up to Chris Byrne's authoritative presence; it may also have stemmed from the fact that I'd abandoned the game of music some years previously to become a playwright. In essence I'd finally taken the advice of the poet, Copernicus, who had many times advised Turner & Kirwan of Wexford to "go to the mountain." He felt that we would never distinguish the forest from the trees, so caught up were we in the day-to-day task of surviving in the music business. In my case he was definitely right.

Playwriting enabled me to catch my breath and start from scratch. In many ways it was like going to college except that I was both professor and student, and the syllabus was wide open. Some four years later, when I began writing for Black 47, the new songs often featured fully drawn characters reacting to dramatic situations. I wasn't even aware of the change until Rolling Stone and other outlets began commenting on it; the discipline of playwriting had apparently added much needed definition to my songwriting.

There are many temptations when creating a play, however, one of which is to get too caught up in research - that definitely happened with *Mister Parnell* but it was to have a long term unexpected, if beneficial, outcome. I was obsessed with the subject of Charles Stewart Parnell, partly because my maternal grandfather's family in Carlow had split over the great man's divorce case in 1891. One side stuck with Parnell, the other favored his opponents including the Catholic Church; the family didn't fully reconcile until the death of my grandfather's much older anti-Parnellite sister in the 1950's.

Although I had a good idea how people spoke in 1891 – after all many Victorians were still alive in the Wexford of my boyhood - I pored over a number of Thomas Hardy novels so as to familiarize myself with the speech patterns. Hardy led me back to Dickens, one of the great loves of my childhood. I was living on East 3rd Street in the East Village at this time and discovered that Dickens had not only visited the legendary Five Points slum, barely a stone's throw away, but had written about it in his *American Notes for General Circulation*.

Dickens mentioned that Irish immigrants and African-Americans performed together in Five Points' dancehalls. Around then I came upon engravings of these bands and the inter-racial couples who danced to them. I couldn't help but wonder just what kind of music these inter-racial ensembles played. Though I had no way of knowing for definite, I figured it would be jigs and reels set to African-American rhythms. That was the first inkling of what would later become the core Black 47 sound – Irish Traditional tunes melded to the Hip-Hop beats of the 1980's.

I decided to make *Mister Parnell* a musical, rather than a straight dramatic play, a mistake in retrospect, as musicals are much more difficult to produce. Though the book still reads well, and the music is sound enough, *Mister Parnell* only received one full production. Whatever, as they say. In the search for theatrical authenticity I immersed myself in the music of the late 19ᵗʰ Century. To my surprise, I'd already heard much of

it sung at parties and pubs before television cast its
dumb pall over Irish life. The treatment of these old
songs, though, had calcified, and they were still
delivered in Victorian parlor fashion. For that reason, I
hadn't given them a lot of thought; they were old-
fashioned and most definitely not cool enough for
someone infatuated with the Beatles, Kinks and the R&B
of the 1960's. Now as I picked them out on guitar and
keyboard, I realized just how powerful, beautiful and
finely crafted they were once the dust had been
dislodged. Stick a Hip-Hop or Rock drum machine beat
beneath them, and *voila*, you were confronted with an
intriguing, effervescent hybrid.

Around this time too I began writing music for
the choreographer, June Anderson. One of the first
pieces was a collaboration with Mark Blandori, a
percussionist and composer. Mark had come up with a
great groove track, not unlike some of the rhythms of the
Nigerian, King Sunny Ade. June had become interested
in Irish music, and so we invited my friends, Eileen Ivers
on fiddle, and John Whelan on accordion, to play over
Mark's track. Easier said than done – such cross-cultural
couplings are common nowadays, but back in 1985 it
was virgin territory – at least for us.

"Finding the one," as James Browne always
proclaimed, was the key. Mark's piece contained a
number of different time signatures, routine enough for
him and June, but we Irish heads only nailed the piece in
the studio when I would count "eights" from a certain
point in the track and Eileen and John would play to my
count rather than Mark's percolating percussive
grooves. It was a great moment for all of us – but me in
particular – for it clearly demonstrated that the music of
all ethnic groups, no matter how divergent, will work
together given a little imagination and encouragement.

Both Eileen and John have gone onto successful musical careers; Eileen, in particular, has continued to experiment with African and African-American rhythms. Mark Blandori was the first percussionist to perform with Black 47. Oddly enough, back in those early days, my idea was that a rotating group of musicians would interpret the songs while Chris and I would be the core of the group. A good idea in theory, but one that didn't hold up to the practicalities of the road!

Black 47 was an open book in that first hurly-burly year of apprenticeship in the bars of New York City. None of it would have been possible without Chris Byrne. Chris was a detective in the NYPD when I jammed with his band, Beyond The Pale, in Paddy Reilly's. The New York of the late 80's is a far cry from today's more sanitized version. The streets were still wild, and being a cop definitely meant putting your life on the line on a daily basis. So to say that Chris brought a whole different element to the mix of an original band would be an understatement.

But then Chris was an unusual person. He was deeply rooted in the Irish-American ethos of New York City: Catholic school, civil service job, he had even married an Irish woman. With a very grounded Irish Traditional music background, he could play tin whistle, bodhrán, and that most difficult of Irish instruments – the uilleann pipes. He was a committed Irish Republican, one of those instrumental in causing an international incident, enraging British and Unionist politicians, by getting the NYPD Emerald Pipe and Drum Band to march in a Republican commemoration in Donegal. His views on the situation in the North of Ireland were straight and to the point – it was time for both the British army and government to leave. He broached that theme very powerfully in *It's Time To Go,* one of the great political songs of our era. Oh, by the way, did I mention that he was also very into Hip-Hop and was a fine rapper? Now NYPD membership and Rap music might seem, on the face of it, to be antithetical, but many cops have an appreciation of Hip-Hop, and why not? Rap has ruled the streets since the 1980's, and cops, whether they like it or not, march to its rugged beat.

The idea that I was now in a group with a cop caused no little stir among my friends, along with various tastemakers in East Village circles – particularly a cop who made no bones about the fact that he was an ardent Irish Republican. Pot-smoking heads kept their distance from cops in general. The cop was still "the man," and as Steven Stills said, "the man come and take you away." My own pot smoking days were over. Four hours of screaming into monitorless microphones in noisy bars puts tremendous stress on your voice – particularly as those bars were then thick with cigarette smoke. From this point on, I had to be careful, even talking too much during breaks could cause vocal fatigue that would nail you somewhere in the middle of the third set – with still a fourth to go.

From playing in Brooklyn and Bronx bars with Turner & Kirwan of Wexford, I was well used to having off-duty cops in the audience. Yes, some of them could be pains-in-the-arse, but such was the case in any profession. I looked on them as working-class guys who were keeping some semblance of order in a city close to skidding off the tracks. The NYPD throughout the 70's and 80's had little interest in a person toting around a dime bag of weed for his or her own consumption. Just don't kill or hurt anyone, go about your business in a fairly orderly manner and you could act out your own chosen lifestyle in New York City. In the years spent with Black 47, I got to know many cops – for the most part they were just like everyone else – trying to make a living and doing the best they could under rough circumstances.

Chris's striking presence and his obvious cop vibe was a godsend in those early days. He would often come straight from work, still packing his piece; with no dressing rooms in Irish bars, all pre-gig preparation took place on stage. Chris would open his black wooden case, remove the pipes, take off his gun, deposit it in the case, and away we'd go. The pub might be stewing with resentment at the mere thought of what they were about to hear, but that deft pipes/gun changeover tended to put some manners on even the rowdiest of elements. What might have been yells and bottles thrown leveled off to a more manageable hostile muttering.

There were exceptions. One snowy night in a Queens bar we had set up on the floor near the entrances to the ladies and gentlemen's toilets. An air of deep-seated depression hung like lead over this very bare-bones joint; the naked sheet-rocked walls barely contained the ripples of tension. With the snowflakes drifting down the crowd was sparse, and yet the band would have to be paid. The bartender made no great show of welcome, but that was hardly uncommon, and so we dug in for another pleasant evening of light entertainment – yeah right!

We only knew one way to play – hard assed and in your face, and by the end of the first set less than a dozen dedicated drinkers remained. With the snow intensifying and three sets still to go, it promised to be another long night in the musical apprenticeship of Black 47. Chris and I nursed a couple of beers at the end

of the bar and kept a wary eye on the drinkers. The pub
was a Connemara hangout – this beautiful area of
County Galway produces some of the nicest people in
the world, but they can be unpredictable, to put it
mildly, and with drink taken, they're often mere sparks
away from volcanic. We gathered that a "couple of the
lads" had just arrived from London and were being
given a welcome party. What with the jetlag, drinking
aboard the plane, and many shots of US alcoholic
hospitality, the guests were, shall we say, well beyond
any acceptable state of inebriation.

During the middle of the second set Chris noticed
a stream of water emerging from the Gents. Had we
been on a stage this would have caused us no particular
worry – such things happen in bars – but the water was
now seeping over the microphone leads. Upon
investigation, the bartender discovered that the urinal
had come loose from the wall. He appeared puzzled by
this occurrence but turned off the plumbing, swept up
the water around us, and so a trifle uneasily we
continued.

The partying in the middle of the bar had now
reached near feral levels. The revelers were not paying
the least attention to us and, in truth, we were treating
the gig as a long rehearsal, although we had already
figured that we'd have to give a break on the fee given
the snow and low attendance. This was never a
welcome prospect – it was hard enough playing to a
crowd of fucking morons for four sets without taking a
cut in pay into the bargain.

During the third set one of the lads from London
careened past us three sheets to some wind or other on
his way to the Ladies' bathroom. I didn't like the look of
him and wasn't comfortable that he was now at our
backs although apparently ensconced in the bathroom.

However, he was in there so long I eventually forgot about him until he came staggering out and collided with the sheet-rocked wall. He was so far gone he didn't even seem to notice us. Some minutes later, however a fresh stream of water surged from the Ladies room and approached my amplifier.

This was no joke. I stopped playing and made my heated concern known over the microphone. The barman ambled down, took a look and followed the source into the Ladies. Chris and I trooped behind him. The sink had been wrestled from the wall. The bartender gazed at it in some awe before turning off the plumbing and sweeping up around us again. It was decided that we should play a couple more songs so as not to "put a dent in the good mood" while he cut off the drinkers – which he assured us would be no easy task as they were "from home" and expected to make a late night of it – and would now have nowhere else to go given the gathering snow.

We were, as one might imagine, a little uneasy with the situation. One of these jerks had just wrecked two bathrooms and from the build of him looked like he could demolish the whole joint and a nascent Black 47 into the bargain. We also figured that he and his mates were no fans of the band and, seeing that they had totally ignored us up until then, perhaps it was best to call it a night before we caught their attention. We had scarcely begun the first song in our finale, which if I remember was *Paddy's Got a Brand New Reel*, when one of the lads erupted from amidst the crowd with a roar that could be well distinguished from our own pounding mix of pipes, guitar and drum machine.

"I hate this fucking music!" He enunciated in the broadest Connemara accent, flecked with broad hints of Cockney. Thereupon, he picked up a barstool and slammed it into the gaily-lit jukebox. The clash of glass and broken metal ricocheted around the bare walls of the pub as Chris and I came to an abrupt halt.

"Are you fucking mad?" One of his mates inquired into the sudden silence.

"That's a fucking band playing, you gobshite!" The barman added in high dudgeon, "not me brand new jukebox."

The perpetrator of the foul act appeared stunned by this revelation. Nonetheless, he gathered himself, extracted the barstool from the jukebox and stumbled down the bar in our direction.

"If he lays a finger on me I'll fuckin' whack him!" Chris announced over the microphone before reaching for his pipes case. The "lad from home" was having some problems negotiating his way but showing no little determination. I watched his progress with some concern – my lovely gleaming new sunburst Stratocaster at the ready although I had no idea what I'd do with it. "You better not kill him, we'll be in big trouble." I warned feebly.

"What do you think we're in now?" Chris didn't even bother looking at me so busy was he searching for his gun amidst the chord charts, lyric sheets and other bric-a- brac that littered his pipes case.

Sensing disaster and a cover story on the next day's New York Post, the bartender leaped in front of "the lad from home" and began to reason with him about musical taste, jet lag, illegal immigration, imminent arrest and other such concerns. In the end, he prevailed and ushered out the protesting party into the gathering blizzard. We stood on guard until the front door was safely locked. The bartender shook his head as he ambled up towards us, pausing for a sorrowful glance at the smashed and silent jukebox.

"That man has problems," he sighed. And so ended another night.

I had no problem with Chris's Republican views. I'd grown up with them for they closely resembled my grandfather's. The British Army had no right to be on Irish soil, the British Government had disgraced itself by supporting an undemocratic, gerrymandered police state; decisions on Ireland should be made by the population of the whole island – not by a manufactured majority in the six North Eastern Counties. Although my beliefs were more in line with Connolly and Larkin on Ireland we had plenty to agree on. We decided early on that we would align ourselves with no political party or movement since we would be much more effective were we seen to be independent. There was plenty of room to roam without nailing anyone else's flag to our mast.

Our first gig was a fundraiser for Bernadette Devlin McAliskey in The Bronx. I had first heard her speak over twenty years previously when she was a young firebrand recently elected to the British Parliament. She'd had some tough years in between, and assassins' bullets had taken a toll, but hardly on her indomitable spirit. Though often vilified and marginalized, she has always been one of the best speakers and clearest thinkers in Irish political life. And that evening in The Bronx in the fall of 1989, she electrified the room with her call for justice in the North of Ireland. We made a bit of a splash ourselves. After playing Bob Marley's *Three Little Birds* in tandem with our own, *Desperate*, some yahoo yelled out, "Play something "Irish."

To which I replied, "I wrote it, I'm Irish, what does that make it Swahili?"

263

But we made our first real mark politically by supporting the Guildford Four. And when released from British prisons in 1989 after fifteen years of a rigged sentence, we became fast friends with Paul Hill, Gerry Conlon and Paddy Armstrong on their first visit to New York. We were particularly close to Paul and stayed with him in London when we opened for The Pogues at Brixton Academy in December 1990; in fact, he was the one who first labeled us a "voice for the voiceless." This was because we purposely set out to represent the views of the Nationalist people in the North of Ireland with such songs as *Free Joe (Doherty) Now, Fire of Freedom, James Connolly,* and *Time To Go,* among others.

1989 was a bleak time in Irish affairs. Sinn Fein were political pariahs, few spoke out for the Republican people of the North, and if you railed against the British system of injustice, as we did, you were labeled a fellow-traveler of the IRA, no matter how nuanced your views. It was an old British tactic - tar everyone with the same brush. After a St. Patrick's Day show at the Ritz, a British newspaper declared that we were "the musical wing of the IRA." Apart from being untrue, that was an incendiary statement as Loyalist paramilitaries had declared war on all "Pan-Republican" organizations. So much so that on St. Patrick's Day 1996 when a shot was fired at a Black 47 gig at The Academy in New York City many felt it was a Loyalist attack.

From my own point of view I was convinced that the only way to gain any kind of just settlement in the North of Ireland was for the US to get involved. Our job was to raise the consciousness of Irish-American audiences and get them to put pressure on their local politicians. There was a folk hatred of England deeply ingrained in many Irish-Americans, but that sentiment by itself was useless, even self-defeating; however, if it

could be honed and politically directed, then it could -
and ultimately did - have a very positive effect. With
songs like *Black 47* you could inform young Irish-
Americans how their forebears first arrived in the US,
while *The Big Fellah* (Michael Collins) demonstrated that
negotiation from strength was ultimately better than
warfare, and with *Bobby Sands MP,* you could show that
the struggle continued even behind bars.

At first we assumed that the "new Irish" (recent
young immigrants) would be a natural constituency for
us, but instead young Irish-Americans flocked to the
shows. Many had grown up listening to The Clancy
Brothers & Tommy Makem, but couldn't relate to the
acoustic nature of their music. Now all of a sudden they
were confronted with a band that expressed some of the
same sentiments but did so from above big fat Hip-Hop
and Reggae beats.

Amazingly, most Irish people, whether from
Ireland or American born, did not know what "Black 47"
stood for. In Ireland it was a phrase that had gone out of
common currency; there was also a desire to get beyond
such events - leave them to molder in history books.
While to us these two stark words were cousins to the
Jewish cry, "Never again." In the US, there was a shame
factor, successive generations of immigrants wished to
assimilate and had purposely withheld family history; in
many cases they had only remotely alluded to their
county or townsland of origin – this led to a great
hunger from young adults to discover their roots. The
one universally accepted truism handed down seems to
have been that "the English were responsible for the
famine."

And of course they were – but not directly. It
wasn't a case of ethnic cleansing, no matter how
convenient an answer. *An Gorta Mór* - The Great

Hunger - was caused by many factors including the landlord system, the penal laws of the previous century that had destroyed the native culture and economy, the ever smaller plot portions on which families were forced to live, and reliance on the potato as the only staple that could feed the people and still provide some rent for the rapacious Anglo-Irish landlord and, even worse, his Irish agent. When the blight struck in three consecutive years of 1845-47 the English authorities, fearing a collapse of the grain market, refused to make the surplus corn, wheat and barley in the country available to feed the people. They were also wary of placing millions of "indolent Catholics" on their welfare rolls. As a result of this reluctance to meddle with a British Laissez-faire free market system, a million Irish died, and more than another million emigrated – and that's a very conservative estimate.

Black 47's idea was to harness and inform the simmering hatred many Irish-Americans had for England so that when an opportunity came, as it did under the Clinton administration, there would be an educated and directed force that could help seek change in the North of Ireland. As a side issue that did not gain as much traction, we were discreetly pointing out to conservative Irish-Americans that over-reliance on the free market to solve social issues could backfire and cause much hardship.

Black 47

Everything is still
Not a chicken not a body
Just an awful sickening silence roaring in my brain
And the fog of death deepens and lies upon the land
An auld one rolls over on her back
The grass stains still green upon her chin
I can still hear her keening and screaming in the wind

"God's curse upon you Lord John Russell
May your black-hearted soul rot in hell
There's no love left on earth
And god is dead in heaven
In these dark and deadly days of Black 47"
God's curse upon you Lord Trevelyan
May your great Queen Victoria rot in hell
'Til England and its Empire
Answer before heaven
For the crimes they committed in Black 47

Paudie says, "C'mon now
Don't look back, she's not living, she's a phantom
And she'll curse us if we look into her eyes!"
Oh God, I think I'm dying - the fever's in me brain
For can't you see that pack of children up ahead
The beards of old men sprouting from their chins
Can't you hear their screams of hunger on the wind

Darlin' Paudie save me
I think I'm sinking fast, me blood is boiling
Don't let me die here in a ditch
If the hunger doesn't get me - the fever surely will

> *Paudie picked me up and threw me 'cross his*
> *shoulders*
> *He nursed me everyday 'til we reached Amerikay*
> *Screaming and shouting like two madmen at the wind*
>
> *"God's curse upon you Lord John Russell*
> *May your black-hearted soul rot in hell*
> *There's no love left on earth*
> *And god is dead in heaven*
> *In these dark and deadly days of Black 47*
>
> *God's curse upon you Lord Trevelyan*
> *May your great Queen Victoria rot in hell*
> *'Til England and it's Empire*
> *Answer before heaven*
> *For the crimes they committed in Black 47"*
>   *(Larry Kirwan)*

It wasn't all politics. We'd come of age in bars
where you were hired to entertain. One of our favorite
bands had been The Clash, but no one would ever
accuse those guys of possessing an overabundance of
humor, onstage anyway. Still, black humor is an innate
part of the Irish psychological make up and, as with the
Jewish people, we employ it as a tool to get us through
the bad times. I never gave it much consideration, but
we could swivel effortlessly from a darkly intense *Black
47* straight into a lighthearted *Funky Céili* romp,
something that surprised critics early on. But to our way
of thinking, the last thing the world needed was a band
giving a history or political lesson onstage. No, far
better that an audience come to whoop it up and in the
process be exposed to songs with a more serious bent. It
didn't matter to us if they "got it" then or later in the

week, or at all for that matter. We weren't out to convert anyone – rather to get them to think about issues. That being said, we took it seriously that they'd paid their hard earned money for a show, so the ultimate goal was to send them away smiling, but perhaps with some questions that might surface later.

Early on I adapted what I'd learned from researching *Mister Parnell* – that you could take hackneyed melodies such as *Sally Gardens*, flush the glut and glue of Victoriana out of them, slip a beat underneath and come up with an anthem like *40 Shades of Blue*. That song told the story of Kevin Donovan, a friend from Wexford, who I found living on my local Spring Street subway stop after his fall from grace. Over the years it morphed into an uproarious song of redemption and became a huge favorite at gigs. I'd never forgotten Eddie Furey's dictum, "If you don't add to the tradition, it just ends up in museums."

With that in mind I never used an old melody in a Black 47 song without enhancing it. Thus, in *40 Shades of Blue* I added a complementary intro and bridge. I found that in so doing you could play with the tension of the song and often heighten the effect of the older tune. Of course, the trick is to come up with a melody that seems as though it's an innate part of the original.

Kevin's been dead a long time now, and I often think of him – he was never a *Sally Garden* type of person, a bit too way out there and complicated; the intro and bridge are more his style. I see his crooked Wexford smile every time I sing this song, cascades of his beloved cigarettes showering down on the stage.

269

Larry Kirwan

40 Shades of Blue

Ah, it's midnight on the Bowery and your feet are soakin' wet
And you've drank your last brass farthin'
You'd sell your soul for a cigarette
And the sounds from CBGB's are comfortin' to you
Then you think of the green fields of Ireland
And you feel 40 shades of blue

Ah you're back on the drink since September
And your head feels like a sieve
And you know that you're goin' from bad to worse
But you just don't give a shit
And the hymns from the Sally Army sound heavenly and true
Then you think of your friends and your family
And you feel 40 shades of blue

Ah you've got a great future behind you
But you're goin' nowhere fast
Just up and down the Bowery from Canal Street to old St
Marks
And you wonder what she's up to now
Did she really find somebody new
How the hell could she just walk out like that
On your 40 shades of blue

And you wonder how it came to this
Was it always in the cards
'Cause workin' is for idiots
And you love the smell of bars
And the letters that you sent back home
Were full of all the things you've done
But they don't say you're down there on Bleecker Street
With your hand out on the bum

Now the dawn's comin' up on the Bowery
And you're heartsick and soakin' wet
With your tongue hangin' out for some Irish Rose
You'd sell your soul for a cigarette
And some day I'm goin' to give up this drinkin'
Maybe someday I'll win the lottery too
Then I'll go back home to old Wexford town
Paint her 40 shades of blue
                                          (Larry Kirwan)

People often ask me what type of music does Black 47 play. And much as I've tried over the years, I can never come up with a label. We had no template. We weren't influenced by any band in particular; when all is said and done, we were making it up as we went along. As Chris Byrne said, "the plan was not to have a plan!" No doubt we were aided by my divorce from popular music for the four years after Major Thinkers because upon forming Black 47 I was an open book and dead keen on filling up the pages.

Our idea was to come up with as many original songs as quickly as possible for the four sets we would be playing nightly in pubs. I often wrote two new songs a week, and Chris would memorize his instrumental lines as we drove to the Bronx; he'd pick up the lyrics from repetition and stage memory. I'd have come up with a suitable drum machine pattern that day and we'd play the new songs early in the first set and late in the last set – in other words, sober and drunk; the end result, we'd have at least a working knowledge of the new song by the time the gig was over.

I spent so many hours writing drum machine patterns. I never used a pre-set as the songs always called for something unique. While merging music and

271

lyrics I would begin to hear the placement of the kick, snare and high hat in my head; I would then try and approximate that pattern on the drum machine. Since we didn't use a bass player I put particular emphasis on the kick drum – often combining three and four different kicks then adding an extra-heavy hip-hop one at the end. As we began to play in bigger venues with more powerful PA systems, soundmen took to calling it "the kick of death." In deference to Phil Spector and his wall of sound, I would usually combine a tambourine in some combination with the high hat. I knew the tempo of all the different patterns by heart and would increase or decrease it as I saw fit depending on the mood of the crowd.

We never rehearsed except immediately before recording a new album. It took a certain type of player to deal with this and fit in – he had to be fearless, willing to go onstage without knowing exactly what was going to happen. He might know the main line of a new song – or he might hear it for the first time onstage and then join in as best he could the second time round. But that only added to the excitement and the sense that each player was coming up with his own parts and adding to the whole. Geoff Blythe (saxophone) and Fred Parcells (trombone) might then work on some contrapuntal figures or harmonies to stick in the verse or chorus while downing pints during the break between sets, or they might not. Either way by the third or fourth time playing the song, the arrangement would gel.

As a songwriter I was fearless, and thick-skinned as any rhinoceros. My only goal for the first performance was to get from A to Z. I never added a song to the repertoire unless I was confident it was going to work – applause or audience indifference didn't affect or interest me until the song had matured and come into its own. The stage was my laboratory because I had stumbled on something of great value: you could mess around with a song for hours or even days at a rehearsal studio, but you still had to take it public. However, if you managed to get through it onstage without any rehearsal, you were immediately way ahead of the game – songs seemed to find much of their own level and nature on that first intuitive outing. You just had to banish the natural preciousness, fears and sensitivities of the songwriter and instead place your trust in the material and the players. And I did, wholeheartedly, for I was in a hurry – as Jim Morrison had prophesized, "the future's uncertain and the end is always near."

Of course, you had to be prepared for apathy and resistance, and hold your head high if the song flopped with the audience and, more importantly, the band. For at some point in this process you would have caught a glimpse of the spirit of the song, and you knew that you'd find it again – perhaps by some band member playing a difficult figure brilliantly, or totally missing what you'd asked for thereby illuminating the way forward.

It was a wild scene back in those early days. We were playing four or five nights a week including Wednesdays and Saturdays in Paddy Reilly's. Even if we got a lucrative Saturday night gig elsewhere, we'd hotfoot it back to Reilly's for a late set. Chris was a detective, Hammy a dispatcher, Fred ran Giant Rehearsal Studios, while Geoff and I were "professionals;" in other words, we had no other sources of income. Three of us were raising families, so the residency in Reilly's was a financial lifeline – a little known music biz fact: Irish pubs pay well, rock clubs often don't.

But there was a promotional method to our madness too. Manhattan was the center of the media universe, and Black 47 had a gripping story: we were a very original – and political – band packing a mid-town joint two nights a week. Instead of going to the world, we felt that the world should come to us – and not to your usual cool rock club either, but to a steaming hot Irish pub where you'd better love your neighbors because you were going to be rammed skin-deep into them for three hours of riotous unpredictability.

Joe Strummer, of all people, threw a spanner in those works! If I remember correctly Bob Gruen, John Lennon's ace photographer and friend, first brought him to Reilly's. Strummer instantly fell in love with Black 47 and the scene we were creating. He recognized all the different strands of music we were pulling together and reveled in the anarchistic nature of the band. Although one of the founding fathers of Punk he despaired of how it had been locked into such a rigid format – blaring guitars, pounding drums, spiky haircuts, and narrowness of vision. The guy's musical horizons were so vast he wanted to knit them all into a grand new vista – or, at least, that was what I gathered from him in some overwrought 4am conversations. He was a Celt at heart: stormy and opinionated, but wide open to outside ideas especially if they made some kind of soulful sense.

He never mentioned that he was indiscriminately preaching the word of Black 47 around New York City. To my amazement I had been receiving inquiries from downtown bookers and promoters, all of which I turned down in accordance with our "promotional" strategy; this was hardly difficult as one merely had to ask for a decent fee to scare them off. Finally, Walter Durkacz of Wetlands called a second time and said, "For Christ sakes, man, name a figure and I'll give you the gig – just get Strummer off my back." That's how we first came to headline a major venue and partially broke away from the Irish pub scene. Always loyal to those who supported us we continued to play Wetlands until it closed in 2001. Our *Live in New York City* and *On Fire* CDs were both recorded there.

Strummer was a dream to play for, and in fairness so too were most celebrities, not so the idiots who will crawl a mile through broken glass to catch a glimpse of their idols. The word had spread that you could catch Matt Dillon, Danny Glover, Sean Penn, Liam Neeson, Brooke Shields, and many other "A names" on any given night at a Black 47 gig. Of course, I wasn't unaware of the cachet this added to the band, but my tunnel vision was to hammer out as much great original music in as quick a time as possible - which necessitated trying out new and unrehearsed songs on a nightly basis. The celebrity idiots jumped up and down with the believers to *Different Drummer* or thrust their fists in the air to *James Connolly* but as soon as we wrestled with new material they'd lose interest.

This did not sit well with me and only upped the general intensity in Reilly's as well as sparking outbursts of profane tongue-lashings. It probably gave rise to the legend of the "angry" Black 47 because in those early days we were still battling hostile audiences in the Bronx so we took the stage in Reilly's more than willing to confront any insult – real or imagined. Although I was the chief provocateur, Chris, after a hard day on the beat, had little patience with poseurs – his one-liners were invariably scathing. Geoff remained stone-faced when not emoting on the sax and cast a "cold eye" better than anyone this side of Drumcliffe Graveyard; while Fred, normally immersed in the music, could be a testy enough drunk late at night - and make no mistake about it, drink flowed like an ocean back in those early dancing days.

I've always been ambiguous about celebrity anyway and never felt particularly comfortable in its presence due to the high maintenance and neediness that comes with the turf. It's one thing to have Neil Young or Ric Ocasek take in your set and then offer you input and advice, quite another for your audience to be ogling Paulina Porizkova - lovely person though she is – while you're spilling your whiskey-proofed soul all over the stage. As far as I was concerned, when you attended a Black 47 gig the band should be the focus and look out anyone who tries to take away from that.

Luckily, we all felt much the same way; we were there to make music - spark off each other, turn the songs inside out, and put pedal to the metal at every performance. That's what good bands are all about. The rest is just incidental when you're a player doing your job.

And what players! Everyone who came into Black 47 added to the band, its ethos and musicality. Each one brought his own background and experience and was given free rein to express it - I had learned that from watching jazz sessions. The key to a successful jam is respect for the other participants, and a desire to groove off your collaborators and take the music to a different place. That's what we did with Black 47.

Fred Parcells and I had played with Copernicus and Chill Faction. He heard that I had started a new band with Chris and just assumed that it was another improv outfit. He didn't even say hello, just strolled into McGee's Pub (in the Ed Sullivan Theatre building on Broadway) in November 1989, took out his trombone and began to play along with the pipes. I could scarcely believe that combination of sounds; it seemed mournfully jubilant like an Irish/New Orleans marching band. Fred had come from a jazz and big band background and added those flavors. His real reason for coming, as he confessed later, was to learn the Irish tin whistle – which he did – adding Coltrane flourishes that in the early days drove traditional players round the bend, until they tried to figure out how he was hitting those notes

Director/screenwriter, Terry George, but back then music editor of The Irish Voice, claimed that Geoff Blythe really put the band over the top – and he was probably right. Geoff had a top-shelf pedigree – founder member of Dexy's Midnight Runners and The Bureau, as well as sax player for Elvis Costello and many others. At that time our following contained a very Irish Republican element. Geoff fit right in – no one hated Margaret Thatcher as much as he did. He caught on instantly that we weren't going for the normal "brass section" sound but that each of the horns, along with the pipes, would be a lead instrument. And so he stepped to the front, positioned himself at my right shoulder, began to blow, and that was that!

At times Fred would take sabbaticals to play with Pierce Turner. By then we'd made a name for ourselves in Irish pubs whose proprietors were very conscious that they were paying for four members of Black 47 and would dock us if we arrived with one member less. Thomas Hamlin had become entranced with West African drumming. As he was one of my closest friends and Major Thinkers' veteran, I would call him up and inform him that there was "a chair open onstage." He hadn't the least problem in adding djembe, timbale, and all manner of percussion (including a large Foster's beer can filled with sand) to the drum machine beats. With his outgoing and friendly personality, he quickly became a fan favorite. One night when Fred came back from his travels, Hammy informed me he wasn't leaving. Nor did I want him to.

When the *Fire of Freedom* CD took off, we had need of a bass player. There was only one man in town we wanted, Dave Conrad, again another Chill Faction/Copernicus alumnus. Dave not only added the funk, he is also one of the most melodic bass players I've ever come across. He had health problems in 1994 and had to leave but after that we were admirably served by Erik Boyd, Kevin Jenkins, Jeff Allen, Andrew Goodsight, Rob Graziano and Joseph "Bearclaw" Burcaw. One night at a festival in Connecticut, we even used a bass player from one of the opening bands, whose name I forget but not his bravery and brilliance. Without ever hearing any of our songs he did a full set and rarely put a foot – or finger – wrong. Now that's what I call Rock 'n' Roll! Thanks, brother.

Rockin' The Bronx

Got a job in a band called Black 47
I was doin' nothin' special after 11
We learned some tunes, wrote some songs
Bought ourselves a drum machine to keep the beat strong

Well we bought the Irish People, The Echo and The Voice
Rang a few bars, said, "We got a new noise
It would please us greatly to come on uptown
Show you Paddies how we get on down"

A History of Irish Music

One o'clock, two o'clock, give us a chance
All we wanna do is be rockin' the Bronx
3 o'clock, 4 o'clock what does she want?
The girl in black leather wants to
Rock The, rock The Bronx

We got a gig in the Village Pub
But the regulars there all said that we sucked
Then big John Flynn, said, "Oh, no, no
You'll be causin' a riot if I don't let you go"

Then a Flintstone from the Phoenix gave us a call
When he heard the beat, he was quite appalled
"D'yez not know nothin' by Christy Moore?"
The next thing you'll be wantin' is Danny boy!

Chris is chillin' on the uileann but he isn't alone
Here comes Freddy on the slide trombone
Add a little guitar, Geoff Blythe on the sax
Gonna shoot you full of our New York fix

Then we went into the studio, made a tape
Frank Murray from The Pogues said, "I think that it's great"
Galigula said, "It could be a hit
And if it falls on its face, who gives a shit!"

Now everywhere we go we cause a fuss
'Cause we play what we like and our sound is us
It's got a whole lot of hell, a little bit of heaven
That's the story so far of Black 47

(Larry Kirwan)

CHAPTER TWENTY

I was checking him out across Rosie O'Grady's Manhattan Club at an *Irish Echo* event. He was giving me back the hairy eyeball like it was going out of style. He looked different than your regular priest, burly, muscular and not quite fitting the cut of his black clothes; one thing for certain, I could tell he'd been around the block a few times, and I'm not talking Vatican City! There was something really familiar about him, but for the life of me I couldn't place it. When he winked at me some of the years flew off him, but he was obviously from another lifetime, far removed from an upscale Midtown Manhattan Irish eatery. Even when he spoke, I couldn't place him. He thought this was beyond hilarious and fed me a couple of tips like The Bowery, Hardcore, and then on the third clue – CBGB's weekend matinees - I nailed him. Father Henry Reid had been a teenage Irish-American bouncer who worked the door and occasionally dove into the mosh pit to rescue some over-his-or-her-head novice from getting their brains trampled in the perpetual front-of-stage maelstrom.

"How the hell did you end up being a priest?" I inquired, not without some justification.

"Long story," he grinned. "I'll tell you about it over a couple of pints."

But in retrospect, Father Henry's story wasn't that out of the ordinary, for Hardcore and Punk were always about being true to yourself. It's beyond strange the effect that Hilly Crystal's dump on The Bowery had on the world, or was American youth already primed and waiting for someplace where it could invent its own music and let off some steam in its own principled company? I first got turned on to Hardcore's pulsing, flailing power by Bad Brains - a band from DC who had moved to the Lower East Side.

They were the most exciting outfit I'd seen since The Clash and in ways they even out-strummed Strummer since I always saw them in small venues at ear-piercing volumes. The fact that they were African-American and tempered their fury with Reggae only added to the mystique. Their lead singer, HR (Human Rights) may have been the most outrageously charismatic American performer I ever encountered, with perhaps the exception of Iggy Pop on a wild night. Coincidentally, Bad Brains' bass player Darryl Jenifer, a friend of Ric Ocasek, added a righteous bottom to Black 47's recording of *Fire of Freedom* as well as the freestyle toasting on the instrumental outro.

Bad Brains was an outstanding bunch of musicians, each one highly accomplished on his instrument, a rarity in the realm of hardcore. In fact, there was almost a pride in only having a rudimentary command of one's axe; but, oh, could Hardcore dudes play fast! The Ramones, renowned for the speed and brevity of their songs, were like sedate marathoners as compared to some of the sprinters I witnessed at CB's matinees. Songs would go by in a blur, the moshers totally tuned in for what seemed like 30-second symphonies of distortion, feedback and angst-ridden bellowing. Whatever their instrumental prowess, all three or four band members could stop on a dime, allow two or three beats of screeching silence before pounding off into some other tortured vortex of Marshall amps and beat-to-hell drums.

I only ever witnessed the Boston Hardcore scene secondhand when Major Thinkers played Gallery East, an actual art gallery by day, but music venue by night in the old leather district by South Station. Amazingly, Michael Patrick MacDonald, author of *All Souls*, happened to be there that night, although we didn't know each other at the time. Major Thinkers was then in its punky incarnation: Pierce Turner, Thomas Hamlin, and a well known Boston bassist, Peter Collins, who had moved to New York to join us. It was a homecoming of sorts for Peter, and many of his musician friends had shown up. Unbeknown to us there had been an altercation of sorts between the club management and some Hardcore fans from South Boston the previous night. I was pleasantly surprised to see that the house was packed for our Boston debut; perhaps it was the fact that Peter had drunk a homecoming bottle of vodka and his pupils were doing their best to focus on the crown of his skull, but in my concern for him, I missed a certain strained mood in the audience.

Despite the full house, there was little or no response after our first song and barely even a pretense at moshing in front of the stage. Usually, a fine, driving bass player, Peter was having difficulty remaining upright, the weight of his Fender causing him to sway unsteadily over the first line of stage-huggers. But such is Rock 'n' Roll, and I resigned myself to the reality that it would be a long hour's performance. I could have spared myself the anxiety. We were barely into our second number when a well-disciplined cadre detached itself from the surly mob and proceeded to systematically smash the exhibition of framed photographs that hung on three walls of the gallery. There are few worse sounds than smashing glass intruding on distorted guitars and overwrought vocals – I'd heard variants of it in sweat-soaked Wexford ballrooms, punky clubs and during drunken barroom brawls. The key is to keep playing, show no surprise and usually someone with an interest in preserving a viable performance space will intervene and throw the offenders out on their butts.

This failed to happen, but to tell the truth, I was somewhat chuffed that Major Thinkers were provoking such passion in downtown Boston. I had no idea we were held in high enough regard to actually provoke an out-and-out riot. I had witnessed a similar occurrence during a Kinks performance in an Irish ballroom when two gangs of local teddyboys went at it with bicycle chains and hammers; the affair had left a lasting impression on my teenage sensibilities. But as the glass splintered and ricocheted around Gallery East, the audience harbored no such fascination – heads down they broke for every possible exit in the darkened room. Nor were women and children put first, punches were thrown, and bottles were flying as they finally divined that there was only one actual exit. A crush of huge proportions formed there as the revenge seekers too decided to make their escape now that every framed photo had been systematically destroyed.

And still we played on. The song was called
They've Fixed The Motor In My Brain; it was of
considerable length and boasted a long melodic
feedback-driven coda. Despite the suspicion that the
repeated title did not particularly suit the occasion,
various Major Thinkers, including yours truly,
considered themselves masters of dichotomy, and so we
soldiered on to a sustained climactic conclusion.

In the silence that followed, I gazed out at the
empty club, smashed frames, trampled photos, slivers of
glass sparkling in the subdued lighting, not without a
certain amount of awe. Words cannot do justice to the
ravaged scene. I had seen many the fight in my Rock 'n'
Roll years, and in their aftermath there would usually be
the comfortingly familiar sounds of women crying, guys
cursing, the siren of an ambulance approaching but
never before this frozen silence. Then from right behind
me, in his even slower than usual almost cartoon-like
delivery, Peter unburdened himself, "They ruined my
fucking party, man."

I suppose it was a perfect summing up although
it seemed a tad self-centered at the time. In actual fact
though, he had a point. We were less than ten minutes
into our set and now standing in a totally deserted club.
There was no owner, nor any person of authority, to be
found. Within minutes, Peter and his soon-to-be-wife,
Jan, had exited too, leaving only the New York
contingent in a deserted club, the door hanging off its
hinges. We had no money; our fee - which we would
hardly be receiving - was supposed to pay for two motel
rooms. We were too drunk and shell-shocked to drive
the two hundred or so miles home. The carpeted stage
was the only glass-free area, and so after scouring the
club for whatever liquor might be still corked, we lay
down next to our amps and after much tossing and

turning passed a few sleep-filled hours until dawn when we made our bleary escape back to the sanity of early 1980's New York.

I doubt if Ken Casey, a founder of Dropkick Murphys, was at Gallery East on that particular night; he would still have been in middle school back in Milton, MA. But Hardcore was already coursing through his veins. Given the times and the sad state of popular music with MTV beginning its slow, glossy but deliberate campaign to drain all the living grit out of Rock 'n' Roll, there was little else to hang your purist hat on but the music of the jagged perimeters: Ska, Punk and Hardcore. Soon enough Ken would be picking up a bass guitar, sitting in his bedroom hammering out Clash, Ramones and Pistols licks, then heading into Boston to catch shows by Eye For An Eye and Wrecking Crew at The Rathskeller. He would take with him another kind of music, however, the ballads that he heard on the jukeboxes of Irish pubs in Milton, Quincy and Dorchester.

Milton, per capita, is the most Irish town in the US, and Ken was steeped in its music. I had played many Irish bars in MA in the 1970's and was amazed at the knowledge of Irish music and how entrenched it was in the various communities. Bands that I hadn't given a lot of thought to back in Ireland, like The Wolfe Tones, and singers like Paddy Reilly were gods in these dark, claustrophobic saloons, most of which sported a rudimentary stage in a back corner; in fact, you were looked at with a great deal of suspicion if you couldn't belt out at least a few verses of *The Wild Rover* or *The Black Velvet Band*, *The Patriot Game* or a hundred other songs of that ilk. The pub was the center of the community, even more so than back in Ireland, but social mores were more relaxed, kids of all ages would accompany their parents on liquid weekend afternoons where they soaked up the rebel songs and ballads from the ever-booming jukebox.

The Black Velvet Band

In a neat little town they call Belfast
Apprenticed to trade I was bound
And many an hour's sweet happiness
I spent in that sweet little town
'Til bad misfortune came over me
That caused me to stray from the land
Far away from my friends and relations
To follow the black velvet band

As I was out walking down Broadway
Not intending to stay very long
I met with a frolicsome damsel
As she came tripping along
A gold watch she pulled from her pocket
And slipped it right into me hand
On the very first night that I met her,
Bad luck to her black velvet band

Her eyes they shone like diamonds
You'd think she was queen of the land
With her hair flung over her shoulder
Tied up with a black velvet band

'Fore judge and jury next morning
The both of us did appear
A gentleman claimed his jewelry
And the case against us was clear
Seven long years transportation

Right on down to Van Diemen's land
Far away from me friends and relations
Betrayed by the black velvet band

So come all you jolly young fellows
A warning take by me
Whenever you're out on the street at night
Beware of that pretty colleen
For she'll fill you with whiskey and porter
'Til you're no longer able to stand
And the very next thing you'll notice is
You've landed in Van Diemen's Land.

(*Traditional*)

Hardcore music has many delights, but no one would ever accuse it of inspiring melodic or enduring songs. The offerings of the singers are more in the nature of rants, with the most emphatic repeated lines serving as choruses. Ken Casey's genius was to marry the idea of Hardcore with the roots of his Irish background - Irish ballads. Looking back it seems a no-brainer, but for something like that to work you have to believe equally in these two very disparate styles; only then will they coalesce in a believable and organic manner. The catalyst is the Hardcore mantra – be true to yourself. That slogan is no stranger to the Irish immigrants of South Boston, Dorchester and Milton, nor is their determination to hold on to the one bit of culture they were allowed to carry with them from Ireland – the songs and ballads of their people.

Ken has such drive, belief, talent, producing chops, and a knowledge of his audience and their taste, allied with not a little marketing skill, that I think Dropkick Murphys would have become successful one

287

way or the other; but it was his harnessing of Irish ballads to the drive of Hardcore that lit a fire for the band around the world. *Finnegan's Wake, Rocky Road To Dublin*, and *The Wild Rover* got a kick in the arse the like of which these venerable songs never received before, and in return, the old songs added depth to musicians raised on *Oi* music and helped to transform their latent songwriting skills. I've played with the Murphs many times down the years - from the early days at Irish festivals to last year's headlining at the Boston Garden - and I've always been impressed by their painstaking professionalism, sonic assault, devotion to fans, and the idea that fourth walls are there for one reason only – to be demolished in the course of a 90-minute, life-affirming gig.

The band is so inextricably linked with Greater Boston it's hard to think of it existing elsewhere. It's the old Yeats conundrum: how do you separate the singer from the song. Ken lives and dies for the Boston sports teams – it's a genuine love – a neighborhood thing. Dare a New Yorker wear a Yankee cap at a Dropkicks' gig – though why someone would be crazy enough to do so is beyond logic. Talk about asking for trouble! That being said, the band has raised the general awareness of Boston around the globe, and it's hard not to notice that as the Murphs have grown more popular, so too have the local teams become more successful. Methinks it's time The Mets, Nets, Jets, Rangers, Knicks and others put some seed money in a local musical group instead of sinking it in another spoiled and injury prone athlete. Couldn't hurt! But that's being facetious. Like all great bands, the Murphs got no handouts. They were bottom of the barrel and had to claw their way up. That's the way it is in Rock 'n' Roll – only the strong make it to the top and only those with an original and burning vision stay there.

Dropkick Murphys have become even more socially aware as their career has progressed, bucking the usual trend in rock music. In many ways the band shares the same working class intellectualism of the writer and social activist, Michael Patrick MacDonald, himself raised in hardscrabble South Boston. Having lost a number of siblings to communal and drug violence, Michael Patrick once told me that he doesn't think he would have survived his adolescence had it not been for Punk's transformative influence. In both Casey and MacDonald, you feel the same burning sense of "do the right thing" and "stick up for your people." I can vouch for MacDonald's values from the years we worked together with Irish American Writers and Artists, a progressive organization, while not so long ago, Casey caused a stir by kicking a renegade skinhead offstage for delivering a Nazi salute.

Ken Casey is also an astute businessman who almost immediately grasped the economics of the music business. At a time when the rest of us were flogging a few CDs and t-shirts after our gigs, the Murphs team would arrive many hours before their shows with a jaw-dropping display of merchandise encompassing everything from a needle to an anchor. The guy truly thinks macro and has moved into bar ownership and, of late, boxing management and promotion. But all this entrepreneurial drive stems from having his finger on the pulse of his people and their neighborhoods. It would not surprise me if in the years to come he went into politics. He would be a deft fit for this roughest of sports and would acquit himself well in the halls of power in DC, Springfield MA, or his own beloved Boston.

Larry Kirwan

CHAPTER TWENTY-ONE

Orphan of the Storm

Get off the plane at Kennedy
Got a dream in your heart
Though it's down in your boots
Got a hundred quid in your pocket
And a couple of addresses
In Woodside and The Bronx
And you fit in like a fist in a glove
With the other hard chaws on the gang
Some are running from themselves
Some are running from God and man

And you drink to dull the memory
Of why you strayed from home
To the concrete fields of New York City
An orphan of the storm

The gangerman looks at you
Respect in his eyes
He knows you'll work until you drop
'Cause there's a black rage eating away inside you
You'd walk through walls, son
Before you'd ever give up

And at night you're like a phantom
Nailing every young one you can
It's better than lying awake in the dark
Thinking of her with another man

But she'll never take your dreams away
That's not why you've come
To the canyoned streets of New York City
An orphan of the storm

You only went back once
You just had to be sure
Kindness in her eyes
You saw only pity there
So drink up your Bushmills whiskey
Wash it down with pints
Obliteration on the rocks
Then out of here in the dawn's hungover light

So you put her far behind you
You hardly think of her anymore
Well, maybe on a rainy Sunday night
You're the gangerman yourself now
Got a new job down the Trades
And every little thing's gonna be alright
Then they blew you to sweet Jesus
On that grand September day
Not a cloud on your horizon
Your heart finally okay

But they couldn't take your dreams away
They were not for sale or loan
On the shattered streets of New York City
This orphan has finally come home

(Larry Kirwan)

B ands that stay together go through phases, and I've often felt that Black 47's career has been split pretty equally by the disaster of 9/11. Chris had left the band the year before to pursue his own fine solo project, Seanchaí and the Unity Squad. It was a big change, especially for me, but it had been coming and Chris, in his honorable fashion, had waited until we finished promoting *Trouble in the Land*. That was on May 1ˢᵗ, 2000. As ever, there was a minimum of rehearsal, Chris left on a Saturday and we played our first gig with Capt. Neil Anderson on pipes the following Friday. Though it felt strange without Chris, there is never a void in music, particularly if your players come from improv backgrounds. Everyone took a step forward on stage and filled in the spaces. Neil played with us while he could and then Joseph Mulvanerty took over on pipes.

This was to herald somewhat of a change in the band's style, as Joseph had come from a Jazz as well as Traditional Irish background and was very much into listening to and riffing off Geoff and Fred. Although we missed Chris' vocals and pipe playing, there was now more fluidity in the arrangements. New York was a great city in those turn-of-the-century years. Although George W. Bush had been elected president, the city still swung to the Clinton expansionist beat. And then it struck!

The attack on the World Trade Center changed everything. What had once been a bustling, optimistic city was, in a few short minutes, turned into a graveyard. Black 47 immediately went back to play in Connolly's on Saturday nights. Times Square was deserted. You could walk across Broadway and 7ᵗʰ Avenue without fear of getting hit by a car. There were nights when you could imagine sagebrush rolling by. Everyone we knew had lost friends. When you consider that Black 47's audience contained large segments of firefighters, cops and financial workers you can estimate the cost in fans and friends. Included was Victim 0001, Fr. Mychal Judge, OFM, Chaplain of the NYFD, confessor and friend to many. But like all New Yorkers, we had a job to do, and for that first year we returned to Connolly's almost every Saturday night; it was important that there was a place for first responders to let off steam and to demonstrate to the world that New York City was back in business, and should you desire a night on the town, then Black 47 would be there to kick out the jams.

Those nights were so intense; you would almost jump for joy when you saw a familiar face enter – at least he or she was alive. When someone wouldn't have shown up for a month or two you feared the worst. In many cases you might not know a name, so you couldn't inquire if they'd made it through. On gigs around the tri-state area people would show pictures of lost ones and request their favorite Black 47 songs. Hard as it was when you recognized a familiar face, strange as it may seem, it was even tougher when you didn't – to think your music had meant so much to someone you hadn't even known.

I stopped writing. Everything seemed trivial when compared with the smoldering pit downtown; besides, we were looked on as ambassadors for the city every time we played outside it. When you stay busy, you can deal with loss by putting it on the back burner with the promise that you'll confront it at the appropriate time. But loss chooses its own time for settlement, and it hit me like a ton of bricks on the first anniversary - the antidote was close at hand. I would

write an album of songs that would show New York
City in the aftermath of the disaster and contrast them
with songs that celebrated the wonderful world we had
been a part of for the ten previous years. As I walked
home from visits to a number of churches that evening, a
song poured forth. All I had to do was pick up pen and
paper and write it down. The melody was already there,
along with chords, phrasings, and arrangement.

Mychal

In New York city I made my home
I loved the streets, the very stones
Cared for my comrades, cherished my friends
Loved all beginnings, had no time for ends

A city's streets are full of woe
I saw suffering where'er I'd go
I did my best to console and heal
Treat each human with full dignity

I never saw a reason to
Hate someone who thinks different than you
Each one has their anointed place
In the love reflected in their god's face

We all have sorrow, our share of trials
We all are sinners in each other's eyes
Love alone can ease the pain
God bestows love in so many ways
I have my failings and I have tried
To look them squarely in the eye
To be there when someone might call
For I know cruel well how hard it is to fall

I love the company of friends
The fire and the music sparkling in their eyes
But I achieved my heart's desire
When I rode beside the ones who fight the fires

As I arise on this September morn
The sun is beaming down, the streets are warm
God's in his heaven and all is well
I will go forth and do His will...

(Larry Kirwan)

That album was like a rebirth. It came out in Feb. 2003 when nerves were still raw. It had been our first album of new songs since *Trouble in the Land*. Many people embraced it though I was a little leery that we might get tagged as the "9/11 band." I needn't have worried. Within a month, on St. Patrick's Night, while playing two shows in The Knitting Factory we came out implacably against the invasion of Iraq. That was to set us on an intense, storm-filled course for the next five years. It had been almost surreal to watch the Bush/Cheney/Rumsfeld troika lie and maneuver the US into another war halfway across the world, even more stunning to realize that so many usually reliable people and institutions, including Hillary Clinton and The New York Times, were willing to accept this deception. But even as late as the afternoon of March 17th while shamrock revelers were whooping it up in the bars of New York, and more soberly attired Hibernians were parading up Fifth Avenue, it seemed as though sanity might prevail.

During the sound check at the Knitting Factory, however, it became apparent that the invasion had been set irretrievably in motion and would not be stopped. Something had to be said, and so I added some words and inserted a new instrumental part into Pete Seeger's *Where Have All The Flowers Gone.* In the midst of the wildness of the St. Patrick's Night revels, I announced that Black 47 was adamantly against this invasion and we broke into Pete's classic; arguments and scuffles broke out as the packed house separated into two camps over this issue. It was a foretaste of what was to come over the next five years.

I wrote *Downtown Baghdad Blues* soon after and it became our most polarizing song. Any number of Black 47 songs the like of *Bobby Sands MP* and *James Connolly* had caused controversy down the years but they were acceptable to many because the enemy was usually Britain; but *Baghdad,* although written from the point of view of a National Guard who had signed up for one-weekend-a-month duty, questioned US policy. This provoked a real backlash: some audience members would walk out, or turn their backs while we played, and sometimes threaten physical action.

Very soon I realized that we were one of the few bands protesting the war on a nightly basis. Others did speak out sporadically, but they were usually preaching to the converted. Black 47's audience contained both a strong Right and Left wing demographic. One thing I learned early on is that Right-Wingers have little trouble making their views known. The Left - at our shows anyway - were much more circumspect. This was to be the case with much of the media and public too up until the first seeds of doubt were sown when Iraqi insurgents began to fight back.

Downtown Baghdad Blues

Got a buddy in Najaf, he's playing it straight
Prays to the Lord Jesus Christ every night
Got a homey in Samarra going up the wall
Every time he hear an Islamic prayer call
Me, I don't care much about Jesus or Mohammed
They don't stop bullets to the best of my knowledge
Later for the both of you, catch you in eternity
Hopefully, towards the end of this century

I didn't want to come here, I didn't get to choose,
I got the hup, two, three, four Downtown Baghdad Blues.

I wish I was back home rooting for the Padres
'Stead of dodging bullets from Mookie al-Sadr
Wish I was back in the land of Giuliani
Instead of taking heat from Ayatollah Sistani
One thing for certain, one thing is clear
Twenty years old, I can kill but I can't buy a beer
Keep your head down, don't get your brain cells fried
You'll be home by Christmas - dead or alive!

I wish I was back in the US of A
Instead dodging bullets in Falluji-ay
There's a lady with my tattoo on her so special
Dream of her and me out in the desert
She riding round in her daddy's Ford Explorer
I'm kicking in doors, hey, I thought this war was over
Sand in my nose, sand in my eyes
But the sand can't cover up the sights of a
Sniper with my number, got his finger on the trigger
Hope my baby's okay, I'm still waiting for a letter
All I get are emails, so much unsaid
It's hot here, baby, but it's so cold inside my head.

> *Mission accomplished, yeah, up on deck*
> *Got no armor for my Humvee, left facing this train wreck*
> *Shia don't like me, want Islamic revolution*
> *Sunni say civil war part of the solution*
> *Maybe someday there'll be peace in Fallujah*
> *McDonald's on the boulevard, Cadillac cruising*
> *I'm trying hard to keep this whole thing straight*
> *Will someone tell me what the hell am I doing here in the first*
> *place?*

> *(Larry Kirwan)*

That first year was tense, to say the least: the two and a half after it were no bed of roses either. We soon added *South Side Chicago Waltz, Stars & Stripes* and *Ramadi* to our repertoire. Many nights going on stage my stomach would be queasy at the thought of the inevitable conflict, and occasionally I'd make up a set list that would contain no reference to the war; but after my customary shot of whiskey half-way through, I'd think of the Black 47 fans carrying a hundred pounds of equipment, slogging through Fallujah in over 100 degrees of heat, with the bullets ripping the earth around them, and I'd think "No way" are we going to let a crowd of bar-stool patriots dictate what we should or should not play.

I often thought of a young man from Chicago – let's call him Kevin. He'd been coming to see Black 47 at our annual Memorial Day Weekend shows at Gaelic Park since he was a boy. He'd often written to me of his love for the band and how we'd influenced his hopes and dreams. In late 2001 he'd enlisted in the Marines as a reaction to 9/11. This pure display of patriotism had not been uncommon among Black 47 fans, and I was

struck by the depth of their conviction. I heard from
Kevin occasionally after the invasion. I could tell he was
a good soldier, solicitous of his comrades and "eager to
get the job done" despite the many hassles in an
unfamiliar country that was rapidly souring against the
occupation.

I met Kevin at a gig in 2004. He still showed
flashes of the crooked boyish grin, but he was now a
more somber grown-up; we spoke for a few moments in
the usual after-gig crush and euphoria. He was tanned,
had filled out and looked very handsome in his uniform.
Although surrounded by friends and family, he seemed
on an island of his own making, distant and somewhat
wary. His three years were up and he was considering
college. You could tell he would stand out in any class
of normal freshmen – apart from his age, there was a
gravity to his bearing, nor was he drinking with the
usual Gaelic Park abandon. He'd brought something
home with him that I was to see on a regular basis –
from wounded warrior to seemingly untouched young
veteran – war in the legion of ways it touches
individuals.

I didn't hear from Kevin for six months or more
after that– neither, apparently, had his wide circle of
friends. He had taken some time off to see the country
and to settle on some kind of route in life. I was one of
the recipients of a terse email he wrote declaring that he
had decided to re-enlist and go back, that his civilian life
hadn't seemed to make a huge amount of sense since his
return, that he needed to finish what he had begun, and
that he would be in touch with us all. He stopped
writing, and he hasn't contacted me in years, but I've
heard from mutual friends that he survived. I often
wondered, while performing this song inspired by
Kevin, just what was at the heart of the bile we were

receiving from certain audience members. Could a song have been more supportive? I suppose in those early days any question about the logic of invading another country in a war of choice was perceived as traitorous.

Southside Chicago Waltz

With the shells going off and the tracers so bright
There are times I can't tell if it's day or it's night
I still feel the St. Christopher's medal you gave me
When you promised me it would get me home safely
I wish I was back in the arms of my family
Memorial Day Sunday all ready to party
When the band hits the stage down in Gaelic Park
With my brothers beside me and you, the queen of my
heart

Mickey's in the fire department, Danny's a cop
I'm here in Baghdad with the marines mopping up
I wish I was home with you, darling, because
We'd be dancing to the Southside Chicago Waltz

With the canons all roaring, the jets in the sky
The flares going off like the Fourth of July
For a moment I held him dead in my sights
I squeezed the trigger and it's later, pal, good night
I think of you lying safely at home
With your arms crying out for me alone
Let's go down Gaelic Park, yell out "American Wake"
Let me be in one piece when I get home for both of our
sakes

Sometimes you gotta be better than you are
Step up on your toes and reach out for the stars
I hope to God what I'm doing here is right

*'Cause I can't take many more of these bloody god-
awful nights*

*Missing Mickey in the fire department, Danny the cop
While I'm here in Baghdad with the marines mopping
up
I wish I was home with you, darling, because
We'd be dancing to the Southside Chicago Waltz*

(Larry Kirwan)

Oddly enough, much of the sting went out of the
vituperation at our gigs around the Fall of 2007 – I've
often wondered if Cindy Sheehan's protest outside
President Bush's farm in Texas was responsible. I had
been introduced to her by Malachy McCourt sometime
before and wrote *The Ballad of Cindy Sheehan*; amazingly,
it became the most hated Black 47 song. I'm not sure
just why this woman who had lost her son in the war
and had the temerity to protest the conflict inspired so
much negative emotion; perhaps it was the last gasp of
those who felt that the authority of the US
administration must be respected even when it is
misguided and patently wrong.

By 2009 people were kicking up their heels to
Baghdad Blues or smooching to *Ramadi*, but Black 47's
reputation had suffered. Up until the war, we had been
the main draw at many Irish festivals – now we were
often not invited. We were no less liked as musicians or
people but we were considered "trouble." Book us and
there could be murmurings from a small, but vocal,
section that we were unpatriotic – even worse that this
small section might not turn up. There was no real way
to combat this perception. and besides, we'd drawn our
own line in the sand. The Iraq War was a drastic and

unconscionable mistake and, to add insult to injury, it was our working and lower-middle class fan demographic that was doing the fighting and suffering.

But in many ways, I think that the *IRAQ* album and the conflict those songs caused was Black 47's finest moment, and I take great pride in the fact that for all the protests, not one Iraq veteran ever came out against the band. In fact, songs from the CD became some of the most popular with troops in Iraq and Afghanistan. When all was said and done, even if occasionally those in the services disagreed with what we were saying, they knew that one band was actually thinking of them on a daily basis and willing to lay its reputation on the line. And in the end, that's all that counts.

There have always been two strands to the Celtic Music tradition – songs of entertainment and songs that talk about our history, politics and cultural identity. We're definitely in no danger of losing the former – as long as there's an *Irish Rover*, a *Wild Rover* or any other kind of rover to be lauded, we'll have entertainment. That goes for the hedonistic Celtic Rock side of things too with songs like *Streams of Whiskey*, *Drunken Lullabies* and *Funky Céili*. But take away the politics, the history and our ongoing resistance to political and economic oppression, then our music loses its life-affirming and, for my money, interesting, quotient. Nor does every song need to be a fist-pumping anthem or political tract set to a four-on-the-floor beat; sometimes you just need to take into account the loss and loneliness of someone far away who is wondering how the hell he ever ended up enmeshed in a foreign culture, and if he'll ever make it home. That's the root of Irish music, and if we lose that, we risk becoming a parody of ourselves no matter what level of professionalism, proficiency, and entertainment we aspire to.

Ramadi

Sitting here in Ramadi
Thinking about you, baby
Wondering what you're doing
Are you thinking about me maybe
Or are you cruising down Main Street
Hanging with your old squeeze
While I'm sitting here in Ramadi
Thinking about you, baby

Ah, the Jihads got me pinned down
But that ain't the worst thing on my mind
Just keep thinking about you, darlin'
Exactly what you're doing
I know he wants you so bad,
It's driving me outa my head
I know you'll always be true,
But it's my third tour and I don't know what to do
But think about you, baby,
While I'm pinned down here in Ramadi

I keep waiting for something concrete
Like a letter or a pack of cigarettes
But all I get is "whatever"
And cold kisses across the Internet
And I know that I've been hesitant
But how can I explain the worlds I've seen
And when I come home
Will this madness follow me?
Will you resist his passionate company?
Waiting for me oh so lonely
While I'm thinking about you, baby
Pinned behind a wall here in Ramadi…

(Larry Kirwan)

CHAPTER TWENTY-TWO

The Saw Doctors had gone past their allotted set time at the American Fleadh back in 2003. I had actually got the idea for this traveling Irish Rock festival while watching half of the audience walk out of the main stage area after their set at the Chicago Gaelic Park Festival the year previously. It was a stomach churning experience; however, the area was full again by the time Black 47 took the stage. A eureka moment followed, for it struck me that if you could get a number of bands not incompatible with each other who would attract different audiences you could have a very successful festival.

All very well in theory, but we were now in Baltimore, Flogging Molly's road manager was furious, his band was itching to get onstage and deliver a full set before the curfew kicked in; yet a fly of major proportions had landed in their ointment: the very popular musician/mayor of the city, Martin O'Malley, was urging his favorite band, the Docs, to do an encore, well-deserved but prohibited by festival protocol.

Martin, a great friend of mine, is nothing if not persuasive - he has since become Governor of Maryland and may yet be President of the US. Veterans of many festivals, the boys from Tuam hesitated to retake the stage. Since the Fleadh was my baby, I should have seized the moment, ran on stage and laid down the law; discretion, however, once more seemed the better part of valor, so not for the first time in my life, in a moment of crisis, I decided this was an opportune moment for a nice cold beer.

A minute or so into my search, the Docs, who were giddily speeding down the N17, went oddly silent. A great clamor erupted out in the stadium corridor with much running to and fro accompanied by unintelligible shouting. I had found a nice cold tallboy and was in the process of draining it when the door burst open and the Docs' manager, Ollie Jennings, face crimson with rage, accosted me and demanded that I apologize to his charges.

"For what?" Said I, incredulously.

"Didn't you see what happened?"

The long and short of it – Flogging Molly's German sound engineer had cut the power to the stage, and when I ventured forth to investigate, he was calmly setting his band up, not a bother in the world on him – while irate Galway managers, future presidential hopefuls and many Saw Doctors' fans were giving him the benefit of their scabrous, unsolicited opinions. If I learned any lesson with my American Fleadh, it was don't mess with Flogging Molly. This band means business!

If the Murphs epitomize Boston, Flogging Molly, the other great Celtic Punk band, are nothing like the Los Angeles of popular imagination. Then again The Doors seemed to have little overt cultural roots in that city either. Go figure! I first met Dave King, chief bottle-washer, singer, writer, and acoustic guitarist at Molly Malone's in LA in 1993 when Black 47 played the Fairfax Avenue establishment. Dave and Bridget Reagan had only recently begun playing together but, as yet, not under the Flogging Molly name. In the interests of disclosure, I should mention that over the years they have become two of my closest friends in the music business and, in a twist of fate, now live mere miles from Wexford town.

Dave impressed me right away – he has that lovely inner city Dublin friendliness spiced with black humor, intelligence and sensitivity. Unlike a lot of people with a poetic sensibility, he downplays his obvious talents, and you have to press him to get details of his successes and achievements. Like many Irish people he's more at home emphasizing the various disasters he's survived, albeit in a hilarious manner. He sometimes reminds me of Ric Ocasek, also a great conversationalist and a really interesting person to be around; they both actually listen to what other people are saying. Having been through many ups and downs in his life, Dave is very empathetic, and I've often found myself opening up and telling him things that I wouldn't dream of relating to anyone else.

And yet, he's no pushover. You don't come from his neck of the woods, travel halfway around the world, and gain Flogging Molly's kind of success without a spine of steel. He was born in Dublin's Liberties where writers such as Jonathan Swift, James Joyce, Brendan Behan and rebels the like of Wolfe Tone and Robert Emmet mixed, matched, plotted and drank in proximity to the Guinness Brewery. His father died young. His mother worked in a factory. Music was Dave's escape.

And yet, he was never a part of Dublin's incestuous and often suffocating rock scene. Like Luke Kelly, another inner city Dubliner, he lit off for England at an early age and became a heavy metal belter – you can tell his influences by how low his guitar is slung from his shoulders. He achieved some success with Fastway, his collaboration with "Fast" Eddie Clarke of Motorhead, but eventually Dave washed up on the shores of Los Angeles, unsure of his future and undocumented into the bargain. We share an ongoing feeling of dislocation – originally fueled by years of being unable to return to Ireland because of legal status. I love *Factory Girls*, the song he wrote about his mother; although radically different from my own *Life's Like That, Isn't It*, yet they're both written from the same vantage point – looking backwards at your mother as a young woman.

Factory Girls

Build a bridge or maybe two
Together held with footsteps she outgrew
But now she sits alone, everyone's long gone

She dances in a photograph
When it was good to joke and have a laugh
But that was yesterday, if only today

Now the walls are crawling faces that still breathe
But before she nods her head what's left but sleep

She hears a chorus of factory girls
Singin' in the streets
Drinkin' their coca-colas
After washing your filthy sheets

Chasin' down the avenue
After a childhood that she never knew
Choking on Woodbine
Cigarettes just kill the time

Now the walls are crawling faces that still breathe
But before she nods her head what's left but sleep

She hears a chorus of factory girls
Singin' aon and all
Empty are their pockets
But their voices are filled with song

"Come day go day
Wish in my heart it was Sunday
Drinking buttermilk all the week
And whiskey on a Sunday"

Slayed Richard and his court of Kings
He stole my heart and many other things
But me I took his crown
Wish he was here to steal it now
(Written by Bridget Regan, Dave King, Dennis Casey, Bob
Schmidt, Matt Hensley, George Schwindt, Nathen Maxwell.
Published by 26F Gellert Hill Music/TwentysixF Music)

I have a lot of time for Bridget Reagan. She's like a sister to me. Maybe it's because I know her roots in the Detroit Gaelic Club – Jesus, what a place! It's this lonely outpost of Irish culture – and all that comes with it – in the middle of downtown Detroit. Talk about Fort Apache in the old wild days of the Bronx. Once that door on the outside world closes and you step into the club, you've entered a little womb-like Connemara of the soul. Maybe it's the siege mentality, but the alcohol flows freely and my memories of playing there are all on the hazy side. How and ever, that's where Bridget - although I think of her as Bridie - was introduced to the wonders of Irish music and dancing.

I've often marveled at how the flame of Irish culture is kept alive in tough, unaccommodating places like The Bronx, South Boston and all the other Southies (why do the Irish always seem to end up on south sides?), but none of these aforementioned outposts holds a candle to the once desolate Downtown Detroit. And yet, it's there that Bridie and her friends trekked to learn their fiddle tunes, to dance and to flirt with the lost old souls of Ireland who congregated for succor and calm at the bar of the Detroit Gaelic Club.

Don't get me wrong about Detroit. Tough as it is, it's still a great music town and always will be – that's built into the local DNA. Motown Records, James Jamerson, Iggy Pop, and Question Mark & The Mysterians hailed from the general area, and it's a joy to play there. One of my fondest gig memories is Black 47 sandwiched between The Neville Brothers and Question Mark at Detroit's Concert of Colors in 2007. I would gladly have carried the members of both bands on and off stage, and shined their shoes to boot, just for the thrill of playing in their presence. *Yellow Moon*, *James Connolly* and *96 Tears* all in one show – that's the kind of town Detroit is.

And yet Bridie quit Motown and moved to LA. She's told me the reasons and the odyssey that brought her there a number of times, but we were usually drinking and the story never seems to stick. Luckily for us all, she met Dave and added her sparkling fiddle to his intensity, metal chops, and insightful songwriting. But it's more than that – she adds an Irish-American sensibility to the whirlwind, moshpitting shenanigans

that FM incites. It's not a world that she would
necessarily have gravitated to herself – in fact, she might
have run a mile from it – but she adds a grace and
gravity to the high jinx and provides a steadying hand
when the craziness threatens to spill over. It's great, too,
to see that Dave finally found the woman of his dreams
when it was obvious to many that she was there beside
him all the time.

Whistles The Wind

Whistles the wind, blowing my way
Sweeping me back, back here to stay
Can winners be losers running on the same track
Some head for glory, others refresh

Well it breaks my heart to see you this way
The beauty in life, where's it gone?
And somebody told me you were doing okay
Somehow I guess they were wrong

My isolation, now there's a sobering thought
A minute alone a lifetime too long
See the face in this mirror, so pale it could crack
Desperately wanting the color it lacks

So you drank with the lost souls for too many years
Time to be right 'cause they'll cripple with fear
Never been righteous though seldom we're wrong
Life's only life with you in this song

Now there's an ocean between us
Where I am and where I want to be
So you pray in doubt, doubt not for me

Oh you'll find your way out, but there's no going now
Every woman and child drags you down for the dive
It's not safe being free, can't give back what you feel
You said you'll always be in heaven with me

(Written by Dave King, Ted Hutt, Dennis Casey, George
Schwindt, Matt Hensley, Nathen Maxwell, Bridget Regan,
Bob Schmidt. Lyrics published by Bob-A-Lew Songs)

I actually wondered about their move back to
Ireland – would they fit in, would they find what they
were looking for? Dave and Bridie seem to have
discovered their own peace there, although when I see
them in Wexford, I recognize the mark of emigration on
them and know that like my father who celebrated his
fifteenth birthday in Russia, or the many returned
emigrants from London and their Cockney children,
they'll never totally fit in. But that's as it should be.
When you travel the world with a high-octane Rock 'n'
Roll band, you inhabit an almost hyper-reality that
makes it difficult to sink total roots again. You always
have your ear cocked for the road manager's call, while
every typed sheet of paper looks like the "book of lies"
that is your itinerary.

It's odd too, this whole status of Irish-American
musicians. We think of Ireland, dream about it, breathe
its imagined air, but we're focused on the place we left,
the politics, the soul, the culture of that particular time.
The present is not nearly as important. Part of that is
due to the fact that when you actually live in Ireland
you're within the cultural boundaries of the UK and
particularly its media. When you leave for the US, you
don't immediately cast all that aside, but it does wear off
gradually.

The change seems to come in three phases: you still snap back like an elastic band to the old country for the first three years. At five years, you begin your big internal battle as the Mets assume the same importance as Manchester United, and Congress becomes as relevant as Dáil Éireann. Unless you're just a total die-hard who clings maniacally to all things Irish, you drift free of your moorings around the seven years mark. This can be either exhilarating or confusing, or both – for you no longer have unquestioned certainties to shore up your fragile emigrant psyche.

This questioning of values and tradition replicates itself in your music too. I definitely didn't come to the US to play Irish music, nor did Dave; and I'm sure Ken Casey in his conversion to Hardcore was probably fleeing the ballads on South Side jukeboxes. But in the end, mainstream popular music doesn't have a huge amount of depth and such roots as it has barely delve below the surface. The mainstream music of your youth may be powerful, even intense, but after its time passes, it can seem dated and stale, easily enough replaced by some new wave. It's at times like that you feel a need for substantive grounding and a mainline to your own soul and culture. I experienced this after surviving the general vapidity of the MTV pop culture of the early 1980's. I had to shut the door on music, then apprentice myself to the discipline of playwriting before I could return to my roots and become a musician again.

I see the same search and longing in the Murphs, FM and B47 – it takes on a different complexion with each band, and we've all added our own particular musical and life experiences to what we perceive as Irish music. Each band too has deep-seated and even class-based political sensibilities. But perhaps that arose out of a moment in time, because for better or worse, I see

very little political awareness in most of the upcoming
Celtic Rock American bands; they seem to have adopted
wholesale the drinking/whoring/bad boy aspect of the
genre but little of the political outlook, though their
commitment to humanitarian and charitable causes is
deeply ingrained and often acted upon.

One thing, however, that all Irish-American
bands embrace is the desire to demolish the fourth wall
between musicians and audience in the shortest time
possible. Shane MacGowan, in speaking about The
Pogues, has a theory for that: "We were a crowd of
drunks playing to a crowd of drunks." For the most
part, Irish-American bands get their start in Irish pubs
and most of us - whether we ever stepped foot in the
place or not – are infected by the spirit of CBGB's. And
that's a good thing, for the palace of punk was all about
equal opportunity, and an in-your-face sense of being
true to yourself and the music you're making. Little did
you know, Hilly, the effect you'd have on Irish-America
when you moved from pristine, overpriced 13th Street in
the West Village to your esteemed dump on the Bowery!

CHAPTER TWENTY-THREE

Meg Griffin and I were laughing and reminiscing in the corridors of Sirius Satellite Radio. Steve Blatter, head of music programming, happened to be passing by. He noticed my accent, called Meg over and inquired if I might be suitable material to host a Celtic Music program Sirius was contemplating. Meg asked me to collate enough songs for a three-hour show and to put some thought into how I'd like to introduce them; but most importantly of all – be myself. Some days later I was in the studio, with Meg at my side, learning to man the controls while spouting whatever came to mind about some of my favorite Celtic tunes. That was almost ten years ago. Celtic Crush has become so much a part of my psyche and thought process it's almost hard for me to imagine a time before it. Suffice it to say, life cannot have been quite as rich.

Meg and I had much to reminisce about. She had invited me up to Sirius for an on-air chat about *Green Suede Shoes*, a memoir of mine that had just been published, and its accompanying Black 47 CD, *Elvis Murphy's Green Suede Shoes*. But we had met many years earlier when she was a host on WNEW-FM and regularly made the scene at CBGB's, Max's Kansas City and many of the other hole-in-the-wall clubs that dotted Manhattan of the 70's and 80's. I often think of Meg, and peers like Vin Scelsa and Ray White of WLIR, as those who didn't distinguish between the dancer and the dance. They were as committed to the musicians as the music. Many people in the Rock Radio business made the scene at prestigious and high profile gigs – that was their job – but the aforementioned and others actually lived much the same lives as we musicians did. The music of the time meant everything to them and, consequently, the musicians' lives became enmeshed with their own.

Everyone should write a memoir, if only because it makes you examine your past and opens up channels to so many discarded memories; likewise, everyone should be blessed to host and produce their own radio show for it makes you examine your tastes and general philosophy of life. I make no bones about the fact that my on-air influences include the old WNEW-FM crew and particularly the free-form ethos of that station. Throw in Jonathan Schwartz, Steve Post and John Schaefer of WNYC, not to forget John Peel and Kenny Everett of the BBC, and you have a well-rounded, if anarchistic posse. As you might gather from these names, I like the idea of framing music with information that can heighten the experience for the listener; I also think an audience is much more engaged when they feel you're flying by the seat of your pants – if you're not sure just what you're going to say nor what's coming next, then they'll be somewhat on edge too and that's the thrill of "under-produced" radio. It doesn't hurt that being a musician I have an insider's view of the world whereof I speak and have a positive distrust, as well as distaste, for hype. This very much helps when interviewing artists. I instinctively know how far I can go while not being intimidated by showbiz - aka bullshit - smoke and mirrors. In any case, I'm not particularly interested in musicians' personal lives except when such details influence the music being created.

There was a time when music was at the cutting edge of society and helped to define and change it. I don't find that to be the case anymore; it's not that artists are not engaged – it's more that marketing and the market place is much more of a factor nowadays. It's a lot harder to make a breakthrough on radio, perhaps because the medium is so compartmentalized and programmed. I remember Alison Steele, rhapsodizing about Turner & Kirwan of Wexford for some weeks on her "night bird" WNEW-FM show – we became instant musical "names" in the tri-state area although we were teased unmercifully by the many who could mimic her quite stilted accent and delivery. That was the power, immediacy and universality of free-form radio in the 70's.

I hear somewhat the same urgency on current Hip-Hop and Rap Radio and am aware of this medium's intimate connection with fans of the genre. Unfortunately I'm also so cognizant of formatting and lowest common denominator marketing that I find it hard to listen to more than fifteen minutes of radio shows that feature this most vital form of current American music. Yet as a musician I find myself still gravitating towards African-American radio when I wish to "find where the one is," as Mr. Brown used to say, and how wide the pocket is on the streets.

But then radio has always been at the nexus of entertainment and information. I adore the medium. I have so many memories of listening with my grandparents to the news, mysteries, commentary, and above all music on their old tube-lit, cloth-covered wireless. This was long before the balkanization of the medium; it's almost surreal now to think how so many different genres co-existed on the BBC or Radio Éireann - it was an education to listen, and yet I never felt less than entertained.

Radio was a lifeline to me as a teenager; it allowed me to dream and be carried away by the explosion of the new sounds of the 1960's. That's what I try to do with Celtic Crush – open up universes for the listeners by playing them music that they will never hear anywhere else and in the unlikeliest of combinations: Ó'Riada next to The Sex Pistols; Stephen Foster butting heads with Van Morrison; the two Joes - Heaney and Strummer going elbow to elbow, how both of them would have loved that!

And why not - I got some of my training doing late night shows for Meg Griffin on her Sirius Disorder Channel. She programmed every song for her genre-breaking channel segueing fearlessly from Stephane Grappelli to Elvis Costello, from the rowdy Kinks to the reedy Nick Drake. When I once mentioned the sonic disparity such choices caused, she darted me a kindergarten teacher's all-knowing smile, and murmured that good music will always fit together – it's the host's responsibility to make that happen. Thus was I introduced to the wonders of the cross-fade and how dissonance can work and even be pleasing when you learn to master and control it.

My chief joy on Celtic Crush, though, is to find great songs and overlooked artists – put them in the proper context and allow them to shine. With the strict formatting on most stations today, it's getting increasingly hard for an artist to get any kind of decent airplay. Thus a middling popular band like Black 47 had to battle it out with superstars like Bruce Springsteen or Bob Dylan for the few spots on NPR or any other kind of national show; I can only imagine how hard it is for new bands and singers. But everyone is treated equally on Celtic Crush – it doesn't matter about your past successes; it's the song I'm after – something original that stops me in my tracks, just like it did when I first heard Them and *Baby Please Don't Go* or Dylan's *Like a Rolling Stone*. Nor do I care if the song is new. It could be something from an album of twenty or even fifty years ago. As long as it's fresh or daring and lights my candle, it has a place on the show.

I'm particularly taken with artists who have a vision and follow that star without any thought of commerciality, for who would have thought on first listen that Van Morrison, Bob Marley or even Bob Dylan would still be enchanting and challenging people fifty or so years after their first, sometimes feeble studio steps. It's also interesting how certain artists have been touched by a master at an early stage of their lives and how that encounter opened up their creative process and propels them to this day.

Iarla Ó'Lionáird is a case in point. He was born in the *Gaeltacht* of West Cork. Although he occasionally does sing in English, he is still at heart a *Sean Nós* singer. It's not just that he sings in Irish but that he reaches back into an age-old tradition for strength, lyricism, truth and musicality. His mother, grandmother and aunt were noted singers, and from infancy he instinctively knew that he was destined to follow in their footsteps. Even more momentous than Mike Scott's influence on the musicians of Galway, Ó'Lionáird's village of Cúil Aodha was roused from its slumbers by the arrival of Sean Ó'Riada in 1964 seeking his own roots in Gaelic culture. Ó'Riada formed a choir, *Cór Chúil Aodha,* and Iarla, along with other locals, joined.

Ó'Riada died while Iarla was still a boy, yet I sense subtle echoes of the master in Ó'Lionáird's music. But the echoes dissipate the deeper you go, for Ó'Lionáird has mainlined into the soul of Irish music – the *Sean Nós* songs that are the expression of unfettered Gaelic Ireland. These songs are not only about the love between a man and a woman but the love of country, homeland, and local culture - the very rocks and stones, heather and grass of each Irish person's surroundings. There's a darkness to the songs too, just as there's a darkness to Irish history; and, yet, what a foundation to build your career and oeuvre upon!

Iarla made a tape of some of these songs and sent them along with a six-page introductory letter to Peter Gabriel at Real World Records who invited the young man over. When Iarla arrived at the Real World Studios in Wiltshire, he was introduced to Simon Emmerson. Out of this union arose Afro-Celt Sound System, one of my favorite Celtic Crush bands. What an original concept – mixing loops, beats, synthesizers, Traditional Irish Music, African *Griot* and *Sea Nós* singing, along with seasonings from many other cultures. Although neither I, nor most audience members, understand the lyrics in these pieces, it makes little difference, for we're touched by something ancient propelled by the beats and rhythms of today.

The band has long been on hiatus, and Iarla has gone his own way, but his solo offerings are still informed by the songs he heard in the kitchens of Cúil Aodha. I don't doubt that the spirit of Sean Ó'Riada is still peering over the shoulder of Iarla - the man who was once a boy soprano in *Cór Chúil Aodha*.

I am forever amazed at the quality of fiddlers I hear on CD or on stage at various Irish Festivals around the country: Eileen Ivers, Ashley MacIsaacs, Winnie Horan (Solas), Natalie MacMasters, Séamus McGuire, and Kevin Burke spring instantly to mind, but there are many other equally gifted lesser-known artists. The rise of boisterous Celtic Rock has paradoxically provided openings for many young lady fiddle players. Not only do they tend to be accomplished technicians, but they also grace the stages with taste, style and beauty. In fact their level of speed, dexterity and, in some cases, ability to use digital effects is stunning.

I'm sure Martin Hayes can saw with the best of them, but he'd seem to play at half-speed if placed back to back with some of the Celtic Rock dervishes. And yet to me, Martin is the fiddler of his generation. For while most of his peers project outwards as though playing on a stadium stage for frenzied thousands, Martin is all about finding the inner source and harmony of his music. He makes no effort to impress; it's as if you're invited into his living room to experience a 90-minute excursion around the far edges of his soul. The noise level drops and you find yourself breathing slower and more quietly than you imagined possible. His partner in these musical meditations, Dennis Cahill, matches Martin with guitar shadings so complementary and perfect you'd think he'd invented the very concept of minimalism.

A far cry from when I first heard them rattle the walls in Chicago's Abbey Tavern with Midnight Court, a Celtic Rock/Jazz ensemble, for want of a better description! There the volume was piercing and the legendary kitchen sink itself seemed to have found its way into the mix. But Martin and Dennis have mastered the Pete Seeger adage – "it's not what you put in that counts, but what you leave out!" For when I finally saw them in their present incarnation, I felt like I was attending a séance – so quiet and still had they become.

In an odd way the word séance suits, for I often get the feeling that while in the midst of a tune, Martin is in communion with something very otherworldly. Just as Iarla reaches back into time with his *Sean Nós* singing, so too does Martin with his fiddling. No surprise, I suppose, seeing that his father P.J. Hayes is a founding member of The Tulla Ceili Band - an East Clare institution. A ceili band's function is to get people out of their chairs and onto the floor to perform set dances like *The Walls of Limerick* and *The Siege of Ennis*. Not everyone was a champion of this form of entertainment - Sean Ó'Riada, uncharitably claimed that ceili bands sounded like "the buzzing of a bluebottle in an upturned jar."

Personally, I've always enjoyed ceili bands and even more so ceili dances – perhaps because young Irish ladies always accepted your offer of a fling around the floor – unlike their sisters at showband and rock dances where one might get refused ten times before finding a partner. I doubt that had anything to do with young Martin at an early age joining his late father in the Tulla Ceili Band, but you never know, music and sex are rarely not intertwined.

Such somewhat risqué speculation aside East Clare has its own style of music, one that's deep and contemplative to my untutored ear, that seems to move slower and more deliberately than Sligo's delightfully ornamental style or the faster-paced *Sliabh Luachra* tradition. Whatever it is, Martin has returned to those roots and burrowed even further into them than the many great local players of his father's generation. The fact that Martin often drops his tuning a tone or more seems to add to the sense of stealth and depth. I was playing Martin and Dennis' *The Lonesome Touch* one evening when a friend arrived. As she was taking off her coat, she stopped with one arm out of the sleeve and listened transfixed for some seconds before murmuring, "That's the sound of fairy music." She may well have been right.

To many ears – my own once included – Irish Traditional Music can seem generic, and I'm careful when programming a tune on Celtic Crush to place it in the most advantageous setting so that the audience can more easily find its way into and delight in the intricacies. I never have such concerns with Martin Hayes, for he touches people in a way that no other fiddler does; small wonder that Martin's fame has spread worldwide. He now collaborates with such craftsmen and composers as Paul Simon. I don't think it will be too long before he becomes a household name – surely an amazing feat for a man who has stayed true to the music of his beloved East Clare.

I am always struck that the songs with the most resonance for Celtic Crush listeners are those that go beyond the surface and connect to some bone-deep idea, event, person, or place. As for myself, I never hear Dominic Behan's *The Patriot Game* without experiencing an almost visceral sense of displacement. Before I knew the background of the song, it used send me on a somewhat generic, if emotional, spin through Ireland's convoluted history of betrayal; but since I discovered it was actually inspired by IRA volunteer Fergal O'Hanlon's death in 1957, I am transported to a cold, dark evening in Wexford when, as a little boy, I stood with my grandfather in a large silent crowd awaiting the remains of Patrick Parle, a local IRA volunteer, who had died in the same landmine explosion.

Old songs can be transformed too by an imaginative arrangement. Whenever I listen to the audience in Hampden Park sing along with Runrig on *Loch Lomond,* I am stunned by the feral power unleashed and am immediately swept up in Scotland's painful history. Because of this recording, I was not in the least surprised by the emotional appeal of the *Yes* vote in last year's referendum on Scottish independence.

Songs don't have to make literal sense – Joyce and Beckett liberated us from such drudgery – the mere sound of words can conjure up feelings and moods. Which brings me back to the Irish language and its ongoing influence on Celtic music. *An Gorta Mór,* The Great Hunger of 1845-47, would appear to have rung the death knell of the language. The Irish speaking areas were decimated by death and emigration; many of those remaining lost faith in the old traditions and made the conversion to English. After all, it was the vernacular of commerce and modernity, and for the most part the language favored by the Catholic Church.

But *an sean teanga* (the old tongue) clung on in remote rural areas of the South, West and Northwest until independence was gained in 1922. Over the years, Irish became a compulsory subject in schools, and by mid-century one had to be a fluent speaker to apply for many state jobs. This led to a great distaste for the language and resentment among native English speakers. We all knew and spoke Irish to some slight degree but were never fluent enough to use it; most of us discarded the language the moment the school doors finally closed behind us.

However, those who came from Irish speaking homes had a great love for the old tongue. I often

envied them – not even so much for the language itself
but because of the web of courtliness and friendliness
the language seemed to spin around its speakers. It was
as if they communed on a different plane than we
English speakers. Irish seemed softer and more
welcoming while there was a brusqueness to the way we
addressed each other. This brings to mind a retort made
by an old *Gaeilgeoir* to his son who had adopted the new
ways: "I hate the sound of the auld English clattering
around in your mouth." There is a pleasing guttural
plangency to the Irish language; oddly enough it
combines amazingly well with rock music.

   I first began experimenting with it while writing
music for the modern dance choreographer, June
Anderson. I've always liked using the voice in an
abstract manner when composing, especially for dance
pieces. However, June didn't want English lyrics – no
matter how disassociated - as it might seem that her
dancers would be interpreting the score a la MTV. So, I
began scatting in my limited Irish over some of the
melodies; at times this practice produced the strangest of
subliminal messages when translated, though more
often than not, pure nonsense was the end result. June,
however, liked the otherworldly effect of the Irish
language, and as she got more interested in Irish culture
she began suggesting texts – one of which was *Caoineadh
Art Uí Laoghaire* – one of the epic Gaelic laments.

   It tells the story of Ó'Laoghaire's murder by a
British official, Abraham Morris, as recounted by his
wife, Eibhlín Dubh Ní Chonaill. I set large parts of the
poem to music and eventually used one of these as the
prelude to the Black 47 song, *The Big Fellah*. It's hard to
put one's finger on it, but the Irish language allows a
glimpse into an alternate reality and I, for one, never fail

but come out enriched by this brush with the ancient culture of my people.

Liam Ó'Maonlaí and Fiachna Ó'Braonáin of Hothouse Flowers are native speakers entirely at home singing in Irish. They have a casualness and ease of expression that I greatly admire – and envy. They began their career as The Incomparable Benzini Brothers busking on Dublin's Grafton Street. I first saw them in a small basement club in that area in the company of their then manager, Lorcan Ennis, and the ubiquitous, Donal Lunny. What a night! By then they had become Hothouse Flowers, grown to a five piece, and oh, how they electrified that small space! Liam brought to mind an unlikely cross between Jim Morrison and Legolas the Elf from Lord of the Rings. Blessed with a strong, melodic voice, and powerful skills on piano and tin whistle, he also possesses an anarchic musical personality very much informed by Gospel and Soul improvisation.

The Flowers had huge early success both in Ireland and the UK but inevitably suffered from the "next U2" tag. Bono was an early supporter and their first single came out on Mother, U2's record label. There was always a chaotic aura to the Flowers that endeared them to me – perhaps because of Black 47's own somewhat shambolic ethos. We first shared the stage with them in the early 90's on a St. Patrick's Day show broadcast by WNEW-FM. They always seemed to be "just about there but not quite caught up" – this may well have been because of Liam's bohemian outlook on life and music. He never took the easy way out. The band's performance depended greatly on his mood, thus giving their shows that unpredictable feeling that often leads to great Rock 'n' Roll. They were one of the bands

I asked to perform on the *American Fleadh* tour along with Flogging Molly and The Saw Doctors.

The one time I ever saw Liam rattled was at that tour's stop in the Electric Ballroom in Philadelphia when heckled by some Flogging Molly fans. He actually stopped the show to have a heated discussion with them. When that didn't work, he merely upped the ante until it felt like the pressure would blow the roof off. That was a strange night, however, as neither Molly nor The Saw Docs would go on last after their battle the previous night in Baltimore, so the tension was thick in the air. Eventually Black 47 had to take the last slot in order to break the deadlock – not a great place on the bill with hundreds of Molly and Docs supporters streaming for the exits.

But I diverge. Apart from Liam's mercurial personality, my favorite part of the Flowers' show has always been their excursions into Irish language songs – I would imagine that this drove their record company, Polygram, crazy. My favorite piece by them is *Sí do Mhaimeo* – a driving reflection on a rich widow and what Liam might do to bed her. As far as I remember, I never heard him introduce the song or explain what was going on but the audience rocked and reeled to it every night. The Irish language is not unlike Yiddish in that many of the words have an onomatopoeic effect – you don't need to know the meaning – you just feel it. After trying to explain the meaning of *Sí Do Mhaimeo* on Celtic Crush one day, I received emails from separate women who both had roughly the same thing to say: "Honey, a woman doesn't need to know the language to know what that guy has in mind."

I don't know if the Flowers will ever perform again. In these days of Spotify streaming it's become almost impossible to keep a band on the road. Besides,

Liam is busy indulging his creativity by traveling to
countries such as Mali to jam with indigent tribesmen;
he also spends time musically directing his
dance/theatre piece, *Rian.* But for me, the Flowers
remain one of the great Irish bands – not only for the
fine songs they have written or performed (listen to their
Gospel version of *I Can See Clearly Now).* No, it's more
than that – they've helped me to reconnect to the Irish
language and the soul of the Irish people that lays
hidden behind the misty scrim of *an sean tseanga.*

    If An tUasal Ó'Maonlaí represents an old chaotic
soul inhabiting a modern day troubadour, then Damien
Dempsey is the personification of Dublin's North Side
and all its attendant modern joys and ills. I was first
introduced to Damo by Chris Byrne of Black 47 who was
blown away by Dempsey's songwriting chops and
working class voice. For months, Chris played a
battered cassette of some lo-fi recordings while we
barreled around the roads of America.

    At first I was more fascinated than impressed
although the song *Dublin Town* had more hooks than a
curtain rail. But it was the unapologetic proletarian
North Side voice that resonated, for you could tell he
didn't give a tosser for Dublin 4's pseudo-sophisticated
preoccupations. Damien was the voice of his people, in
much the same way that Bob Marley spoke for the
shantytowns of Kingston. Speaking of Marley, his
influence permeates Damien's work, but in an odd way
– for if Bob is supple to the extreme, Damo is far more
stolid; and yet the man from Donaghmede has his own
peculiar North Side Rocksteady lilt.

    Chris was so taken with Damien that he invited
him over to New York City where he took up residence
at Rocky Sullivan's on Lexington Avenue – much to the
titillation of the local ladies, for Damien is very

handsome and a gentleman of the first order. In fact, that's the first thing you notice – the gentleness that one often sees in ex-boxers. His overt sincerity can be startling at first, but unlike many musicians and entertainers, Damien is exactly what you see and he makes no bones about it. He began to sing at Rocky's – taking to the stage in between bouts of bartending. He was a curiosity at first, for no one had ever heard anything like him. A true original, it was hard to classify him – although he played an acoustic guitar, he seemed far removed from your typical Manhattan singer-songwriter. There was a slight element of Christy Moore to him but, that being said, Damien already had his own voice.

His output was phenomenal. He seemed to write a song or two every night. In fact, he was turning them out at such a rate you couldn't remember the names of songs, for he would often drop one that you were just getting the hang of and replace it with that morning's inspiration. Gradually, though, the songs began to solidify: you would find yourself humming a line here, a lyric there. He was an imposing performer – dominating Rocky's minimal stage with his 6′2″ frame, his eyes closed, positively emoting sincerity and commitment. Every song, nay, every syllable meant the world to him. You'd catch rockers and trad heads gape at him almost in disbelief. The ladies gaped for other reasons – sometimes the purring was so loud it threatened to drown out the man's guitar.

He's come a long way since those distant days, headlining concerts around the world, but he remains a very humble person, as likely to buy you a pint as to accept one. I sometimes listen to his songs when I'm feeling a bit ungrounded. They take me back to the times I spent drinking in The Hill, a pub near the Mount

Pleasant Buildings in Rathmines. There's a comfort level
you find when accepted by Dublin working class people
– their great sense of humor puts you at ease, and the
delight they harvest from their beloved surroundings is
infectious. That's Damien for you, and I can't help but
think that he must be a great role model to the North
Side youth as they strive to find their place in an Irish
society that is under-employed and over-mortgaged.
For his songs urge you to enjoy the beauty of existence
that lies beyond the banality and drudgery of everyday
life.

He's writing songs in Irish now – another artist
seeking his roots and recognizing that there's a vast
uncharted world of ideas, history, personalities and
pain, lurking behind the old language, only waiting to
be tapped. But whatever, Damo is well ahead of the
game for very early on he found that most important
element that goes into the making of an artist – his voice
- and we're all the richer for it.

Sing All Our Cares Away

*Mary loves to grouse, hides the bottles round the house,
She watches chat shows and the soaps, broken-hearted but she
copes,
Michael's out of work, feels he's sinking in the murk,
He's unshaven and a mess, finds it hard some days to dress
Stevie smashes the delf, 'cause he can't express himself,
He's consumed by rage, like his father at his age
Rita's little child, has a lovely little smile,
This means nothing to her father, because he's never even seen
her.*

We sing, sing all our cares away
We'll live, to fight another day

Joey's off the gear, he's been clean for half a year,
He gets bored out of his mind, but he's tryin' to toe the line
Maggie's in a chair, 'twas joyriding put her there,
She puts the kettle on the boil, and she's always got a smile

We sing, sing all our cares away
We'll live, to fight another day
We sing, sing all our cares away,
We'll live, to love another day,

We grow strong, from it all,
We grow strong, or we fall,
We grow strong, from it all,
We grow strong, or we fall,
We grow strong.
(Lyrics courtesy of Damien Dempsey &BMG
Rights Management US)

CHAPTER TWENTY-FOUR

Tramps Heartbreak

When I was young, I knew it all
But I didn't even know the time of the day
I laughed at you and your forebodings
Made fun of all you held dear.
I was ashamed of your peculiarities
So old fashioned always out of phase
So one night I left you aching
Took the light from all your days.

I played with life like old chess pieces
Discarded rooks for kings and queens
Seared the hearts of those who loved me
Ah, those faraway hills looked green.

I'm going back to where I come from
Though I don't fit there anymore
I've got some friends and blood relations
They won't turn me away from their front door.

It's a long road with no turn in it
It's an odd love without a portion of heartbreak
And if I hadn't laid all of that hurt upon you
I wouldn't be stuck out here like a fool
Cruising down along tramps heartbreak...
(Larry Kirwan)

But there's no going back. You set out on a journey, and you follow it to its conclusion. Besides, the place you set out from no longer exists. The template is still there but the façade is very different. Late at night, walking the narrow streets and back lanes of Wexford, I still can feel echoes of the town I grew up in, but by dawn those shades have fled back to where they belong – the past. Where once I often shed a silent tear crossing Wexford bridge on the way to the airport, now I save it for a last visit to Crosstown cemetery; for the truth is - when one's parents pass on, bonds once forged in steel become frayed, and by the time the plane is taxiing down the runway, I'm already engrossed with New York, its continuing scintillation and, of course, its many demands. I still carry the soul of Wexford inside me though, and can summon it up at an instant; the old town, its spirit, substance, and memories are always a source of strength in times of crisis.

When home I try to make time for a drive down to my grandfather's old farm in Tacumshane. Unlike the town, nothing much has changed, and I can retrace my boyhood steps along the coarse sandy dunes between the grassland and the mighty Atlantic beating along the graveled beach. Occasionally, out of the corner of my eye, I fancy I see the flash of an elderly woman's scarf arising from her favorite picnic spot in a secluded dune and recall my grandmother serving tea from a hot thermos flask along with thin mustardy ham sandwiches, but it's only wishful thinking.

As ever, that restless beach is deserted, and in the wind I hear strains of the old songs I learned from the men who worked the farm. But I've forgotten most of these screeds from the past myself, so why should I expect any of the locals to remember. And yet, an occasional old soul does, treasuring them like ancient artifacts in a museum, taking them out and dusting them off at some commemoration or recital; these songs still retain their latent power, though they seem lonely and unmoored in an inter-connected world. They speak of a different age and sensibility; nonetheless, if you allow them time to settle and take their ease next to a glass of Jameson's, they can haul you back to a graphic era of blood, revolution, emigration and a thirst for freedom.

Who knows, maybe a generation of earnest young folk singers will seek them out again as we did, and build careers on their sturdy backs, but for now Wexford town and county throbs to an ubiquitous Techno beat. There's little room or time for the old songs in country pubs where I used to catch wind of them; flat-screened cable TV beams down keeping us forever up to date with year round sporting events and the latest banal celebrity sighting or transgression, and if there is a song playing, then it's usually accompanied with a solid four on the floor, a beat too robust and rushed for the nuances and complexities of stories from a more reflective time and place.

But of course, there is great music about, always has been since some caveman or woman cracked two sticks together and hummed along to the rhythm. And there always will be because we have an ineffable need to reach into the depths of the human condition and frame our discoveries in meaningful terms; songs still provide the best vehicle for this expression. They don't cost anything to create, and you need only a minimum of technique to get started. I write plays, novels, memoirs, and newspaper columns; each of which provide their own rewards, but let me write a good song and I'm unequivocally on top of the world. That high may not last long, but I come out of the experience lighter in spirit and closer to my own particular gods from this small act of creation.

I know my creativity was first kindled on the medieval streets of Wexford, and it's inextricably linked to the violent history of the town. The very stones seemed to speak to me of days gone by, and those voices were always accompanied by shards of ancient songs floating past from dank alleyways and back lanes. You only had to reach out and touch these stray melodies and words to experience the joys and losses of previous generations. Sometimes you'd hear a snatch of such songs in the quayside pubs or at variety concerts out in the small village halls that dotted the countryside. Many dealt with what used to be known as "the national question" and the desire to be free of English rule. These issues provided a backdrop to everyday life and only intensified for me with the last great outbreak of the "Troubles" in the North and my membership in Black 47.

In so many ways I'm glad that the situation in the North of Ireland has improved and stabilized. For the most part, people can get on with their lives without the discrimination and sectarianism that blighted previous generations. And yet, there was a richness to the tradition of resistance that songwriters and poets could draw on. Even those who rejected this tradition made a conscious creative decision to do so and were thus influenced by it. Where will the inspiration come from now? Is it to be found in a Facebook consumerist society? Undoubtedly, but the imagery may suffer and the poets and songwriters will need to plunge deep into the heart of the human condition to get beyond the current surface banality.

The arts, however, always tend to do well in lean economic times; if so, there should be an eruption of creativity on both sides of the Atlantic soon. And yet, I know it was a lot easier to create an album about Iraq rather than one about bankers and gangsters. The big, violent, soul-searing issues are always more inspiring than the day-to-day grind of venality and greed – no matter how much damage was wreaked in the latest recession across broad swathes of society.

I'm always surprised by the dearth of meaningful commentary on current events in modern songwriting, either from a serious or comedic aspect. One would think that the economic situation in Ireland and its effect on youth emigration would spur some incisive political songwriting but, to the contrary, it seems instead to be producing a bumper crop of fine pop bands and Roots Americana influenced combos. While over here, the fact that the US is going through its greatest economic transformation since World War II appears to have little resonance in the Rock, Folk or Rap worlds either. The rich getting richer while everyone else treads water, at best, has elicited little comment except from rappers who either claim to be part of the gilded 1% or will be just as soon as you download their latest "dropped" masterpiece. Meanwhile, the Celtic Rock world seems stuck in a groove of revving up fiddle tunes, or delivering anthems about getting messed up on booze, or turning the bad girl they met in the pub into a virgin so that they can marry her and take her home to mother.

An over-simplification, I'm sure, but few songs I hear speak of any desire to break the chains of economic slavery that vast segments of the county are fast becoming accustomed to.

Whatever! It seems to me that popular music, and the arts in general, are somewhat on hold at the moment, perhaps taking a bit of a breather while coming to terms with the huge societal changes of the last twenty years. That situation rarely lasts for long, and I'm looking forward to some new outbursts of creative originality. Speed the day, for almost everything I hear is referential. I can tell the influences of a composer within the first few bars of practically any modern recording. There are few surprises. Rock music has become so standardized that I can barely listen to the radio for fear of fading away to rust; and even in the field I helped create, Celtic Rock, I hear little but shades of Shane, Ken and Dave. When asked for advice, I'm continually forced to say, "Throw away your Pogues, Murphs and Molly. Go back to the root source and give us your interpretation of Sean Ó'Riada, Seosamh Ó'Heanaí, Dominic Behan, Maggie Barry. Find out what The Clancy Brothers & Tommy Makem were listening to; they didn't arrive on this earth fully formed; they researched and edited songs they heard in the Ring Gaeltacht in County Waterford or from Tommy's folklorist mother, Sarah, up in Keady, County Armagh.

The greatest artist of our time, Bob Dylan, created his joker/outlaw persona by immersing himself in Civil War newspapers in New York's Public Library. Contemporary songwriters are a mouse-click away from Iraq, Afghanistan, Vietnam, Wall and Main Streets, but they seem hopelessly glued to Facebook and Twitter.

If I have to suffer through another carbon copy version of *Galway Girl*, *Wagon Wheel*, or a dozen other of their worn-out ilk, I'll go up the bloody walls. Bands reply, "That's what the promoters and punters want to hear." To which I have one standard reply, "Fuck the promoters and the punters. An artist's brief is to push the boundaries not cower behind them!" I suppose if you want to make a career ploughing the same furrow as someone you're in awe of, that's fine, but if you want to add some small enhancement to the poetry and music of life, then find your own un-trodden path and open our eyes to it. Life is short; leave something of value behind you. You may not create an *Astral Weeks* - that took a confluence of Van's talent, the tenor of the times, and a lack of awareness that such a thing of beauty could be created. But, by God, you can come up with something better than a watered-down version of a Steve Earle song, bless his soul; and I don't care how many fiddles and accordions you tack on to it.

These are the best and the worst of times for creativity. The old order is gone. I've recognized that for many years. You couldn't create a band like Black 47 now and play up to 2500 gigs across a quarter of a century. The venues are not there anymore. The CD sales that kept Black 47 and other independent minded bands on the road are drying up – why should people buy from bands at gigs when they've already downloaded the songs for free, or can listen to them gratis on Spotify, Pandora and the many other streaming, artist demeaning forums?

And yet, new bands will come along and adapt to the changing circumstances. The mantra now is – give away your music for free and people will pay to come and see you play. That may work, but only for the American Express acts at major venues, for costs have continued to spiral for the regular band on the road. There'll still be openings for those willing to survive on peanuts while sleeping on borrowed couches. But that gets old after a time – and do you really want to become an itinerant intern musician? In fact, don't even think of becoming a professional musician unless there's so much fire in your blood, you can't even think of doing anything else. And if that's the case, then before you do take the leap, for god's sake, acquire a skill that can net you a couple of hundred bucks a day, so that you can actually make choices in your musical career and not be forever dealing with the debt, doubt and insecurity that paralyzed most of my peers.

The old template of making a record and then touring is caput and has been for some time. The new road warriors will be those who can harness the current Facebook and interactive culture - they will create at home and travel digitally as in a William Gibson novel. Instead of making albums, they'll release digital singles every couple of months – not unlike The Beatles or groups from the 1950's. When a song gets traction, then they'll tour. They may be a little stage rusty at first, but an enthusiastic audience in each city will soon cure that.

A new Bob Dylan is quitting high school right now. Like Dylan, he's finding his inner Woody Guthrie – but not at Hootenannies or song-swapping open microphone nights. No, he's trawling the web, a lick here, a note there, a lyric somewhere else, a look from some fashionable catalogue or museum site; and when he puts all that together, you won't even recognize the influences, the finished whole will seem original – just like Dylan did when he emerged from three months of creating his persona in New York's Public Library. And our digital Bobby will continue to borrow - just like Mr. Zimmerman did - until, before you know it, you'll stumble straight into the blinding heat and once-in-a-lifetime originality of his *Like A Rolling Stone*.

People are always asking me what's the new thing? And believe me I keep my ears open. I don't know, but I can feel it barreling down the pike; it's just not quite here yet. In the meantime, I've heard some really fine bands and artists that are very much worth experiencing and exploring.

Villagers is a project driven by Conor O'Brien from Dublin. There's a 60's type quality to this young man's work. His tunefulness is remarkably self-assured: his melodies get under your skin on first listen. You can tell he will not be restrained by genres – that he'll take a shot at any style in his desire to create great pop songs. I sense a tad of a Brian Wilson in him, and how bad can that be.

The Strypes are another band that should do something major. These guys from Cavan town quit secondary (high) school years before graduation, but they have a grasp of R&B that's startling. It's as if they swallowed whole each LP of Dr. Feelgood and everything The Yardbirds ever listened to. Somewhere in this band there's a major intelligence working out his plan for world domination and he already has a solid foundation to build upon. I hope they're managed well and given the opportunity and time to fail every now and then. There's greatness in these teenagers; if it's allowed to blossom, god only knows where it will end up.

I love Irish traditional music, and the players seem to get more brilliant by the year, but I often feel the genre has become stuck in time. It's as if it never quite recovered from the turbulent brilliance of The Bothy Band. And then you hear Beoga, and you realize that Trad can be so much more. The piano base tends to send them off on less common rhythmic paths, but it's their joyful willingness to incorporate everything from

Piazzolla's jazzy tangos to Dr. John's New Orleans funk, with many the tangent in between, that sets them apart and, perhaps, shines a light on where Irish Traditional music might eventually end up.

Gerry Diver's Speech Project may be one of the most intriguing albums I've heard for many a year. Gerry, a multi-instrumentalist, who cut his teeth playing with everyone from Shane MacGowan's Popes to Laurie Anderson, runs with the idea that every person speaks in a key, or two or three. On his groundbreaking first CD, he loops snippets of meaningful speech from the like of Shane MacGowan, Christy Moore, Damien Dempsey and, in particular, the great street singer, Margaret Barry. He then adds chorales of sympathetic music that sometimes merge with, and other times highlight, the voice. It's strangely heart-wrenching at times, and you find yourself listening to music and the human voice in a way you did in your childhood but had long forgotten about.

Put Martin Hayes and Iarla O'Lionaird together then add Dennis Cahill, Caoimhín Ó'Raghallaigh, and Thomas Bartlett, and you have The Gloaming. Their eponymous album is a revelation and perhaps outlines one of the main roads that Irish music will travel in the years to come. I've already dealt with the first three members of the group in other chapters, and there's little need to say that each one brings their considerable talents and perceptions to the band. Ó'Raghallaigh plays no second fiddle to Hayes; rather he adds a vista of sounds courtesy of his instinctive exploration of a new instrument that he commissioned – a fiddle with five bowed strings and five sympathetic strings – that is somewhat of a cross between a Norwegian *Hardanger* fiddle and a five-string violin. The sounds he coaxes from this strange instrument are often ghostly with a

hint of the long dark nights of the Scandinavian winters.
It truly has to be heard to be believed!

Bartlett, on the other hand, brings more than a
touch of New York minimalism to the mix, but his
contribution is far from the worlds of Philip Glass or
Steve Reich. There's a restrained simplicity in his
playing that allows him to get to the real heart of Irish
melodies, while his chord voicing and arpeggios provide
the perfect foundation from which the other players can
soar. You're never less than aware that these five
players delight in their comrades' contributions and are
keenly listening to each other. It's an album for the ages,
and I have little doubt that it will provide a roadmap to
a new generation of players while giving the rest of us a
bounty of pleasure.

Two Dublin bands that I'll be keeping an eye on
are Lynched and The Spook of the Thirteenth Lock.
Each is taking old elements and reimagining them, while
dusting their songs and arrangements with new colors
and sounds. Their original take on things makes you sit
up, listen, and long for more. Bring it on!

What of the veterans? Well, *Appointment With
Mr. Yeats* is one of the finest Rock releases of many
years. Mike Scott has re-imagined William Butler Yeats
poetry by setting it to some powerful melodies and
innovative arrangements. Though respectful, he wades
into Yeats' translucent work, unafraid to not only blow
away the considerable dust that has come to calcify it,
but also to cut and edit where he sees fit. He may not
even know it, but he appears to be guided by Yeats own
dictum that "poetry should be as cold and passionate as
the dawn." When Scott senses whimsy, he attacks with
earthy electric guitars to regain artistic balance, and
when Yeats occasionally becomes obtuse Scott relocates
the center by welding the ungainly words to beautiful

341

melodies. Mike Scott has done us all a favor and turned the illustrious poet into a first class lyric writer – something Mr. Yeats always aspired to.

And what will I be up to myself? Who knows? I never expected Black 47 to last 25 years, yet I always felt certain that when the time came to disband, I'd know. It had nothing to do with the music. That was always a joy – no matter how low I felt before going onstage, I always came off transformed. The original idea of the band was to infuse the songs with your mood and, most importantly, be unafraid to fail. We could have kept going indefinitely, created new songs and played many more gigs; but times change, and what's life without new challenges?

Even in my early days playing folk and pop, music was always about the Rock 'n' Roll experience. By that, I mean the transcendent moment onstage when everything comes together. The poet Federico Garcia Lorca called it *Duende*. You can't wish it or force it – you just have to put all the elements in place - great band, inspiring song, total commitment - and then wait for the spark. It's as good as sex when it arrives.

Rock 'n' Roll, by my book, is very different from Rock music, which is more about entertainment. I've never even really aspired to the idea of entertaining an audience, though I'm happy when it happens; rather, music to me is more about an almost Dionysian/Shamanistic catharsis where you try to take things to a different level. The intent is to get the members of an audience to partake, become part of the process, and thereby transform both themselves and their surroundings. Showmanship and onstage experience are essential to this mission, but I'm always more concerned with moving an audience rather than merely entertaining it, for touching hearts and even souls is much more gratifying than tickling fancies or expectations.

The song has to be interesting – either in lyrical content, musical innovation or just sheer tribal resonance. With Black 47, we had three basic song types: uproarious, political / historical and those dealing with memory – although many songs contained traces of all three elements. Thus *Rockin' The Bronx* fits the uproarious, *James Connolly* the political, and the song that begins this chapter, *Tramps Heartbreak*, deals with memory. Because each of our songs had a different narrator or protagonist, this called for at least a modicum of method acting. Problems could thus arise on any given night; for instance, I might not always be in a mood for figuratively getting shot in a chair while performing *James Connolly*. However, I found that a belt of Irish whiskey can ease you into any role and it sure helps obliterate all manner of artistic preciousness.

And as regards commitment? Well, 100% is not worth talking about, everyone can aspire to that. What counts are those magic points between 110% and beyond. They call for huge bursts of energy and, strangely enough, restraint; for when so fired up, you can have trouble coming down after a performance, which inevitably leads to burn out – never a pretty thing.

Whatever I do after Black 47, I hope to be inspired by these elements. I'm already digging deeper into musical theatre – I very much enjoyed re-imagining Stephen Foster's songs in the musical, *Hard Times*, and trying to make sense of Foster himself - the enigmatic father of modern songwriting. I learned a lot about my own limitations in deciphering his genius. For some years I've wanted to turn the Black 47 *IRAQ* album into a musical – it seems one way to come to terms with an ongoing burning issue in American life. Likewise, I don't believe we've yet got to the heart of the Northern Ireland historical and political situation. Finding an artistic way to do so would be both exciting and meaningful.

I'm sure I'll write new music to perform, perhaps of an acoustic nature, for a change – I've been listening to Liam Clancy of late. I'm still moved by the last conversation I had with him when we both knew he wouldn't be coming back to New York. I told him then that no one ever put silence between lyrics in the way that he did. He smiled and nodded gravely, perhaps remembering the first time he noticed his unique gift. I hope some of it rubs off on me and that I'll be able to come up with my own individual notion of *Duende* in solo performances. But more than anything, I want to enjoy a little time off the glorious spinning top of Black 47 that I've been perched atop these last 25 years so that I can re-examine, and perhaps re-imagine, what I've done myself. With the rigors of touring and managing a controversial band, I've had little time for reflection. It's always been onwards and upwards, put out fires, steady yourself then leap for the next rung of the ladder.

But I won't stay away long – there's forever something new to learn, some new challenge, a different drummer to march to. As an old man with fiery eyes once said to me long ago in a decrepit Bowery saloon, "You might think I'm a bum, but you're missin' the point, Mack. I was in the arena – that's all that counts."

That's all, indeed.

America 2014

*Hey kid, I got a job for you, now you're finally out of graduate
school
Here's your desk, your computer, Excel sheet, and roto rooter
You be workin' 9 to 7, occasionally past 11
But that's okay, me oh my, jobs these days so hard to find
What you talkin' about, cash in the hand, you think this is a
rock & roll band
You're my intern, get with the program, your Daddy pay your
health care and your futon*

*Welcome to the new republic
Say hello to your American dream
And you better know who you're talking to
You better be born with a silver spoon
In the US of A 2014*

*The NSA is on the phone, they want to know if you're at home
Beg your pardon for the intrusion, but terrorist plots ain't an
illusion
Heard you bitchin' about the CIA, the FBI, the NBA
Wanta save your democracy but freedom don't come easily
We know what is best for you, stay the course, kid, don't get
fooled
Next thing you know – they wanta let the freaks out of
Guantanamo, oh no!*

*They sold out Iraq, next up Pakistan, now they wanta exit
Afghanistan
I ain't no interventionist, but hey yoh, who whipped the
communists
Cut defense, you gotta be kiddin', bombs make jobs for my
constituents*

345

This the real world, get with the program, gassin' the Syrians
while you out partyin'
Be a good boy, go back to bed, pull that pillow up over your
head
Plug in your earphones, listen to some moron hallucinate
about his hoes and his hard-ons

I'm out of here, hey it was a blast, Black 47 soon a thing of the
past
So many gigs, could go on but I might end up repeating this
song
Thanks for the praise, love and all, especially the alcohol,
Called it like we saw it, so sorry if we occasionally played out
of key
This ain't no 1989, what the hell happened to my life
Asked all the questions – nobody knows
Who stole the scent from the American rose, nobody knows

Welcome to the new republic
Say hello to your American dream
And you better know who you're talking to
You better be born with a silver spoon
In the US of A 2014

(Larry Kirwan)

About The Author

Larry Kirwan was the leader of Black 47, the Irish political rock band, for 25 years. The band played over 2400 gigs, released 16 CDs and appeared on many major TV shows including Leno, Letterman, O'Brien and Fallon.

Kirwan also released two solo CDs. He has written 14 plays and musicals, five of which are collected in the book, Mad Angels. His most recent musical, Hard Times, is in workshop for a major production. He has written two novels, Liverpool Fantasy and Rockin' The Bronx, along with a memoir, Green Suede Shoes.

He hosts and produces Celtic Crush for SiriusXM Satellite Radio and writes a regular column for The Irish Echo. He is currently President of the Irish-American Writers and Artists. Despite all these distractions, he still finds time for his most important activity – sampling and savoring fine pale ales.